Guilt and Punishment in "Law and Literature"

International Studies in Law and Literature

VOLUME 6

The titles published in this series are listed at *brill.com/isll*

Guilt and Punishment in "Law and Literature"

Cervantes, Dostoyevsky, and Kafka

By

María José Falcón y Tella

Translated by

Pablo Falcón Dieguez

BRILL | NIJHOFF

Originally published by Marcial Pons Ediciones Jurídicas y Sociales in 2026 under the title *Culpa y castigo en "Derecho y Literatura". Cervantes, Dostoievski y Kafka.*

ISSN 2773-191X
ISBN 978-90-04-76599-3
ISBN 978-90-04-76600-6 (PDF)
DOI https://doi.org/10.1163/9789004766006

Library of Congress Control Number: 2026938292

Brill Nijhoff and Koninklijke Brill BV are part of De Gruyter Brill.
www.degruyterbrill.com

Questions about General Product Safety Regulation: productsafety@degruyterbrill.com

To my family

The first punishment of the guilty is that his conscience judges him and never absolves him.

Juvenal

•••

It is ugly to be worthy of punishment, but inglorious to punish.

Michel Foucault

∵

Contents

CHAPTER 1

Introduction

This work attempts to connect two related themes: guilt and punishment, analyzing them in general terms as well as, specifically, their reflection in world literature, particularly in the works of three writers who excel in this topic, such as Miguel de Cervantes Saavedra, Fyodor Mikhailovich Dostoyevsky, and Franz Kafka. The topic of guilt and punishment is analyzed from both a theoretical and general perspective, as well as in its application to the lives and writings of these three distinguished figures in the history of literature.

We have already addressed these issues in some of our previous works.[1] This study attempts to provide a more global and comprehensive overview of them.

The book will be published in its original language, Spanish – like our two previous monographs on Law and Literature – by Marcial Pons, Madrid-Barcelona-Buenos Aires-São Paulo. There will also be this English translation, by the De Gruyter Brill's series *International Studies in Law and Literature*, which was launched in January 2024 with an excellent volume by Martín Laclau, professor emeritus at the University of El Salvador in Buenos Aires, and which in 2025 featured two magnificent new works, one by the legendary Richard H. Weisberg, and the other by Pedro Talavera, professor at the University of Valencia, Spain. Volume 4 followed later that year, written by the Belgian professor François Ost, with a compilation of nine of his celebrated

1 María José Falcón y Tella, *Derecho y Literatura*, Foreword by François Ost, Madrid-Barcelona -Buenos Aires-São Paulo, Marcial Pons, 2015. Reviewed: – In *International Journal of Education and Social Science*, vol. 2, no. 12, December 2015, pp. 41–43. – In *International Journal of Arts and Humanities*, vol 1, no. 4, December 2015, pp. 38–39. – By Nuria Cuadrado Gamarra, in *Las Torres de Lucca. Revista Internacional de Filosofía Política*, no. 7, 2015, pp. 325–328. – By Cristina Fuertes-Planas Aleix, in *Foro. Revista de Ciencias Jurídicas y Sociales. Nueva Época*, vol. 18, no. 2, Year 2015, pp. 528–531. – By Isabel Araceli Hoyo Sierra, in *Iuris Tantum. Revista de la Facultad de Derecho. Universidad Anahuac*, Mexico, year XXX, no. 26, Tercera Época, 2015. There is a translation into English, *Law and Literature*, Foreword by François Ost, Leiden-Boston, Brill-Nijhoff, 2016. *Id.*, "El progreso de la Humanidad: Dostoievski y Kafka," in Tribute to Manuel Nuñez Encabo, *In varietate concordia. Anuario de Derechos Humanos. Nueva Época*, supervised by Cristina Fuertes-Planas Aleix and Fernando Falcón y Tella, Instituto de Derechos Humanos – Departamento de Filosofía del Derecho, Facultad de Derecho, Universidad Complutense de Madrid, vols. 13 and 14, 2012 (released in May 2017), our contribution in vol. 13, pp. 213–233. *Id.*, "Delito y castigo en la Literatura," in *Anuario de Filosofía Jurídica y Social. Asociación Argentina de Derecho Comparado. Sección Teoría General*, Buenos Aires, Lexis Nexis, Abeledo-Perrot, no. 40, 2020, pp. 213–240.

 | HTTPS://DOI.ORG/10.1163/9789004766006-002

legal tales, originally published in French by Éditions Dalloz, with translations into Brazilian Portuguese, English, Italian, and Spanish. The fifth volume of this collection is an essay by M. Paola Mittica, professor at the University of Urbino, that will be published in 2026.

We would like to thank all the members of the Editorial Board of this series for their invaluable help. Without them, this undertaking would not have been possible. We extend our gratitude to the members of the editorial team at De Gruyter Brill, whose professionalism makes each of their products unique.

This book will also be published in Italian by Giuffrè, Milan.

CHAPTER 2

Guilt

1 Psychological Perspective[1]

The topic of punishment has been extensively examined by psychiatrists and psychologists.[2] Are criminals, or at least a subset of them, mentally ill individuals?[3] The response to this inquiry is contingent upon the definition of ailment that we employ.[4]

---

1 María José Falcón y Tella – Fernando Falcón y Tella, *Fundamento y finalidad de la sanción: ¿Un derecho a castigar?,* Foreword by Antonio García-Pablos, Madrid, Marcial Pons, 2005. Reviewed in *Foro. Revista de Ciencias Jurídicas y Sociales. Nueva Época,* Facultad de Derecho, Universidad Complutense de Madrid, no. 1, 2005, pp. 374–375. Also reviewed by: – María Eugenia Pérez Montero, in *Anuario de Derechos Humanos. Nueva Época,* Instituto de Derechos Humanos, Facultad de Derecho, Universidad Complutense de Madrid, vol. 6, 2005, pp. 790–798. – Ana Valero Fdez. de Palencia, in *Foro. Revista de Ciencias Jurídicas y Sociales. Nueva Época,* Facultad de Derecho, Universidad Complutense de Madrid, no. 2, 2005, pp. 461–463. There is a translation into English, *Punishment and Culture: A Right to Punish?,* by Peter Muckley, Leiden-Boston, Martinus Nijhoff Publishers, 2006. Reviewed in: – *Foro, Revista de Ciencias Jurídicas y Sociales,* no. 2, 2005. – Martinus Nijhoff Publishers, *Catalog Spring 2006, "Human Rights & International Law,"* pp. 28 and 89. – Martinus Nijhoff Publishers, *Catalog Spring* 2007: *"Human Rights & International Law,"* cover and p. 34. Also reviewed by: – José María Carabante Muntada, in *Archiv für Rechts-und Sozialphilosophie,* Band 94, Heft 4, 2008, pp. 547–549. – Carissa Byrne Hessick, in *New Criminal Law Review,* vol. II, issue 3, pp. 498–503. And also a translation into Portuguese, *Fundamento e finalidade da sançao. Existe um direito de castigar?,* by Claudia de Miranda Avena, supervised by Luiz Flavio Gomes, Brazil, Editora Revista dos Tribunais, 2008. And a translation into Italian, *Fondamento e finalità della sanzione: diritto di punire?,* by Raffaello Dal Col, Milan, Giuffrè, 2008. Reviewed by the doctoral student Faen.

2 Cf. Gregory Zilboorg (1890–1959), *The Psychology of the Criminal Act and Punishment,* New York, Harcourt, Brace, 1954; London, Hogarth Press, 1955; New York, Greenwood Press, 1968.

3 José María Rodríguez Devesa (1916–1987), "Tratamiento psiquiátrico en la delincuencia," in *R. E. P.,* 1970, pp. 1121 ff. Günter Stratenwerth, "Strafrecht und Sozialtheraphie," in *Festschrift für Bockelmann,* 1979.

4 Cf. James Boyd White, *The Legal Imagination: Studies in the Nature of Legal Thought and Expression,* Boston, Little Brown and Co. 1973; there is a 2nd abridged edition, *The Legal Imagination,* Chicago, University of Chicago Press, 1985. Wolters Kluwer brought out a *45th Anniversary Edition* of this book, Aspen Publishing, 2018, with a new preface written by the author. Chapter 3, B, p. 173 of the 1985 ed., about the Insanity Defence and the problem of defining the criteria of irresponsibility. David Abrahamsem, *The Psychology of Crime,* New York, Columbia University Press, 1960. Gibbens, "Les problèmes posés par le traitement psychiatrique des délinquants," in *Revue de Science Criminelle,* 1958. Peter Robert Hofstatter

HTTPS://DOI.ORG/10.1163/9789004766006-003

1.1 Criminality as Deviant Behavior

In English Law, from 1843 to 1957, McNaghten's Rules unequivocally delineated the circumstances under which a mental condition might serve as a defense against criminal charges. To be deemed abnormal in relation to a specific conduct, an individual must have been experiencing a mental disturbance that inhibited their awareness of the nature of the act they were undertaking, and the act itself must be deemed wrongful. The mental anomalies mentioned pertain to insanity or cognitive impairment.

Mental aberrations, despite their diverse manifestations, can be classified into two primary types based on their physical or psychological basis. Dementia is categorized as a physical condition. Confusion, delirium, and cognitive impairment, characteristics of dementia, may arise from a medical condition, a stroke, some forms of drunkenness, hereditary predisposition, among other factors. The category of the physical also includes abnormalities such as imbecility or idiocy.

The second group, of a psychological nature, can be subdivided into subgroups. The initial category includes emotional problems such as anxiety, depression, and mania. A second subgroup comprises schizoid states, distinguished by disturbed cognition or atypical behavior. A third grouping would encompass compulsive or obsessive states, diverse manifestations of hysterical diseases, along with psychopathologies. Psychopaths are a prevalent category among criminals, particularly among recidivists.

Not all criminals are afflicted, despite the breadth of disorders. This is the consensus of numerous physicians. An offender qualifies as "mentally ill" just if their situation is documented in psychiatric literature and manuals. A different approach to the topic is the Freudian perspective. This addresses the unconscious, fundamental instinctual drives, sublimation and repression, the Oedipus Complex, the Pleasure Principle and the Reality Principle, or Super-Ego development, among other concepts.[5] In accordance with Freudian theory, criminal behavior can be analyzed as a result of deviant emotional states in relation to normal conduct. Criminals are perceived as individuals afflicted by character deficiencies, arising from a dysfunctional interplay of the Id, Ego, and Super-Ego. Due to a poor emotional environment or childhood traumas,

---

(1913–1994), "Pena y reprochabilidad desde el punto de vista social-psicológico," in *Sexualidad y crimen*, Spanish translation by Enrique Gimbernat, Madrid, Reus, 1969. Nicholas N. Kittrie, *The Right to Be Different: Deviance and Enforced Therapy*, Baltimore-London, The John Hopkins Press, 1971.

5 Cf. Jacques Lacan (1901–1981), "La metáfora del sujeto," in *Introducción teórica a las funciones del psicoanálisis en criminología*, Buenos Aires, Homo Sapiens, 1978.

an individual may cultivate a deficient Super-Ego. From this viewpoint, criminals resemble large infants whose fundamental instincts are unregulated, or who possess an inadequately resolved Oedipus Complex, resulting in a pathological reaction to authority. There are instances in which an individual may commit a crime due to a desire for punishment. The shame evident in these examples may stem from early sexual experiences. Additionally, an individual may have a focus on the infancy stage or familial relationships, which could motivate theft.[6]

Other analogous theories exist that possess a broad applicability. Consequently, numerous individuals associate criminal tendencies with a deficiency of affection during childhood, such as maternal separation, experiences of rejection, or an absence of love. Any one or all of these causes may precipitate a psychological dysfunction or engender criminal behavior at a subsequent time.

Alternative ideas attribute aberrant behavior to an individual's physical constitution. In this context, we may reference the theory of reflex actions as reactions to external stimuli. When an external stimulus affects our senses, such as a breeze on the open eye, the sensory stimulation reaches the brain and elicits a reaction, in this instance, blinking. Inhibition also serves as a defense mechanism against stimulation. Both processes – excitation and inhibition – represent two facets of a singular phenomenon. If, in the provided example, I were to perceive an explosion each time my eye encountered a stream of air, there would eventually be a point at which I would automatically correlate both events and blink upon hearing the sound, even in the absence of wind. Similar phenomena occur in general human behavior and criminal activity, akin to the act of blinking. When a youngster is penalized for every misdeed, he will eventually link the wrongdoing to the punishment, see it as an aversive sensation, and strive to evade the latter by refraining from the former. He will acclimate to experiencing pain and dread in response to the offense and, subconsciously, endeavor to evade it. If we did not experience such condemnation from childhood, we would not link wrongful actions to their consequences.

Additional factors that may affect aberrant behavior include genetic inheritance and environmental influences. Both influence our behavior and reduce the extent of freedom in our responses to stimuli. An illustrative example could involve an individual exhibiting neuroticism or having developed detrimental behavioral patterns and a predisposition to criminality due to genetic

6 Diego-Manuel Luzón Peña, "Prevención general y Psicoanálisis," in *Derecho Penal y Ciencias Sociales*, Barcelona, Ed. Mir, 1982, pp. 149 ff.

inheritance or environmental influences, such as being raised in a marginalized community or one characterized by criminal activity, which subsequently affects their behavior. Individuals typically engage in illegal behavior due to exposure to deviant patterns and failure to adhere to the established legal norms of conduct.

Individual and social elements frequently interact in a complex manner. Criminals are shaped by both individual and societal influences. This can be elucidated equally well through Freudian concepts or the sociological notion of anomie. If the delinquent exhibits Freudian problems, psychoanalysis and treatment are warranted. If crime results from societal issues, then behavioral therapy would be appropriate.[7]

Medico-psychiatric interpretations of crime characterize it as deviant behavior, utilizing terms such as "hyperactivity" and "sociopathology," and employing assessments like the Minnesota Multiphasic Personality Inventory (MMPI) in the United States, alongside causal frameworks grounded in deprivation theory in Great Britain. In both nations, as well as in several others, it is posited that educational elements within a subculture, or a deficiency of affection and maternal care throughout early childhood, incline individuals toward criminal behavior. Children who are not enrolled in school, those from single-parent households or homes where the mother is frequently absent, as well as those with an incarcerated father, are more susceptible to vulnerability and a propensity for criminal behavior.[8]

1.2 Punishment as the Intentional Infliction of Suffering

Miguel de Unamuno, in his work *Del sentimiento trágico de la vida en los hombres y en los pueblos* (The Tragic Sense of Life in Men and Nations) (1913), stated:[9]

> Pain serves as the conduit of conscience, enabling sentient beings to attain self-awareness. Self-awareness and personality include recognizing and experienc-

7 Ted Honderich, *Punishment. The Supposed Justification,* Harmondsworth, Baltimore, Maryland, Penguin Books, 1969, pp. 96–103. Also, in Harmondsworth-Baltimore (etc.), Penguin, 1976. Original edition, London, Hutchinson, 1969; also in Harmondsworth, Penguin Books, 1984; and in Cambridge, Polity, 1989.

8 Barbara Hudson, *Justice Through Punishment. A Critique to the "Justice" Model of Corrections*, London, MacMillan, 1987, p. 135.

9 Quote in Antonio Beristain, *La pena-retribución y las actuales concepciones criminológicas,* Introduction by Elías Neuman and Eugenio Raúl Zaffaroni, Buenos Aires, Depalma, Criminología Contemporánea, 1982, p. 121, n. 13.

> ing oneself as unique from others, a distinction that can only arise via shock, varying degrees of pain, and the awareness of one's own limitations.[10]

The administration of punishment, under the legal system, entails inflicting intentional suffering. This directly contradicts our core value system, which encompasses forgiveness and mercy. How can these two incompatibles be reconciled: paying for one transgression by inflicting another, which entails intentional suffering? What justifications are provided for this deliberate application of punishment?[11]

Subsequently, we will address pain, notwithstanding the challenges in precisely defining and quantifying it. Literature is replete with heroes who endure suffering with fortitude and with cowards who evade it. We may examine the physiology of pain from a medical perspective by analyzing the body's nervous system, thereby determining what is most painful for particular individuals. That is a potentiality. Nonetheless, in assessing pain, it is imperative to account for psychological, moral, religious, and societal considerations. All these factors may mitigate what ought to have been intense pain or exacerbate what should have been minor discomfort. Consequently, we refrain from quantifying pain to determine if specific types are more severe than others, nor do we assess whether pain levels have escalated or diminished globally.

Some may assert that suffering fosters personal growth, enhances one's connection to the Transcendental, cultivates maturity, facilitates rebirth, and provides a deeper perspective on reality. In some instances, this is undoubtedly accurate. Some of us have likely encountered such advantages. However, we have also encountered contrary effects: pain that immobilizes, pain that fosters bitterness, obstructs personal development, and dehumanizes.

A conclusion may be: In uncertain situations, one should refrain from causing suffering or, at the very least, minimize the infliction of pain. This pertains to punishment. We should seek alternatives to punishment rather than various forms of punishment. Although suffering is unavoidable, a constructed Hell is not.

In contemporary civilizations, a stigma exists regarding the expression of pain, suffering, and profound sorrow. The manifestation of suffering must be

---

10 José S. Lasso de la Vega, *El dolor y la condición humana en el teatro de Sófocles*, CESIC (Instituto Arnaldo de Vilanova), 1958. Barcelona, 1971, pp. 65–66.

11 Cf. C.S. Lewis, *The Problem of Pain*, Great Britain, 1940, Fontana Books, 1980. By the same author see also "The Humanitarian Theory of Punishment," in *Res Judicatae*, 6, 1953; and in Sir Leon Radzinowicz – Marvin E. Wolfgang (eds.), *Crime and Justice*, vol. 2, New York, Basic Books, 1971. Ulf Lindblom, "Smärtbehandling under omprövning," in *Nordisk Medisin*, 95, 1980, p. 75.

regulated in terms of both duration and severity. This applies to grieving the loss of loved ones. Likewise, it is acknowledged that punishment is detrimental; yet the examination of the pain, suffering, and anguish it inflicts is often overlooked. It represents the concealed aspect of punishment; however it is the most crucial and authentic dimension for the one enduring it. Legal texts refer to "punishment," yet it would provoke considerable controversy if Criminal Codes were to designate them as "laws of pain," or if we were to assert that Professors of Criminal Law should elucidate "the Law of Pain." Judges would likely disapprove of being assigned the role of "sentencing to pain," and correctional facilities would prefer not to be perceived as "places for inflicting pain." Framing the subject in this manner would be deemed "politically incorrect." Pain and suffering have been omitted from textbooks, yet they persist in the experiences of the penalized, the fearful, the ashamed, and the wretched. It is assumed that anyone who endures punishment experiences suffering. Should it be revealed that they derive pleasure from it, the approach would necessitate modification.

Discomfort is inherently associated with the concept of therapy. Treatment also induces pain, similar to its impact on cures and rehabilitations following an accident or illness. However, the latter does not aim at pain as its ultimate objective; instead, it endeavors to discover a remedy. Prisons are populated with individuals requiring therapy, care, and rehabilitation – those experiencing psychological distress and lacking education, who are effectively "warehoused" while awaiting appropriate intervention. Prisons should not solely function as venues for punishment and infliction of pain; rather, they should primarily serve as institutions that mitigate suffering, addressing both the distress produced by the offense for which the inmate was penalized and the anguish resulting from the punishment itself.

It is futile to assert that we, those in positions of power, are not responsible for initiating the conflict, so alleviating our moral culpability. We cannot only assert that the perpetrator initiated the actions that activated the coercive State machinery. That is certainly accurate; yet, what prompted these individuals to violate the law? Is it plausible that society is entirely unrelated to social ostracism, substance use, and the various factors that contribute to criminal behavior? *We detach ourselves from the anguish of others and, from a secure distance, we respond with additional sorrow.*[12]

---

12 Nils Christie, *Limits to Pain*, Oxford, Martin Robertson, 1982. We use the Spanish translation by Mariluz Caso, *Los límites del dolor*, Mexico, Fondo de Cultura Económica, 1984, pp. 7–124.

1.3 Guilt as a Manifestation of Depression: Antipsychiatry

A school of antipsychiatry, originating in England with figures such as Cooper, Laing, and Esterson, advocates for the rehabilitation of the mentally ill. In this perspective, the individual is not perceived as an aberration to be altered through methods akin to "brainwashing," whether for personal benefit or in response to societal expectations. Conversely, he is perceived as an innocent victim of a frequently abusive society, a pathological system rife with self-contradictions that, in some manner, "induces madness as a form of defense." This perspective regards feelings of guilt as symptomatic of depression and advocates for assisting the individual in rediscovering his authentic self rather than merely readapting him to an environment he neither comprehends nor is comprehended by.[13]

1.4 Emotions and Psychological Mechanisms Driving Punishment

1.4.1 Psychological Ambivalence regarding the Punishment of Others: The Contributions of Norbert Elias and Petrus Cornelis Spierenburg

In Elias' work, civilization denotes a certain evolution in human behavior across time, representing a transformative process that has influenced Western cultural practices and emotional experiences from the Middle Ages to the present day. The most compelling elements of Elias' work, pertinent to our inquiry, are primarily his psychological arguments rather than his sociological ones, which innovatively endeavor to integrate historical analysis with Freud's theory of the psyche. Elias posits that individuals internalize their fears, anxieties, and the constraints imposed by their parents and societal environment to cultivate a super-ego that, with varying degrees of effectiveness, suppresses instinctual expression, aligning it with cultural expectations. This induces alterations in the individual's psychological structure, particularly in the cultivation of self-regulation and inhibitory processes, such as guilt, fear, or sensitivity.

A crucial aspect of punishment, as emphasized by Elias in his work, is the management of the privatization of unsettling and troublesome occurrences. Some elements of daily life are obscured from public awareness and exist

---

13 Norberto Álvarez González, *La tendencia a sufrir el castigo: una contribución a la teoría de la culpa,* Alcalá, Universidad de Alcalá de Henares, Servicio de Publicaciones, 1996. Ignacio Muñagorri Laguía, *Sanción penal y política criminal. Confrontación con la nueva defensa social,* Foreword by Antonio Beristain, Madrid, Reus, Biblioteca Jurídica de Autores Españoles y Extranjeros, 1977, pp. 155–156.

beyond the social realm, restricted to the domain of the personal. Sex, violence, bodily functions, disease, suffering, and death progressively transform into sources of embarrassment and are increasingly relegated to the private sphere, specifically within the domestic confines of the nuclear family, as well as in beds, prison cells, and hospitals. Although Elias does not articulate it explicitly, this societal inclination to conceal the humiliating aspects is merely a corollary to the psychological mechanism of repressing instinctual wants, which are relegated to the unconscious for private and guilt-ridden enjoyment in dreams and fantasies.

In his book *The Spectacle of Suffering*, Spierenburg presents a particular argument of Elias regarding the decline of public executions as societal sensibility evolved over time.[14] The assertion is that, during the 16th and 17th centuries, when public safety was limited, individuals typically carried weapons, and remnants of feudal codes of honor persisted; violence was not regarded as abhorrent, although there were diverse emotions of pity, sympathy, anger, and disgust toward specific victims facing execution. Beginning in the 17th century, attitudes toward violence gradually evolved over several centuries. Spierenburg posits that when aversion to violence among the ruling classes intensified, these elites gradually privatized punishment and ceased to display pain. By the onset of the 19th century, numerous historical horrors had ceased to exist.

The most evident illustration of this civilizational process within the criminal justice system is the expansion of empathy, or intersubjective identification, with the victim. Deviant individuals and offenders are extricated from the realm of normative social existence; they are sent off-stage. Likewise, the evolution of civilization is reflected in the humanization of punitive measures. These are no longer as severe and do not involve physical or corporal penalties; instead, they entail restriction of liberty or the withdrawal of financial resources.[15]

During the process of civilization, both individually and socially, humans tend to repress or sublimate their instincts, particularly their aggressive impulses. Nonetheless, this process of repression does not entail the complete eradication of such inclinations, as evidenced by the Holocaust and the wars of the 20th century. These instincts are displaced from the realm of awareness and confined to the unconscious. Freud and Elias assert that repressed impulses and unconscious drives persist and manifest, either through dreams

14 Petrus Cornelis Spierenburg, *The Spectacle of Suffering: Executions and the Evolution of Repression*, Cambridge, Cambridge University Press, 1984.

15 David Garland, *Punishment and Modern Society. A Study in Social Theory*, Chicago, The University of Chicago Press, 1990, pp. 193–238.

and fantasies or through pathological and aggressive behavior. Civilization engenders a conflict within the person between primal instincts and the constraints of the super-ego, a conflict with profound psychological and societal implications. Consequently, while a societal rejection of what some consider instinctual pleasures (such as aggressiveness or sadism) is enforced, it constitutes merely a partial renunciation; the unconscious desire persists. Elias characterizes the repression of these tendencies as a cause of distress. Civilization renders us all hypocritical, with several attitudes stemming from unconscious conflicts rather than rational considerations. A manifestation of civilization's emotional repression is the angry tone often seen in moral admonitions. This is abundantly demonstrated, for example, in the adult's reaction to a child who has acted inappropriately, which parallels the attitude of the "good citizen" when confronted with a criminal.

The menace presented by the criminal – and the anxiety and animosity he incites – possesses a significantly deeper unconscious dimension than the actual danger to safety that the crime signifies. The "fear of crime" sometimes stems from irrational and occasionally disproportionate causes, including phobias. Ironically, a paradox emerges in which we abhor crime yet derive pleasure from the media's accounts of the most atrocious and brutal occurrences. These frequently elicit interest and dread in the general populace, which are only distorted feelings. The disparity in the resentful response and animosity against the offender only illustrates the psychological ambiguity over the punishment of others. We are gratified that crime is penalized, since it compensates for the energy and effort we expend in abstaining from unlawful behavior. Consequently, the punishment of others frequently elicits a sense of joy and covert pleasure in persons who have suppressed and repressed their own desires. Freud posits that this engenders a sense of guilt in the person, as their instincts conflict with societal norms. This sensation of guilt constitutes a variant of sadomasochism, arising from the conflict between the super-ego and the ego. In 1915, Freud posited that certain criminals are shaped by their feelings of guilt, thereby integrating psychoanalysis into the realm of criminality. He was alluding to individuals who perceive a necessity for punishment due to the internal struggle between their unconscious wants and an excessively stringent super-ego. The inclination of civilized cultures to incarcerate offenders, distancing them from our view and recollection, may be seen as an attempt to erase the psychological ambivalence we experience toward the punishment of others.[16]

---

16 David Garland, *Punishment and Modern Society…*, *op. cit.*, pp. 238–241. Cf. on the subject, also by David Garland, "Durkheim's Theory of Punishment: A Critique," in *id.* and Peter

1.4.2 Émile Durkheim and Adam Smith: Resentment

In his seminal work, *De la division du travail social* (1893), in "Deux lois de l'évolution pénale" (1902), and in numerous subsequent lectures compiled in *L'éducation morale* (1902–1903),[17] Émile Durkheim perceives punishment as a manifestation of society's moral framework and the mechanisms via which this framework perpetuates itself. Durkheim's perspective on punishment is more relevant to primitive civilizations than to modern ones. Numerous references he cites pertain to historical civilizations or small-scale communities – such as aborigines and the ancient Hebrews – and he addresses ceremonial rites with religious significance and context.

According to Durkheim, crimes constitute transgressions of a society's holy moral code, which is why they incur punishment. Criminal acts violate the fundamental rules of communal conscience, prompting a legal response.

Young (eds.), *The Power to Punish,* London, 1983. *Id., Punishment and Welfare: A History of Penal Strategies*, Aldershot, Gower, 1985. *Id.,* "The Criminal and his Science," in *British Journal of Criminology*, 25, 2, 1985, pp. 109–135. *Id.,* "The Punitive Mentality: its Socio-Historical Development and Decline," in *Contemporary Crises*, 10, 1986, pp. 305–320. *Id.,* "British Criminology Before 1935," in *British Journal of Criminology*, 28, 1988, pp. 131–147. *Id.,* "Criminological Knowledge and its Relation to Power: Foucault's Genealogy and Criminology Today," in *British Journal of Criminology*, 32, 4, 1992, pp. 403–422. *Id.,* "Penal Modernism and Postmodernism," in T. Blomberg – S. Cohen (eds.), *Punishment and Social Control*, New York, Aldine de Gruyter, 1995. *Id.,* "The Limits of the Sovereign State: Strategies of Crime Control in Contemporary Society," in *British Journal of Criminology*, 36, 4, 1996, pp. 445–471. *Id.,* "Governmentality and the Problem of Crime: Foucault, Criminology, Sociology," in *Theoretical Criminology*, 1, 2, 1997, pp. 173–214. *Id., The Culture of Control. Crime and Social Order in Contemporary Society*, Chicago, The University of Chicago Press, 2001. David Garland – Peter Young, *The Power to Punish: Contemporary Penalty and Social Analysis*, London, Heinemann Educational Books, Atlantic Highlands, N.J., Humanities Press, 1983.

17 Cf. Émile Durkheim (1858–1917), *De la division du travail social,* Paris, Alcan, 1893; Paris, Presses Universitaires de France, 5th ed., 1998. *Id., Les règles de la méthode sociologique*, Paris, Alcan, 1895; Paris, Presses Universitaires de France, 10th ed., 1999. *Id.,* "Deux lois de l'évolution pénale," in *L'Année Sociologique*, 4, 1902, pp. 65–95; also in *Émile Durkheim on Institutional Analysis*, ed., translation and introduction by Mark Traugott, Chicago, The University of Chicago Press, 1978, pp. 153–180 : "Two Laws of Penal Evolution"; reedited as Chapter 4, "The Evolution of Punishment," in Steven Lukes – Andrew Scull (eds.), *Durkheim and the Law,* Oxford, 1983. *Id., Les formes élémentaires de la vie religieuse* (*Le système totémique en Australie*), Paris, Alcan, 1912; Paris, Librairie Générale Française, 1991, foreword by Michel Maffesoli. *Id., L'éducation morale*, Paris, Alcan, 1924; translation into English, *Moral Education*, New York, 1973; translation into Spanish by M. L. Navarro, Buenos Aires, 1947. On this author, cf., Anthony Giddens, *Durkheim*, Hassocks, Sussex, 1978. London, Fontana, 1986. Gregorio Robles, "Émile Durkheim (1858–1917)," in *Juristas universales*, comp. by R. Domingo, Madrid, Marcial Pons, 2002.

What is the rationale for punishing crimes rather than pursuing other actions? Durkheim posits that the explanation resides in the violation of sentiments and emotions profoundly embedded in the majority of society's constituents. It affects their moral integrity. This assault elicits psychological responses, even among individuals not immediately impacted. It incites fury, wrath, indignation, and a fervent need for retribution. In contrast to abstract concepts, which we superficially embrace and tolerate conflicts, profound moral sentiments possess such significance and intensity that they allow for no dissent. According to Durkheim, passion constitutes the essence of penalties. This is seen in less developed communities that impose punishment solely for punitive reasons. In contemporary society, the spirit of vengeance is less apparent; nonetheless, it still persists. While it is constrained within specific boundaries and extreme violence is disapproved, irrational retribution persists in the essence of punishment.

Thus, Durkheim posits that the purpose of punishment, in both primitive and contemporary civilizations, is not a rational mechanism aimed at crime control; rather, it is an irrational force driven by passions and emotional responses that emerge when fundamental social sentiments are threatened. It constitutes a genuine act of retribution. Although most legalists regard punishment as involving only two parties, the controllers and the controlled, Durkheim emphasizes the significance of a third component, the observers, whose sense of indignation underpins the punitive process. Consequently, it may be asserted that, for him, punishment possesses a primarily psychological and emotional dimension, including a realm of social values and a surge of psychic energy. Punishment lacks a definite target; it is not instrumental in achieving an outcome. It is inherently a characteristic of existence, like to the sparks generated when one interacts with an electric current, a spontaneous response of the individuals comprising society, a moment that amplifies collective moral fervor, hence reinforcing these very sentiments.

The moral framework of society – and its cohesion – entirely depends on its ability to enforce punishment. Although he emphasizes the emotional, expressive, and non-utilitarian aspects of punishment, Durkheim ultimately ascribes an objective function to it. It serves to automatically reinforce solidarity, spontaneously reaffirming shared values and social relations of unity. Although punishment manifests as an emotional, unconsidered, automatic response, it does have a purpose. This position, however, is not typically associated with punishing the guilty or intimidating potential imitators. From this viewpoint, its efficacy is questionable and arguably subpar. Its actual function is dual in nature. It is simultaneously a personal emotion and a societal reinforcement of morals. Both elements operate reciprocally to foster social cohesion in both primitive and contemporary communities. In addition to punishment, other variables contributing to social cohesion are involved. They encompass religious rituals, familial structures, educational systems, and, in contemporary communities, the allocation of labor.[18]

Durkheim identifies two principles governing the evolution of punishment: one quantitative and the other qualitative. Over time, forms of punishment have evolved, primarily due to a decrease in the severity of penalties and a transition from capital or corporal punishment to incarceration. Primitive societies employed draconian punishments due to their stringent collective conscience and inflexible moral standards. These manifested as transcendental religious laws, sanctioned by the deities. Crimes were regarded as offenses against the deities, rather than, as subsequently perceived, against humanity itself. Consequently, they were subjected to the harshest form of punishment. The transgression of one individual against another cannot be adorned with the same severity as that perpetrated by one individual against God. Additional exacerbating variables for punishment include the emergence of absolutist political regimes, which are inclined to employ exemplary punishments. Durkheim illustrates that the zenith of absolute monarchies aligns with an era of significant repression. In the context of criminal punishment, absolutism functions analogously to the desire for retribution.

In addition to the aforementioned, Durkheim addresses the intensity or magnitude of punishment, emphasizing the quality of punishment and the abandonment of techniques such as execution with torture or mutilation in favor of imprisonment. This aligns with his perspective on the appropriate moral framework for contemporary schooling. It must be secular, rational, and the educational institution should cultivate a new communal consciousness among children. It must be devoid of mysticism and uncritical faith, while remaining receptive to reasonable discourse. With the emergence of a new consciousness, punishment has shifted from a mechanism of retribution to a means of engaging with an audience. The audience must perceive the significance and impact of punishment; hence, punishment must align with the sensibilities of that audience, which is essentially society.

Specific elements behind Durkheim's concept may be subjected to critical analysis. For instance, the value of discussing a collective conscience is questionable since the present world prominently displays intersocietal conflicts related to group, class, ethnicity, gender, religion, and ideology. While it is accurate that a consensus can be achieved, a fundamental level of societal agreement is necessary. It may be more appropriate to discuss the governing

---

18 David Garland, *Punishment and Modern Society…, op. cit.*, pp. 23–35.

ideology instead of the collective conscience, as, according to Marxists, we are addressing the ethics of the dominant class, the ruling class that maintains hegemony over others. The validity of criminal laws that prescribe punishment as a manifestation of collective conscience is debatable, particularly because such laws frequently contradict rather than align with societal sensitivities. The link is reciprocal: social sentiments not only impact legislative decisions, but existing laws also shape those sentiments. The concept of a sacred social order may be more effectively replaced by what Max Weber termed "charisma."

It is essential to address the societal imperative for retribution. Durkheim considers it primarily a matter of governance rather than management. The distinction between both conceptions is that the latter implies efficiency, the achievement of objectives at any cost, and is characterized by the predominance of the administrative. Governance, however, transcends mere administration; it pertains more to the realm of political decisions rather than administrative functions. It is not confined to mere efficacy. It encompasses a somewhat broader and more intricate application: the maintenance of the entire social order. Governance pertains to the objectives established and the methods employed to achieve them.

In this context, punishment is employed solely as a last resort when compliance cannot be achieved through alternative means. In contexts with weak authority, the focus should be on cultivating respect for that authority rather than imposing punishment, as punishment fails to establish authority, regardless of its severity; the moral order can only be reinforced where authority is already present. Punishment is less effective when authority is either feeble or absent. Increased authority diminishes the necessity for punishment and displays of power. This avoids the Nietzschean extreme of seeing a society so robust that it can forgo the punishment of criminals.[19]

Similar to Durkheim, Adam Smith references the indignation, repulsion, and desire for retribution that the criminal act engenders in the hearts of other members of society as justifications for punishment. He sharpens his description by pinpointing resentment as the sole sentiment fundamental to punishing action.[20]

Smith posits that resentment is the pleasurable sense experienced by the impartial viewer upon witnessing the agony endured by the perpetrator of

---

19 David Garland, *Punishment and Modern Society…, op. cit.*, pp. 47–61.

20 *Ibid.*, pp. 62 and 63. Adam Smith, *The Theory of Moral Sentiments* (1759), Oxford, 1976; Svend Ranulf (1894–1953), *Moral Indignation and Middle-Class Psychology. A Sociological Study*, Copenhaguen, Levin & Munksgaard, 1938.

a wrongful act. Resentment can be differentiated from sentiments such as hatred or aversion, as it represents a more active emotion than the latter. It is driven by the belief that action must be taken to rectify the wrong. Smith, in conjunction with Durkheim, attributes a moral significance to resentment. This distinguishes it from mere retribution or personal hostility. Smith refutes the notion that resentment could be the most malevolent of emotions, if it remains commensurate with the victim's suffering. Any punishment surpassing this moderate pursuit of justice would be unacceptable. According to Smith, while most of society may lack the necessary moderation, in civilized societies, individuals responsible for administering sanctions can effectively calibrate resentment.

1.4.3 Friedrich Wilhelm Nietzsche, George Herbert Mead, and Sigmund Freud: The Role of Psychoanalysis

Friedrich Wilhelm Nietzsche presents a somber analysis of the emotions that drive punishment.[21] For him, instead of a moral obligation to punish, there is a distinct enjoyment in administering punishment. Inflicting punishment on others serves to gratify the sadistic and cruel impulses that arise from the sense of power over others in the human psyche. Inflicting suffering on others results in gratification. It is an antiquated human impulse. According to Nietzsche, the most despicable emotions are prevalent among the lower classes. The enjoyment is heightened when the sensation of power is infrequently encountered. In the context of punishment, the less powerful experience an unusual sense of euphoria derived from subordinating another individual. Such is Nietzsche's conviction. Although modern civilizations assign punishment to the state, the populace indirectly partakes in the exercise of authority. Nietzsche asserts that these desires persist beneath the guise of hypocrisy – what Freud may refer to as the unconscious. Even now, the enjoyment of cruelty persists; for the most part, it has been suppressed and cloaked in an aura of delicacy. A critique of Nietzsche's thesis may contend that it is erroneous to possess a partial and unilateral perspective when identifying the emotions and feelings encapsulated in the punishing spirit during the administration of punishment. In this context, as in numerous other domains, it is necessary to address ambivalence, characterized by the coexistence of conflicting impulses and feelings.

21 Friedrich Wilhelm Nietzsche (1844–1900), "The Genealogy of Morals," in *The Birth of Tragedy and the Genealogy of Morals*, New York, 1956; original edition in German, 1887. Jeffrey Minson, *The Genealogy of Morals: Nietzsche, Foucault, Donzelot and the Eccentricity of Ethics*, London, 1985.

George Herbert Mead examines the intricate psychological aspects of public reactions to criminal offenses.[22] Similar to Durkheim, Mead posits that animosity against criminals reinforces mutual solidarity and affection among law-abiding residents. In contrast to him, Mead posits that, fundamentally, we encounter the psychological forces of mutual antagonism and self-assertion.

This identical ambivalence underpins Freud's theory.[23] Psychoanalysis regards innate mechanisms, inhibition, repression, and similar concepts as aligned with Mead's perspective.[24] From this perspective, punishment serves as recompense for the limitations imposed on one's own sadism. Freud says that this phenomenon is evident in the public's morbidity and eagerness to consume news of criminal activities. For him, this is mere pleasure for suppressed aggressions and repressed sexual impulses that persist within the civilized individual.[25] Crime and punishment evoke a spectrum of conflicting emotions: interest, profound curiosity, and the enjoyment derived from guilt. Sublimated desires and certain cultivated attitudes, such as philanthropy or humanitarian endeavors associated with prison facilities, manifest sympathy, love, and compassion, fostering kindness, forgiveness, and generosity. In summary, there exists a complicated amalgamation of sensations and emotions rather than a singular, unified desire.

These sentiments undoubtedly exist. The media's daily coverage of crime and punishment, the influence of words such as "law and order" on voters, and the throngs of spectators at trials all vividly express these feelings. These feelings are softened and concealed by culture; for example, the desire for retribution is currently disapproved of as a driving force behind the administration of punishment. Courtesy, political correctness, and a sense of shame compel these "unhealthy" feelings to conceal themselves beneath a facade of greater "acceptability." Nonetheless, they persist.[26]

---

22 George Herbert Mead (1863–1931), "The Psychology of Punitive Justice," in *American Journal of Sociology*, 23, 1918, pp. 577–602.

23 Sigmund Freud (1856–1939), *Civilization and Its Discontents*; first edited in London, 1930; New York, 1962. *Id.*, "Criminality from a Sense of Guilt," in "Some Character-Types Met with in Psycho-Analytical Work," in *id.*, *Collected Papers*, IV, ed. by J. Riviere, New York, 1959; first edited in *Imago*, 4, 1915–1916.

24 Guglielmo Gulotta, *Psicoanalisi e responsabilità penale*, Milan, Giuffrè, 1972. John Gunn – Anthony Maden – Mark Swinton, *Mentally Disordered Prisoners*, London, Institute of Psychiatry, 1991. Jäger, "Strafrecht und psychoanalitische Theorie," in *Fest. Henkel*, 1974, pp. 125 ff.

25 See Philip Rieff (1922–2006), *The Triumph of the Therapeutic: Uses of Faith after Freud*, Chicago, University of Chicago Press, 1966.

26 David Garland, *Punishment and Modern Society…*, *op. cit.*, pp. 65–66.

1.5 The Influence of Punitive Rituals as Architects and Manipulators of Emotions

The rituals of penal justice – the trial, the sentencing, and the execution of the penalty – constitute the exterior manifestations that comprise the essence of punishment. Punishment rituals not only convey emotion but also facilitate the expression of these emotions, instructing the public on appropriate feelings and behaviors. They influence emotions and serve as a form of sentimental education, cultivating a specific attitude and sensibility. In certain instances, we may refer to displays and high drama that symbolically reinforce order and authority. They facilitate the association of punishment with sensations of breathlessness, insecurity, or the development of disorders that frequently culminate in criminal behavior. Citizens experience a form of catharsis as direct or indirect witnesses of punitive ceremonies. The rituals serve as symbolic forms that educate and reinforce the audience's public and private sensitivities, providing a moral framework, behavioral patterns to emulate, and a shared language. The court ceremonies affirm the public's dual sentiments toward the twins: reverence for the law and animosity toward the perpetrator. The government and the state appear to position themselves as champions in the legal conflict between criminality and public order. This struggle, this public spectacle, is evident in instances where the death sentence is enacted, where the condemned is manipulated akin to a gladiator in the Roman arena or a bull in the ring. The significance of execution rites is emphasized in the works of Spierenburg for Amsterdam, Foucault for France, Masur for the United States, and Zeman for Puritan Massachusetts.

Michel Foucault contends that contemporary punishment rituals are characterized more by management than by governance. They constitute a system of *surveillance* rather than a spectacle, pertaining more to private regimes of sentence execution than to public rituals. David Garland deems this perspective potentially excessive, asserting that public rituals remain significant now, as evidenced by observing American presidential elections or a coronation in Great Britain. For Garland, what is presently seen as a private issue would pertain to the enforcement of sentencing. The public aspect of punitive rituals is most evident in the overtly public form of the sentencing announcement. This circumstance differs from earlier periods when public executions were most prominent in the punitive process. In contemporary society, the courtroom serves as a public arena for discourse, capturing the audience's focus, whilst the subsequent imposition of punishment has become a mere technical procedure. It has increasingly transformed into a question of management rather than governance. This is particularly evident in the context of jury trials, since it is specifically the public that determines the verdict.[27]

1.6 The Experiment Conducted by Stanley Milgram

Stanley Milgram clearly demonstrated that the deliberate infliction of misery became increasingly easy as the victim or subject of the pain was distanced further away.[28] How often have we witnessed actions where we could have mitigated harm through humanitarian assistance or protest, yet remained silent and complied with the system, believing the situation was too distant, that our individual efforts were futile against humanity's evils, or that these issues would not impact us personally? Similarly, during the administration of punishment, individuals need not feel personally accountable; they are merely agents within a hierarchical structure that commences with the legislator who formulates the criminal law, followed by the judge who enforces it, the police who apprehend the offender, and the prison administration that implements the prescribed punishment. Nonetheless, there are instances when the individual should endeavor to halt the machine, disrupting the chain administering punishment, a chain that cannot be sustained if its links are not cohesively connected.

Stanley Milgram demonstrated this using a straightforward experiment. Various participants were summoned to a sophisticated laboratory at Yale to create a simulation examining the impact of punishment anxiety on individuals' test responses, whether correct or incorrect. Each time the subject erred, another individual was required to administer pain with an electric shock, the severity of which ranged from minimal to maximal.[29] The true objective of the experiment was to determine the extent to which the volunteers would give a final, high-intensity electrical shock, inflicting severe pain, solely based on the directive of the "experimenter" to comply for the sake of scientific advancement.[30] Milgram sought to elucidate – rather than justify – the barbarous

27 Michel Foucault (1926–1984), *Surveiller et punir: naissance de la prison*, Paris, Gallimard, 1975; translation into English by Alan Sheridan, *Discipline and Punish: The Birth of the Prison*, New York, Vintage Books, 1979; translation into Spanish, *Vigilar y castigar*, Mexico, Siglo XXI, 1966. *Id.*, "La pussière et le nuage," in *L'impossible prison*, Paris, Du Seuil, 1980. David Garland, *Punishment and Modern Society…*, *op. cit.*, pp. 67–74.

28 Stanley Milgram (1933–1984), "Some Conditions of Obedience and Disobedience to Authority," in *Human Relations*, 18, 1965, pp. 57–75.

29 Cf. on pain, Jonathan Millar, *The Uses of Pain*, introduction by Peter Cadogan, London, South Place Ethical Society, 1973.

30 Stanley Milgram, *Obedience to Authority*, New York, Harper and Row, 1974. José Félix Tezanos, "Los límites de la obediencia. Consideraciones sobre el experimento de Stanley

occurrences that happened in Nazi death camps during World War II through his experiment. How can individuals collectively inflict suffering on innocent beings solely due to directives?

Erich Fromm's contributions to the topic are significant. Fromm asserts that from early life, institutions such as schools, families, the military, and workplaces have instilled the notion that compliance is virtuous while disobedience is a vice.[31] We acquiesce because it is frequently simpler to conform rather than oppose the prevailing consensus, which jeopardizes our group support. This is Fromm's "The Fear of Freedom." In this psychoanalysis, freedom is manifested in the demise of the authoritarian conscience, epitomized by paternal directives and imperatives – the super-ego – and its replacement by the humanitarian conscience – our intrinsic moral voice. Consequently, we ought to adopt the following principles: *Sapere aude* (dare to know) and *omnibus est dubitandum* (everything is subject to doubt). Doubt should not be the objective or aspiration. It serves as a mechanism to liberate us from biases and entrenched "truths." It is the critical mindset that interrogates established wisdom, which frequently requires scrutiny and enhancement. It is the methodological skepticism referenced by Descartes.

This is evidently relevant to the topic of punishment, where its necessity and societal utility are frequently assumed, and, more concerning, where the existing methods of administering punishment are regarded as optimal. We must reflect, with empathy and solidarity toward people who endure suffering. To what extent is punishment inevitable, and to what degree is society, collectively, culpable for permitting subhuman living conditions that render crime unavoidable, making the rarity of its occurrence noteworthy?

Milgram," in *Sistema*, 12, 1976, pp. 99–114. María José Falcón y Tella, *La desobediencia civil*, Foreword by Fernando Garrido Falla, Madrid, Marcial Pons, 2000, pp. 29–34. There is a translation into English by Peter Muckley, *Civil Disobedience*, foreword by Martti Koskenniemi, Boston-Leiden, Martinus Nijhoff, 2004.

31 Erich Fromm (1900–1980), *On Disobedience and Other Essays*, London, Routledge & Kegan Paul, 1984, pp. 3–8.

2 Legal Perspective

2.1 Penalties

2.1.1 Free Will

An elaborate and secular dispute exists on whether human actions stem from free will or, conversely, are merely a continuation of a causal chain of events beyond individual choice. One of these possibilities affects the reasoning of sanctions. Penalties and retributive philosophy are founded on the concepts of desert and justice, as well as the notion of human freedom. A man should justly be held accountable for his crimes if he is at liberty when he does them and chooses to misuse that freedom. Where there is freedom, there exists responsibility and accountability. Conversely, if an individual has not had the opportunity to make a choice, responsibility for any actions is not attributed to that person; thus, they are not culpable for those actions. This applies to actions executed under duress or force majeure. An unlawful conduct is criminal only if executed with volition. Retributive theories of punishment assert that the origin of crime is in the freedom that the criminal misuses, rather than in the individual themselves. Consequently, the sentence should focus more on the offense itself rather than on the culpable individual, as it reflects the person's exercise of free choice.

2.1.2 Guilt as a Moral Appraisal

Assessing an individual as morally accountable for an action entails evaluating the moral significance of that action, particularly when it involves an offense or an infringement upon the rights of others, which may manifest as moral condemnation. When a moral condemnation is issued, the personal accountability of the individual is asserted for the execution of that particular act. The individual is culpable for the consciously executed act. He may only be legally exonerated due to circumstances that mitigate his culpability, such as asserting it was a mistake, executed in ignorance, under duress, and similar factors.

Guilt serves as both the foundation and the constraint of punishment.[32] One may alone penalize the culpable individual and must do so commensu-

32 Antonio Quintano Ripollés (1905–1967), "Culpabilidad y retribución como premisas de la justicia penal," in *Homenaje al profesor Luis Legaz y Lacambra. Estudios Jurídico-Sociales, Universidad de Santiago de Compostela,* 1950, pp. 1027 ff. Cf. *Id.*, "La evolución del Derecho penal moderno ('contra corriente')," in Anuario *de Derecho Penal y Ciencias Penales,* 1957.

rate with the degree of their culpability and to the extent of that culpability.[33] The role of the guilt principle as the foundation and "maximum" threshold for penalties is unequivocal. The contentious issue emerges regarding the extent to which the penalty may be mitigated below the level of culpability, considering the objectives of special prevention. Consequently, the inquiry emerges regarding the degree to which institutions such as penal substitutes, overriding reasons, amnesty, reprieve, or the forgiveness of the offending individual aligns with the idea of guilt.[34]

The contemporary notion of guilt has faced several significant criticisms. The concept of guilt is currently in a condition of crisis, to the extent that its future appears to be one of eventual obsolescence, whether in the near or distant future. The discourse surrounding determinism and indeterminism assumes significant relevance here. If we deny free will, the concept of guilt will be called into question. The abstract concept of free will cannot be assumed for an individual inside a specific social context. Consequently, a deficiency of freedom prevails. It is necessary to examine the degree to which the individual perpetrator of a crime possesses the autonomy to act differently than they really did. That is, in accordance with his capabilities and personal circumstances, as well as the external environment and his interior condition.

The relative aspect of guilt, concerning value judgments and assessments of social character, also emerges. According to Francisco Muñoz Conde:

> Guilt does not exist as an isolated issue for the individual; rather, it manifests in relation to others. Guilt invariably pertains to human cooperation... Coexistence necessitates communication among societal members, manifesting in mutual behavioral expectations, thereby establishing a system of anticipations. Penalty is invoked when anticipated behaviors are thwarted; thus, it also constitutes a process of interrelations inherent in cohabitation.[35]

33 José Antonio Choclán Montalvo, *Individualización judicial de la pena: Función de la culpabilidad y la prevención en la determinación de la sanción penal*, Foreword by Siro García, Madrid, COLEX, 1997, p. 59.

34 *Ibid.*, p. 65.

35 Francisco Muñoz Conde, "El principio de culpabilidad," in *III Jornadas de Profesores de Derecho Penal*, Santiago de Compostela, 1975, p. 4. Cf. also Herbert Morris (1928-2022) (ed.), *Freedom and Responsibility*, Stanford, Stanford University Press, 1961. *Id.*, "Persons and Punishment," in *The Monist*, 52, 1968, pp. 475–501; reprint in *On Guilt and Innocence…, op. cit.*, pp. 39–58. *Id.*, "Guilt and Punishment," in *Personalist*, 52, 1971, pp. 305–321. *Id.*, *On Guilt and Innocence: Essays in Legal Philosophy and Moral Psychology*, Berkeley, University of California Press, 1976. *Id.*, "A Paternalistic Theory of Punishment," in *American Philosophical Quarterly*, 18, 4, 1981, pp. 263–271.

Consequently, guilt serves a predominantly negative role, assessing whether specific factors – such as mental illness or coercion – exempt individuals from personal accountability, as informed by disciplines such as Psychology and Psychoanalysis. Consequently, it might be asserted that while free will exists in theory, it is unfeasible to demonstrate whether an individual in a particular context has freely perpetrated a specific crime. The empirical reality of guilt, as a concept, is an unprovable presupposition. Rather than grounding penalties on culpability, they should be established on necessity from a legal-social perspective, ensuring proportionality between the severity of the offense and the corresponding punishment. Consequently, penalties may be an unfortunate necessity, helpful in fostering community coexistence and mitigating criminal behavior, to the extent feasible.[36]

2.1.3 Imputability and Ethical Accountability

The concept of penalty, as articulated by the Spanish Classical School, pertains to the metaphysical essence of sanction, which arises from equally metaphysical assumptions: an illusory conception of humanity (the criminal as an individual endowed with total freedom), of conduct (crime as an expression of Free Will), and of the nature and purpose of Criminal Law (the legal framework as an embodiment of rational order, essential for the attainment of absolute justice).[37] All are theoretical approaches, oblivious to reality: Human beings are accountable due to their freedom; thus, their actions can be attributed to them, rendering them ethically responsible.

2.2 Deterrents

2.2.1 Determinism

Determinist theory posits that humans lack the autonomy to act freely and, hence, do not merit punishment. They should not face penalties; rather, they should be subjected to deterrents.

A radical kind of determinism might be argued in which individuals are entirely governed in their actions by external causes, rendering them devoid of freedom. However, not all forms of determinism extend to such extremes. Moderate theories assert that human actions are, to a limited degree, determined. This represents a feeble iteration of deterministic theory that recon-

36 José Antonio Choclán Montalvo, *Individualización judicial de la pena..., op. cit.*, pp. 60–61.

37 Ignacio Muñagorri Laguia, *Sanción penal y política criminal..., op. cit.*, pp 58 ff.

ciles natural causality with freedom. Human actions are determined, although among the determinants are human freedom and volition. Freedom and causality are not incompatible. Compulsion unequivocally negates the possibility of freedom and stands in opposition to it. This exemplifies the distinction between the common thief and the genuine kleptomaniac, who, regardless of intent, is unable to cease stealing. Freedom entails the capacity to deviate from one's inherent nature and, in accordance with current aspirations, to perform deliberate rather than instinctual actions.

In contrast to strong, extreme, or absolute determinism – which asserts a complete lack of causality and is therefore difficult to justify – we encounter the moderate, relative, or weak variant of that concept, set against the context of human freedom. In specific instances, it acknowledges the potential for behaviors influenced by motives external to the agent's will. We believe that only the eclectic, intermediate, or moderate variants may possess scientific backing. They represent the sole defensible forms of determinism.

What does it signify to assert that an activity is determined and not autonomous? Stating that something is the cause of an effect X means, unequivocally, that it is a sufficient element for producing that result. In this context, we can assert that, contingent upon the presence of a cause or a sequence of causes, a specific effect must inevitably follow. To assert that all actions are causally determined – strong determinism – would imply that every choice, decision, and human action is an inevitable result of a prior cause. Consequently, it is asserted that certain mental states result from mental causes, which, according to the most extreme thinkers, may even be physical causes. This occurs to such a degree that altering the cause or physical stimulation also modifies the behavior. Recent advancements in psychiatry and neurology have demonstrated that specific chemical or electrical modifications can influence emotions, mitigate anger, fear, or obsession, and induce well-being, relaxation, enjoyment, or satisfaction. This can be accomplished through pharmacological agents or neurological interventions. This poses a challenge to conventional notions of responsibility and agency, particularly if we infer from these trials that all mental diseases stem from a prior cause, typically a physical one. Nonetheless, we can also harmonize freedom and determinism as not entirely irreconcilable realms. Although our actions and choices exhibit an element of causation, we yet retain a degree of freedom in both. In weaker formulations, determinism and causality are congruent.

To have a clearer understanding, we must revisit the definition of the term "freedom" and its associated concepts. Proponents of the conciliatory theory assert that free signifies unrestrained rather than obligatory. A deliberate decision is not invariably a needed decision. The possibility that my decision was influenced by a reason does not imply that I did not wish to make that decision. Historically, a man was considered free if external forces did not impede his desires. The quintessential illustration of deprivation of freedom was incarceration. Consequently, freedom signified the antithesis of coercion. An individual is considered free if he is not coerced by a bigger force that leaves him without options or the capacity for choice, a force that necessitates actions contrary to his desires. For example, he is not free if he is incarcerated, restrained, or coerced by a firearm, compelling him to act against his will. Conversely, he is free if he determines his actions without external or internal coercion, and if such decisions align with his inherent nature and disposition. The assertion that a decision is made freely entails both an explicit and an implicit component. It is clear that he is not subject to coercion. The implication is that his decision was not a causally requisite outcome of any factor.

Another argument exists, pertaining to the aforementioned, that renders freedom and determinism compatible. This argument posits that the essential criterion for determining the freedom of an action is whether we might have acted differently had we chosen to do so. In this regard, there is no justification for claiming that free actions are feasible if we adhere to determinism. Similarly, if we equate determinism with "mechanicism," it implies a form of determinism that denies freedom, asserting that actions are physically determined in an automated or mechanical manner, leaving no room for liberty. This, however, cannot be true. Scientists may eventually discover physical and mechanical solutions for all physical inquiries; nevertheless, not all inquiries are of a physical nature. Just as chess is regulated by its rules, which dictate the permissible movements of each piece, yet each player may execute varied moves based on courage, intellect, or folly, human actions can also be free and accountable to the individual, despite occurring within specific causal constraints. The same applies if there exist any regulations governing prose composition, grammar, or orthography. They would not inhibit the individual author from cultivating his own style.

The distinction between movement and action is similarly applicable: one is mechanical, while the other is autonomous and deliberate. It is erroneous to regard physical or psychological factors of bodily movement as determinants of actions. Consequently, while the physical and causal rationale for the movement of limbs is informative, human beings, as entities endowed with intellect and volition, may also move their extremities simply because they desire to. The causal explanation for raising a hand involves an impulse originating from the brain that activates that specific part of the body in response to a stimulus. Nonetheless, a mechanical explanation for the hand's "movement" often fails to elucidate the underlying intent behind the act of raising the hand. This may have been an attempt to gain attention, resolve uncertainty, and articulate a compelling question, among other motives. No aspect of humanity inherently arises from motions that are solely physiologically or biologically induced. Intelligence, volition, and autonomy are significantly related to humanity. Consequently, we can restrain instinctive responses such as hatred, humiliation, or resentment toward, or forgiveness for, an individual's malevolent behavior, particularly when that individual cannot be held accountable for their actions. Our response is causally unexplainable. Causal explanation is inadequate when addressing the authentic human and spiritual elements involved in action.

This section elucidates the potential presence of "judgments and opinions." If only absolute truth existed – unambiguously black or white, entirely true – it would be illogical for individuals to express their own interpretations of that reality; thus, relative truth emerges, or "my truth." If strong determinism were real, the formation of judgments or the making of decisions would be impossible. Truth or falsehood is contingent upon the correspondence or lack thereof with the facts. What currently captivates our attention, however, is not the circumstances of reality. Rather, it is to emphasize that an individual can hold a belief and render a judgment, irrespective of their alignment with truth. To acknowledge the possibility, it is essential to concede a degree of autonomy. This buffer enables us to detach ourselves from the axiomatic validation of the veracity of such judgments.[38]

Additional objections may be raised against determinism in its robust version. One perspective posits that all scientific knowledge is inherently "approximative," as scientific theories invariably permit certain minor features to elude explanation. Consequently, a domain for indeterminism is perpetually available.

The deterministic theory suggests that the "future" can be perceived as readily as the past, despite the inherent differences between the two temporal states. The past is defined by that which follows it. The accurate definition is as follows: the past resembles an unalterable granite rock. In contrast, the future is markedly different. It is receptive to the exploration of possibilities and to the construction by active individuals. The future is neither located in any present moment nor entirely predetermined. The future, in contrast to the past, remains open, but the past is irrevocably closed. We can influence the future.

Thus, we must reiterate that recognizing the existence of determinism is one matter, however asserting that the universe is entirely determined is an

38 Ted Honderich, *Punishment. The Supposed…, op. cit.*, pp. 113–158.

entirely different proposition. This last concept lacks scientific validity. If it were different, what domain would then be available for human innovation and autonomy? We should not presume that absolute indeterminism is a reality. There are evidently predictable occurrences. Our cosmos is partially deterministic, partially probabilistic, and partially open; it is emergent. Radical determinism faces criticism from the fields of Sociology, Philosophy, and Psychology. Sociology critiques it for its inability to elucidate significant phenomena such as conflict, social change, and unintended consequences. Understanding such realities necessitates consideration of concepts such as choice, decision, anticipation, and freedom. The same applies to the psychological domain. In that context, the existence of compulsive behavior is acknowledged, but it is asserted that such behavior is uncommon (deemed unhealthy) and typically associated with psychological deficiencies. Often, individuals may not perceive their actions as compulsive but instead believe they possess a considerable degree of autonomy. Daily life presents several opportunities for selecting one response from a variety of options. We are rarely overtaken by intense rage and relinquish control over our actions.

Criminals can be categorized into three primary classifications: those who are not accountable, those who are entirely accountable, and those who are partially accountable. Decisions are deemed free when made by individuals possessing knowledge and free will, enabling them to discern between good and evil, and who are not compelled to act contrary to their desires. Nonetheless, the freedom of a decision does not suggest that it is devoid of external influence. This influence is not compelling. A criminal's accountability is mitigated when their capacity to resist temptation is compromised by several reasons, including immaturity, poverty, drunkenness, and circumstantial pressures, among others. Juvenile criminality is viewed with greater leniency due to the challenges youths face in regulating their emotions. For an impoverished individual in urgent need, it is more challenging to honor the property of others than it is for a wealthy individual who possesses abundance. Controlling one's emotions is more challenging when intoxicated than when sober. Resisting certain temptations is challenging. Nevertheless, the possibility of doing so remains. Acknowledging the freedom of criminals is to acknowledge their dignity as human beings. To deny an individual's capacity for rational choice is to negate their identity as a person.[39]

---

39 Maurice Cusson, *Pourquoi punir?*, Paris, Dalloz, Collection Criminologie et Droits de l'Homme, 1987, pp. 110–117.

2.2.2 Dangerousness as a Probabilistic Evaluation

Determinism, especially in its modest form, influences the articulation of moral condemnation and value assessments. Recognizing that human behavior is influenced by causes outside individual control renders only utilitarian judgments feasible. This is accurate regarding the threat posed by the individual to society, a concern that preoccupies the authorities responsible for enforcement. When considering the criminal's future, they must determine the likelihood of the individual reverting to a life of crime. This constitutes a probabilistic assessment.[40]

Given that reactive attitudes such as gratitude, resentment, forgiveness, esteem, and indignation are prevalent in social interactions, we can focus on resentment as society's predominant response to crime.[41] It can be argued that humans possess the ability to alter or even mitigate this reaction when confronted with an abnormal or morally incapacitated offender – an individual whose criminal behavior is influenced by factors beyond their control.

2.2.3 Social Responsibility or Necessity

The concept of social necessity governs the implementation of deterrents. Considering that the criminal is predominantly conditioned to engage in criminal behavior, crime is perceived as an inherent necessity in all cultures. It is the State's responsibility to address the social necessity of safeguarding itself against actions that violate the law.

3 Religious Perspective

3.1 The Offender as a Malefactor Requiring Rehabilitation

Numerous thinkers perceive retribution as a reprehensible drive of Biblical origin, unleashing society's archaic parricidal impulse: the Cain complex,

40 Jean E. Floud, "Dangerousness and Criminal Justice," in *The British Journal of Criminology*, 22, 3, pp. 213–228. Jean E. Floud – Warren Young, *Dangerousness and Criminal Justice*, London, Heinemann, 1981.

41 Peter Frederick Strawson, "Freedom and Resentment," in *Proceedings of the British Academy*, XLVIII, 1962, pp. 1–25.

which transforms the offender into a form of scapegoat (*Sündenbock*) suffering for both personal and external grievances.[42]

Eschatology presents this "eon," human time, as unfinished and approaching climax. It instructs us to permit wheat and the tares to flourish, as, until the conclusion of the world, transgressions and abuses of authority will persist, despite the fact that the perpetrators have already forfeited the struggle. The Biblical Original Sin has been eradicated; however its repercussions persist in individuals and societal frameworks. The four eschatological themes are Death, Judgment, Hell, and Glory.[43]

3.2 The Christian Faith: Balancing Retribution and Forgiveness – The Doctrines of the Bible

Retributionist desires, to some extent, resemble drives for vengeance, the reciprocation of malevolence for malevolence. Numerous authors denounce the surrender to mindless, vindictive tendencies as despicable and trivial. Certain theologians reach the same conclusion, particularly among Protestants. They assert that the throne of punitive justice is only reserved for God. This conclusion is derived from numerous sacred writings that emphasize justice as only the prerogative of the Lord, rather than that of humanity.

This belief is not novel. Chapter 22 of Exodus places in the mouth of God the commandment "Thou shalt not kill," and Chapter 13 of St. Matthew tells of, and comments upon, the parable of the wheat and the chaff: "Men do not rip them up… That is a task for the Father along with his angels." There are many other Biblical quotations which could be used to back up the contention that punishment is the negation of Christianity, whose essence is, on the contrary, forgiveness. Thus: "Judge not that ye be not judged"; "Do not allow yourself to be overcome by evil, rather strive to overcome evil with good"; "Love thine enemies"; "Do good unto those that hate thee, pray for those who persecute and revile thee"; "Do not return evil for evil, nor curse for curse, rather indeed offer blessings"; "Do not take justice into thine own hands, beloved, give first place to the wrath (of God)"; "For it is written, Vengeance is mine, I shall do justice – saith the Lord; Rather, if thine enemy is thirsty, let him drink, if he hungers, let him eat"; "Whosoever doeth thus, heaps up burning coals upon his own head." Here is the idea that evil is not wiped out by another evil (*malum*

42 Arthur Herbert Gray (1868-1956), "The Christian View of the Use of Punishment," in *Howard Journal*, 2, 1929, pp. 296 ff.

43 Antonio Beristain, *La pena-retribución y las actuales concepciones criminológicas, op. cit.*, pp. 130–132.

pasionis), quite the opposite, evil is only conquered by the good (*bonum actionis*). Below, we shall examine some Biblical texts,[44] which serve as basis for the right to punish, as also with the idea of forgiveness, and we shall distinguish between the teachings of the Old and the New Testaments.[45]

3.2.1 The Old Testament

Sacred Scripture, in multiple passages, acknowledges *ius puniendi*; for example, Chapter 22 of Exodus, which prescribes the death penalty for idolaters and for those who kill a thief during daylight hours, among others. Generally, contemporary exegesis of Biblical texts, with few exceptions, concurs that the Old Testament does not condemn retributive justice.[46]

3.2.2 The New Testament

Regarding the New Testament, exegetes engage in extensive dispute concerning the concept of punishment. Indeed, there are New Testament passages that exhibit punitive characteristics. Consider, for example, the well-known citation from Saint Paul to the Romans:

> For the Prince is a Minister of God for your good. But should ye work evil, tremble, because not in vain hath he unsheathed the sword, as the Minister of God, to exercise his justice, punishing he who worketh evil. (13. 4)

Christ's statement to Pilate is: "Thou wouldst not have power had it not been given thee from on high."

One distinguishing feature of the New Testament, in contrast to the Old, is its foundation on love rather than fear, portraying a God who has become Man

44 For an in-depth analysis of biblical texts interpreted considering law, see the interesting study by James Boyd White, *The Gospel as Conversation: Texts, Sermons, and Questions for Reflection: A Study Guide*, Wipf & Stock Publishers, 2013.

45 J. Arthur Hoyles, *Punishment and the Bible*, London, Epworth Press, 1986. N. Lillie, "Towards a Biblical Doctrine of Punishment," in *Scottish Journal of Theology*, 21, 1968, pp. 449–461. Jeffrie G. Murphy – Jean Hampton, *Forgiveness and Mercy*, New York, Cambridge, 1989.

46 Cf. Richard Adamiak, *Justice and History in the Old Testament: The Evolution of Divine Retribution in the Historiographies of the Wilderness Generation*, Cleveland, J. T. Zubal, 1982.

and a friend, rather than a wrathful Father, emphasizing forgiveness and mercy over vengeance and retribution.[47]

Indeed, the Evangel advocates for forgiveness, while acknowledging the requirement of human criminal justice:

> If thy brother offends thee, see him and make him see, alone together, the two of ye. If he hadeeths thee, thou hast won over thy brother. Should he heed thee not, call upon another or upon another two, so that the whole question be cleared up, supporting thyself with two or three witnesses. Should he not heed them, tell it to the community, and, if he heeds not the community, consider him as a pagan or as a tax collector. (Matthew, 18:15–17; Luke, 17:3)

Along the same lines of forgiveness and mercy, the Scriptures say: "Do not repay evil with evil, nor insult with insult, but answer with blessings, for this are ye called upon"; "Should thine enemy be hungry, give him to eat, should he thirst, give him to drink, thus shalt thou bring out the colours to his cheeks"; "Do not be overcome by evil, overcome evil with the force of good" (Peter I, 3. 9; Romans, 12, 20ff). Forgiveness is thus presented as the remedy between victims and offenders. *Homo faber* engages in labor, yet if he forsakes *homo pius*, he fails to create.

How can one reconcile the conflict between texts that advocate for *ius puniendi* and those that promote perpetual mercy? According to Beristain:

The New Testament prohibits retribution concerning individuals as private people, removing the characteristics and responsibilities of social power. Conversely, in the context of social interactions, punitive authority is explicitly permitted.

The Biblical mandate to forgive does not preclude punitive measures. Forgiveness alleviates the punitive obligation associated with guilt, yet it does not negate the necessity of punishment for reparation. While forgiveness mitigates the punitive expectations of external parties, it does not absolve the offender's self-imposed obligations or those pertaining to the collective welfare. The State is obligated to acknowledge and fulfill the requirements of punishment.[48]

Vengeance is unworthy and cruel, distinct from social vindication or punishment. Greek mythology illustrates this through the dichotomy of *Nemesis* and *Themis*, which lead to opposing outcomes. Private revenge stems from the

---

47 Antonio Beristain, *La pena-retribución y las actuales concepciones criminológicas*, *op. cit.*, p. 127.

48 *Ibid.*, pp. 31–35; quote on p. 35.

unrestrained emotion of the aggrieved, whereas retribution arises from the personal, legal culpability of the offender. Individuals, who are not inherently superior to the offender, enact private revenge, while retribution is administered by public authority, endowed with divine legitimacy through the populace. Private revenge is characterized by caprice, force, and unchecked passion, while retribution is constrained by proportionality between crime and punishment. The ultimate aim of private revenge is to inflict maximum harm on the offender, whereas retribution seeks to achieve restitution and restore the legal order and societal harmony.

In conclusion, when considering contemporary exegetical perspectives alongside the text of Holy Scriptures, one can assert that the objections raised by those who reject retributive justice, citing Scriptural passages, are inconsistent. Reason prohibits private vengeance while endorsing public, social retribution. An individual is never permitted to administer punishment, regardless of the severity of the crime or their status as a victim. The right to impose punishment is unequivocally denied to private individuals, although legitimate self-defense is acknowledged. Otherwise, the individual would be compromised by serving as the judge in their own case.

Nonetheless, theologians, particularly those from the Spanish Theological School of the 17th century onwards, endorse the concept of retribution administered by legitimate authority, which derives the *ius puniendi* directly from God, rather than from mere subjects – albeit through them. This theme is also evident in discussions regarding the legitimacy of the Death Penalty and warfare, as well as in debates about whether masters may physically punish their servants, teachers their pupils, or husbands their wives, with the somewhat shocking assertion today that such actions are permissible “only and always when necessary.”[49] This encapsulates the notion that:

> Authority “may” impose punishment as it has been granted power by God, the Lord of All.
>
> Authority “is compelled to” impose punishment due to the necessity of societal preservation and the maintenance of the legal order in response to criminal acts.

---

49 Cf. Francisco de Vitoria, *Relectio de potestate civili. Estudios sobre su Filosofía Política*. Edition by Jesús Cordero Pando, Madrid, Consejo Superior de Investigaciones Científicas, 2008.

CHAPTER 3

Punishment

1 Punishment: Balancing Retribution and Prevention through Penalties and Deterrents[1]

Legal sanctions are classified into two main categories: penalties and deterrents. Penalties address a *static* interpretation of the law, focusing on *logical* factors. Deterrents, conversely, adopt a *dynamic* viewpoint, incorporating *teleological* or finalist components.[2]

1.1 The Basis and Rationale of Punishment

The foundation and justification of penalties involve *free will* and *guilt*. Penalties come about as a *value judgment*: because man is free, he can be subjected

1 María José Falcón y Tella, *Lecciones de Teoría del Derecho*, Madrid, Servicio de Publicaciones, Facultad de Derecho, Universidad Complutense de Madrid, 1st ed. 2001, 2nd ed. 2003, 3rd ed. 2006, 4th ed. 2009, 5th ed. 2011, 6th ed. 2014, 6th ed., 1st reprint 2018, 7th ed., 1st ed. by Tirant lo Blanch, 2020, 8th ed., 2nd ed. by Tirant, 2023, 9th ed., 3rd ed. by Tirant, 2025. See pp. 60–65 of the 8th ed. There is a translation into English by Howard Shneider and Jon Randall Walden, *A Three-Dimensional Theory of Law*, Leiden-Boston, Martinus Nijhoff-Brill, 2010. And translation into Portuguese by Claudia De Miranda Avena and Ernani De Paula Contipelli, in the series "Direito Europeu," directed by Antonio García-Pablos de Molina, *Liçoes de Teoria Geral do Direito*, Brazil, Revista dos Tribunais, 2011.

2 Cf. on the subject, Alan H. Goldman, "Toward a New Theory of Punishment," in *Law and Philosophy*, l, 1982, pp. 57–76. Fernand Schockweiler, "Fondement du droit de punir. Réflections sur l'évolution des conceptions," in *Revue de Droit Penal et de Criminologie*, 1982, pp. 467–482. Jean Louis Vullierme, "La fin de la justice pénale," in *Archives de Philosophie du Droit*, 1983, pp. 155–180. Paul Hirst, "The Concept of Punishment," in *Law in Context*, 1984, pp. 73–88. P. F. Hooft, "Filosofía del castigo," in *Boletín AAFD*, 20, 1985. Francesco D'Agostino, "Giustizia e misericordia. Fondamenti filosofici e teologici della sanzione penale," in *Rivista Internazionale di Filosofia del Diritto*, 66, 1989, pp. 3–23. *Id.*, *La sanzione nell'esperienza giuridica*, Turin, Giappichelli, 1989. Ted Honderich, *Punishment; the Supposed Justifications*, Cambridge, Polity Press, 1990, 3rd ed. David Nelken, "Why Punish?," in *The Modern Law Review*, 33, 1990, pp. 829–834. Mario A. Cattaneo, "Un tentativo di giustificazione della pena giuridica. Nota su un libro di Igor Plimoratz," in *Rivista Internazionale di Filosofia del Diritto*, 2, 1991, pp. 414–427. Wesley Cragg, "H. L. A. Hart and the Justification of Punishment," in *Canadian Journal of Law and Jurisprudence*, V, 1, 1992, pp. 43–55. Jerónimo Betegón, *La justificación del castigo*, Madrid, Centro de Estudios Constitucionales, 1992.

 | HTTPS://DOI.ORG/10.1163/9789004766006-004

to a criminal trial and found guilty.[3] Penalties involve the idea of *morality being attributable to an individual*: because a person is free, it is possible to attribute responsibility to that person for his or her actions. On the other hand, deterrents are based on *determinism* and *social necessity*. Crime is viewed as something inevitable, not as the product of a free choice. Rather than the idea of guilt, which serves as the foundation for penalties, the notion of *danger* serves as the foundation for deterrents. It is no longer a question of a value judgment, but rather a *judgment of probability*. Rather than speak of morality being attributed to an individual's actions, the notion of *social responsibility* is what is at issue. The underlying idea is that because man's actions are predetermined and not free, we cannot punish him for his actions. However, in any case, *social coexistence* demands that someone respond to bad acts, because the lack of a response results in danger for society at large.

The rationale for penalties is *justice*: to allocate to everyone what they deserve. The principle underlying deterrents is *utility*: to prevent an individual from reoffending. Penalties are primarily based on an *objective* perspective, addressing a crime that, in its legal context, is deemed a violation of a legal norm. Conversely, deterrents emphasize a *subjective* viewpoint, focusing more on the offender and the societal implications of the crime. In essence, deterrents regard crime as a disruption of social order.

1.2 The Purpose of Punishment

In terms of function, penalties look more at the reason, the *why* of the sanction, while deterrents look more to the ends, to the *what for* of the sanction. They say that the function of penalties is fundamentally *retributive*, while the function of deterrents is *preventive*. Penalties are in theory repressive, and lend themself to atonement, and to *revenge*. It involves the concept of "an eye for an eye, tooth for a tooth" – the idea of resolving one wrong with another wrong, and that he who lives by the sword must die by the sword. On the other hand, deterrents focus more on the idea of *security*. In theory, penalties look to the *past*, and deterrents toward the *future*. Penalties punish because a person has broken the law ("*punitur quia peccatum est*"). Deterrents punish so that a person does not break the law again ("*punitur ut ne peccetur*"). But if we leave aside these abstract conceptions of penalties and deterrents, and instead focus on positive Spanish law, we can see that in Article 25 of the 1978 Constitution it is established that "Prison sentences and deterrents shall be oriented towards

3 Cf. Liborio Hierro, "Libertad y responsabilidad penal," in *Anuario de la Facultad de Derecho. Alcalá de Henares*, 1991–1992, pp. 161–173.

reeducation and social rehabilitation." In this context, the focus is on looking toward the future, even in the case of penalties.

1.3 Theoretical Frameworks Advocating Punishment

A series of theories exist that advocate penalties and deterrents. The initial category is termed "absolutist theories," as penalties are considered an *end in themselves*. Conversely, the thesis supporting deterrents pertains to "relativist theories," wherein punishment serves as a *means to an end*.

1.3.1 The Absolutist Theories

The principal absolutist doctrines are those articulated by Kant and Hegel. For Kant, penalties are an *ethical imperative*, a categorical necessity: even if society were to collapse, we must punish every criminal, as failing to do so would render us complicit in the crime. In Hegel's framework, penalties are not an ethical necessity but a *logical* one. They arise from the *dialectical method*, which legitimizes them: there exists an initial phase or thesis (the law), its antithesis (crime), and, as a synthesis, a punishment. Alternatively, this can be perceived as the negation of the negation of the law. These absolutist theories are typically associated with religious interpretations of existence.

1.3.2 The Relativistic Theories

Relativist doctrines focus on prevention, categorized as general deterrence theories and special deterrence theories.

1.3.2.1 Theories of General Deterrence

The theory of general deterrence pertains to the *populace at large* and encompasses *intimidation* and psychological coercion, achieved by threats or by exemplifying an individual.

1.3.2.2 Theories of Special Deterrence

Conversely, the thesis of special deterrence pertains directly to the *active perpetrator* of the crime – the criminal. These doctrines can be categorized into religious and secular theories. *Religious* theories aim for the *moral correction* or enhancement of the criminal, as exemplified by Krause's "Besserugs Theorie" and the Spanish Correctional School of thought represented by Luis Silvela, Concepción Arenal, and Pedro Dorado Montero. In contrast, *secular* theories are content if the criminal exhibits *external compliance,* regardless of genuine internal rehabilitation.

In the *secular* realm, according to the type of criminal, it is necessary to distinguish between three aims or purposes.[4] If it is the case of an *occasional* offender, the end to be achieved is individual intimidation, which is to say, persuading the criminal not to break the law again. If it is a person in the current condition of *being* a criminal ("Zustandverbrecher"), the aim is reeducation, re-socialization, and social reentry. Finally, if it is a habitual, *incorrigible* criminal, what is attempted is his or her incapacitation, in other words, preventing that person from harming society again by imposing the death penalty or a life sentence. This would occur in the case of what Lombroso called the born criminal, "l'uomo delinquente." There are those, however, like Concepción Arenal, who do not believe in the existence of so-called born criminals. Instead, such thinkers believe that human beings are always able to improve themselves – that it is one thing to not yet be fixed, and another, very different thing, to be unfixable.

1.3.3 The Eclectic, Mixed, or Union Theories

There exists, together with the absolutist and relativist theories, a third class of theories – the eclectic, mixed, or union theories. These theories hold that there is not a solution in a singular sense. Instead, the theories distinguish various *stages* in which punishment acts. More specifically, there are three such stages: first, there is the moment of the legal threat, put forth by the "legislature"; the second phase involves the application of the sanction or the realization of justice, through the "judge"; finally, there is the execution phase of the punishment, which is carried out by the "prison administration." Each of these stages corresponds to a predominant *function* and goal of punishment. The first phase corresponds to the notion of general deterrence. The second phase corresponds to the idea of retribution. And the third phase corresponds to special deterrence. Analyzing the different stages in this fashion allows us to see how different functions of punishment are reflected in a particular phase. Sometimes there even emerge conflicts between the first and the third functions – conflicts between what is beneficial for the collective unit as a whole and what is beneficial for the specific criminal.

---

4 On the subject, Joel Feinberg (1926–2004), "El argumento de la graduación moral de los castigos," in Agustín Squella (ed.), *H. L. A. Hart y el Concepto de Derecho,* in *Revista de Ciencias Sociales. Universidad de Valparaíso,* 28, 1986, pp. 355–366. Antonio Osuna Fernández-Largo, "Pertenencia de lo jurídico a lo moral. Reflexiones sobre una teoría iusfilosófica clásica," in *Anales de la Cátedra Francisco Suárez,* 28, 1988, pp. 305–329.

1.4 Dispute among Philosophical Schools

Upon reviewing the fundamental theories underpinning penalties and deterrents, it is noteworthy that these theories have engendered a conflict among various schools of thought. The *classical* school has historically advocated for penalties, whereas the *positivist* school contemporaneously champions deterrents.

1.5 Concept of the State

In turn, each of the doctrines discussed corresponds to a conception of the state. Absolute theses are linked to a *theocratic* notion, such as the absolute state. In this state, power flows from the top down, from the divine to the monarch and from the monarch to his representatives, who are appointed or named unilaterally, not democratically elected. The relative theory of general prevention corresponds to a configuration of the state as a *liberal* state governed by the rule of law, of a non-interventionist nature. This is the type of state that emerged after the French Revolution. In it, there would be negative freedom, according to which everything would be permitted except what is expressly prohibited. Finally, the relative theory of special prevention would be expressed in the development of the state as a *social and democratic* state, a consequence of the concept of positive freedom. It is not enough to refrain from interference. There is no "invisible hand" that self-regulates the functioning of state institutions. Intervention is necessary to ensure the reintegration of offenders.

In a liberal state, punitive intervention by authorities is constrained by a minimum threshold – punishment may only be enacted in response to a crime – and a maximum threshold – punishment must correspond proportionately to the severity of the crime. Conversely, in an absolute state, there are no constraints on governmental power. In a social state, medical professionals operate without limitations, implementing deterrents as alternatives to penalties, such as the application of lesser penalties, sentence suspension, parole, or confinement in psychiatric or specialized rehabilitation facilities.

1.6 Dimension of Existence

1.6.1 Divergences from the Ideal

Transitioning from theoretical frameworks to practical realities reveals the following situation. Deviations from the ideal in various doctrines indicate that absolute theories may engender a purely retributive and mechanistic interpretation of legal application, potentially enforced in a nearly mathematical manner. General deterrence could instigate a climate of criminal terror through the imposition of severe penalties, reminiscent of Enlightened Despotism ("everything for the people but without the people"). In terms of special deterrence, a common deviation involves treating offenders as experimental subjects, a kind of guinea pig, creating an optimal environment for diverse forms of experimentation.

1.6.2 Critique

Additionally, a critique can be directed at the diverse frameworks proposed. For instance, absolute theories lack coherence concerning sporadic offenses. Moreover, they fail to mitigate criminal behavior. Conversely, they necessitate a belief in the myth of an absolute, metaphysical order, wherein humanity is created for the Sabbath rather than the Sabbath serving humanity. Furthermore, it is illogical for punishment to be exclusively malevolent; the context changes if it is accompanied by malevolence.

The critique of general deterrence doctrines is that they may terrify individuals who do not require such measures. This is exemplified by capital punishment, which exerts a demoralizing influence on the populace, even though fulfilling the objective of general intimidation.

Special deterrence may contravene the principle of legal certainty, which is paramount in a rule-of-law state. Indeed, where lies the legitimacy to impose punishment? For what objectives and which society are we addressing? Are we not risking the totalitarianism of the majority? Moreover, special deterrence needs substantial resources and suggests that traditional methods, such as incarceration, which often serves merely as a breeding ground for criminality, are ineffective. To mitigate these issues, it is essential to uphold the fundamental rights of prisoners as much as possible, for instance, by implementing visiting regimes and establishing open systems for serving sentences.

Furthermore, although these theories of special deterrence are humanistic in that they address the specific individual rather than an abstract being, they do not transform the individual's very nature or unique life. On the other hand, they emphasize the ideology of differentiation, the sharp distinction between black and white, good and bad, forgetting that what generally predominates in reality are the middle ground and the range of grays, that things are not always good or bad in themselves, but depend on the color of the glass through which they are viewed. It should be added that when re-educating criminals, the principle of ideological freedom recognized in Article 16 of the Spanish Constitution of 1978 must not be violated, which prevents any religious or ideological creed of any kind from being imposed as dominant. No matter how convinced we are that our ideas are correct, we cannot, and must not, force anyone to share them. In their innermost being, human beings must be free and autonomous.

Conversely, resocialization of offenders is not universally requisite. This applies to occasional offenders, those driven by passion, and individuals who are otherwise well-socialized, such as white-collar criminals, who, despite receiving conventional education and socialization, violate specific regulations, including tax offenses like capital flight. Furthermore, while re-education and social reintegration are essential, they are not always feasible. Their efficacy hinges on the offender's willingness and intention to adhere to societal laws rather than personal inclinations. However, there are instances where individuals refuse to cooperate, rendering successful outcomes unattainable.

2 Advancing a More Compassionate Criminal Law: The Privatization of Criminal Law[5]

When Cervantes authored *Don Quixote*, punitive measures were exceedingly severe: it was thought that criminals would be deterred by draconian penalties, including corporal punishment such as flogging, mutilation, humiliation, and even torture to elicit confessions. In this harsh criminal justice system, there was no consideration for contemporary principles such as non-retroactive

5 María José Falcón y Tella, *La justicia como mérito*, Foreword by Martín Laclau, Madrid-Barcelona-Buenos Aires-São Paulo, Marcial Pons, 2014. Reviewed: – By prof. María de los Ángeles Nogales Naharro, in *International Journal of Humanities and Social Science*, vol. 4, issue 9, July 2014, pp. 134–136. – By prof. María Eugenia Pérez Montero, in *Foro. Revista de Ciencias Jurídicas y Sociales*, vol. 17, issue 1, 2014, pp. 410–414. – By prof. José López Hernández, in *Daimon. Revista de Filosofía*, 66, 2015, pp. 172–173. – In *Iuris Tantum. Revista de la Facultad de Derecho. Universidad Anahuac*, Mexico, year XXIX, no. 25, Tercera Época, 2014, pp. 389–405. – In *Anuario de Filosofía del Derecho*, XXXI, 2015, pp. 290–294. There is a translation into English, *Justice and Law*, Leiden-Boston, Martinus Nijhoff Publishers, 2014. *Id.*, *Cuestiones de Filosofía del Derecho*, Madrid-Barcelona-Buenos Aires-São Paulo, Marcial Pons, 1st. ed., 2020, pp. 118 ff., 2nd. expanded ed. 2025. Reviewed: – By prof. María Eugenia Pérez Montero, in *Foro. Revista de Ciencias Jurídicas y Sociales. Nueva Época*, Facultad de Derecho, Universidad Complutense de Madrid, vol. 23, issue 2, 2020, pp. 405–410. – By prof. María Ángeles Nogales Naharro, in *Dereito. Revista Xurídica da Universidade de Santiago de Compostela*, no. 2, Year 2021. There is an English translation, *Challenges to Contemporary Legal Thinking*, The Haghe, Melrose Legal Publishers, 2026 (forthcoming).

applicability, rehabilitation, social reintegration, reeducation, or the principle of *nullum crimen, nulla poena sine praevia lege poenale*.

Cervantes's remarks, reflective of his era, unequivocally articulate a critique of the atrocities associated with torture and corporal punishment as means of procuring legal proof (*Don Quixote* I, 43, on torture, and II, 26, on flogging).[6]

2.1 Historical Context

A contemporary trend in global criminal and procedural law is the privatization of criminal justice, often referred to as the establishment of consensus on criminal justice reform. Some civil attorneys assert that this phenomenon represents a "civilization" of criminal law, highlighting the impact of civil law on criminal law.[7]

This process entails the relaxation or relativization of the system of strict criminal legality, in which the principle of legality loses its basis. This is partly owing to the phenomenon of globalization, which introduced new risks linked to modern societies and a tendency toward "punitive inflation." This made it necessary for the victim to be at the center of the conflict and forced criminal law to take a greater interest in events leading up to the crime, seeking alternatives to incarceration for conflict resolution. This dissuasive method – predicated on mediation, reconciliation, and redress – involves far more than mere "monetary" restitution and can also include "symbolic" reparations for a crime, such as rendering personal services, offering explanations or apologies... in short, anything that can serve to rectify the wrong and find a peaceful solution out of court by allowing mediators, psychologists, social workers, and other agents outside the criminal justice system to intervene. This is a particularly valid option in the juvenile justice system, because young offenders often have limited resources and find themselves in a vulnerable position if monetary reparation is the only way of making amends. Criminal mediation is more com-

6 José Manuel Pérez-Prendes Muñoz-Arraco, "Cervantes y los juristas (esbozo de una guía historiográfica)," in *Foro, Nueva época*, 2, 2005, pp. 125 ff.

7 On this subject, see, among others, Antonio García-Pablos de Molina, *Criminología. Una introducción a sus fundamentos teóricos para juristas*, Valencia, Tirant lo Blanch, 1996. Gonzalo Quintero Olivares, "La llamada privatización del Derecho penal," in *Revista de Derecho y proceso penal*, 6, 2001, pp. 13–21. Alberto Alonso Rimo, *Víctima y sistema penal: las infracciones no perseguibles de oficio y el perdón*, Valencia, Tirant lo Blanch, 2002. Ricardo Manuel Rojas, "El poder represivo del Estado: ¿Se justifica la existencia del Derecho penal?", in *Themis*, 35, 1997. Elena I. Highton – Gladys Stella Álvarez – Carlos G. Gregorio, *Resolución alternativa de disputas y sistema penal*, Buenos Aires, Ed. Ad-Hoc, 1998.

plex than civil mediation, as the parties generally do not know each other and there is a considerable power imbalance between the victim and the offender.

It is essential to remember that prior to the emergence of the modern state in the 18th century, the sole recognized criminal system was an "accusatory" one, wherein the accuser and the accused engaged in a literal private conflict. Historically, in the absence of a centralized state authority, tribes and familial units existed, with the victim initiating the criminal proceedings to pursue justice, while the court, composed of popular assemblies or juries, rendered a verdict. With the advent of states, criminal law transitioned to a public domain, and the punitive authority of individuals or groups was ceded to the state.

Currently, the prosecutorial function of the state is undergoing significant transformation, facing a crisis. Individuals are increasingly assuming a central role in conflict resolution and may decide whether to pursue criminal proceedings concerning private assets or rights. Innovative negotiation methods have emerged, including summary proceedings, settlements, discontinuances, and plea bargains. Additionally, there has been a notable increase in private prosecutions, where individuals or organizations initiate criminal actions. Nonetheless, this development does not indicate a regression to a system of retaliation and private retribution, wherein victims sought justice independently.

Contemporary criminal law is ineffective in numerous respects, having transformed into a mechanism that prioritizes the purported interests of the state over the genuine concerns of the aggrieved party, resulting in an abusive and infrequently effective system. Restitution is pursued not for the individual but for the state, which arbitrarily decides whom to prosecute or refrain from prosecuting. I contend that a significant portion of criminal cases should be privatized, allowing individuals to assess the potential costs and benefits of initiating legal action and seeking restitution. I do not concur with the notion that the state should possess the authority to impose penalties on its own behalf, a concept referred to by Zaffaroni as "subjective criminal law."

2.2 Comparative Law

The Spanish Criminal Code of 1995 broadened the applicability of public accusations, private complaints, and pardons necessary to initiate or terminate legal proceedings to a significant array of offenses: crimes against personal honor and sexual autonomy, familial abandonment, negligence-related damages, violations of privacy, corporate offenses, and those pertaining to intellectual and industrial property, markets, and consumer rights, among others.

The concept of "restorative" justice emerged in the English-speaking realm, particularly in the United States, during the late 1970s. In the U.S., the crime victims' rights movement has tackled issues such as condonation, the resolution or amalgamation of minor offenses, and the aggregation of crimes. In Germany, victims can initiate *Antragsdelikt* or *Privatanklagedelikt* proceedings. Similarly, the Italian legal system allows for *querela*.

2.3 Restorative Justice and Probation in Criminal Law

In contrast to retributive justice, restorative justice seeks to mend harm, restore relationships, and rectify specific damages through the correction of wrongs and the making of amends, akin to the actions of Don Quixote. It is imperative to remember that the primary objective of the law is to attain social harmony, which, like the private domain, can frequently be achieved by fostering reconciliation between the perpetrator and the victim.

A court may postpone judgment for several years and place the accused on probation, intending to dismiss the case if the individual refrains from further criminal activity, compensates for the harm caused, and adheres to specific conduct regulations during that time.

2.4 Ameliorating Damage: Toward a Reconciliatory Framework

There are those who suggest that convicted criminals sentenced to pay compensation or damages should be able to work for the same wages they would receive outside of prison, with part of their income going to the victim. However, this solution poses an immediate problem: the harm done by the crime is social in nature, even though it directly affected the victim. While private compensation may satisfy the victim's legitimate interest, it overlooks the fact that the harm was public, and restitution must be equally public. Some say that we should avoid privatizing criminal punishment, as this would constitute a reversion to the darker days of our past, and the public nature of the penalty must not be forgotten. Even so, Beristain, Christie, and others have suggested that criminal reparations be considered a third type of penalty for crime, in addition to prison sentences and deterrents, to compensate the victim and thereby restore public order and social protection. If this were done, however, such reparations should be considered partial and ancillary to the primary sentence.

In daily life, when we cause harm to others, we endeavor to rectify our actions. Therefore, why should the states of developed nations not adopt a similar approach? At the very least, why should we not facilitate the ability of aggressors to compensate their victims, thereby minimizing the involvement of the state and the criminal justice system, relegating them to a last resort when all other avenues for a peaceful resolution have been exhausted? In systems devoid of a robust state apparatus, victim compensation appears to be the most customary remedy.[8] The populace must engage actively as participants rather than passive observers, formulating solutions instead of awaiting them. We should strive for resolution rather than imposing authority, offer compensation rather than seek retribution, and promote benevolence rather than inflicting harm.[9]

The matter of restricting the right to impose punishment presents two fundamental inquiries:

Firstly, if a victim is determined to pursue retribution, is it justifiable to permit them to inflict suffering on the perpetrator? Clearly not. Vengeance is morally indefensible. Ontologically, two wrongs do not equate to a right; malevolence can only be rectified via benevolence.

Secondly, if the victim is inclined to forgive, should we invariably permit the victim to exhibit compassion and absolve the offender, even in instances of grave transgression? Can the community insist that the perpetrator atone for his misconduct despite the victim's forgiveness? Once more, the resolution appears to reside in ethical considerations: forgiveness is an individual affair, yet a public violation of societal norms needs retribution. However, what underpins this rationale? Furthermore, what if the likelihood of reoffending is nonexistent?

Due to individual variations in cruelty, the state implements measures to ensure fairness. However, as the generality of law often necessitates the intervention of equity and case-specific justice to prevent excessive legalism, punishments are frequently customized to the individual. Since neither individu-

---

8 Nils Christie, *Los límites del dolor,* Mexico, Fondo de Cultura Económica, 1984, pp. 128 ff, has an explanation for why we tend to resort to the punitive criminal justice system rather than trying to compensate victims.
- Because the system is how officers of the court and their auxiliary staff make a living.
- Because offenders are generally poor people who lack the financial means to compensate their victims and can only offer what they have, which is time, to be wasted in prison. But, Christie says, even the poorest individuals own some possessions that could be handed over to the victim. Why isn't this done? Why are property rights better protected than the right to freedom?
- Because otherwise the strong victim would squeeze the poor offender out of all proportion, and this could lead to vendettas, the all-out war and anarchy typical of the state of nature. To this Christie replies that many crimes take place among equals.

9 On this subject, see Mark S. Umbreit, *Crime and Reconciliation: Creative Options for Victims and Offenders*, Nashville, Abingdon Press, 1985.

als are identical, equal punishments are unattainable. A careful equilibrium must be maintained between abstract, universal justice and equity by analyzing the details of each case within defined parameters. The offender should neither be made a scapegoat nor treated as a guinea pig. Once again, a system of oversight is essential to monitor those in power, establishing checks and balances to constrain the punitive authority of the state.

2.5 What if We Eliminated Punishment?

Regarding punishment, the prevailing assertion that it is indispensable for the survival of any society, serving to maintain order and prevent chaos and social anarchy, appears to be irrefutable. However, is this assertion entirely accurate? I propose to present certain considerations that may, at the very least, introduce skepticism regarding the absolute truth of this ostensibly incontrovertible doctrine.

The perennial dilemma of society is this: what constitutes our most effective defense? Should we erect formidable barriers of mandates and prohibitions, accompanied by penalties for noncompliance? It is crucial to recognize that barriers can be dismantled, surmounted, or evaded through subterfuge, much like the mechanisms of criminal punishment and prison walls if the offender is apprehended. Individuals who are socially well-adjusted provide a more reliable safeguard for a secure society than imposing high prison walls. Would it not be more efficacious to cultivate a society of autonomous individuals who are prepared to be accountable for their actions, fostering trust that people will adhere to rules and laws due to their inherent fairness rather than the fear of punitive consequences for transgression?

I realize that, in saying this, I run the risk of being dismissed as an idealist, a dreamer, an advocate of impossible utopias. However, let us examine the issue on a smaller scale, in the sphere of personal family relationships. In the long run, which is more effective: a metaphorical prison system, where parents set strict curfews, dress codes, and countless other rules for their children who, exasperated, and sometimes justifiably so, will systematically flout those rules whenever possible and conceal their actions; or a system of trust and freedom, of raising responsible individuals, where the parents lay down a few basic ground rules but leave the rest to their children's discretion so that, through constant trial and error, they will develop strong characters and learn to be accountable and free? In the first scenario, the children will grow up overly sheltered or wildly rebellious. In the second scenario, they will most likely turn out to be responsible human beings, capable of making their own decisions. The same can be said of the state and its system of punishment.

Allow me to propose an alternative metaphor: which is more likely to endure gale-force winds, a century-old oak trunk or a lakeside reed? Rigidity or flexibility? The tree trunk appears more formidable, yet it also presents greater resistance to the wind, which could lead to its toppling or uprooting. Conversely, the reed will bend, offering diminished resistance, and its pliable structure will more effectively withstand the assault of opposing forces. This analogy parallels a rigid, totalitarian society with a purely retributive view of criminal punishment, in contrast to a liberal democratic system that adopts a relative, individualized approach to criminal treatment.

Some may contend that, in such circumstances, individuals will act according to their whims, rendering social coexistence unfeasible; however, I dissent. Although it is occasionally accurate that chaos represents the utmost injustice and that force supplants law when legal authority wanes, why would a punitive system that enforces minimal penalties be less efficacious in combating crime?

When the safety valve of a pressure cooker is sealed, steam accumulates within, leading to a potential explosion and significant disorder. If we analogize society to a pressure cooker, the steam represents dissenters, including both those who protest peacefully and the minority who reject the entire system. Dissent requires a safety valve, a regulated means of expression. While some dissidents may misuse their liberties and engage in criminal behavior, the advantage of freedom is that it permits some pressure to dissipate, thereby preventing societal upheaval.

This mechanism is analogous to that employed in vaccines to inhibit the transmission of specific diseases. Vaccines function by inoculating a healthy organism with a minuscule quantity of the pathogen responsible for the disease, a dosage insufficient to induce illness yet adequate to provoke the synthesis of antibodies capable of combating the disease. Consequently, the organism is better equipped to confront that threat in the future. Likewise, society must accommodate a regulated degree of dissent, which should not be violently repressed but appropriately directed.

2.6 Managing Conflict as an Inescapable Reality

It is crucial to recognize that not all conflicts require resolution. Many individuals persist in the puritanical notion that every dispute must yield a solution. To transcend this mindset, an initial step is to prioritize conflict management over conflict resolution. While conflicts can be resolved, we can also adapt to coexist with them. The subsequent logical progression involves engaging with conflict, as this underscores the process rather than the result: "It's not whether you win or lose, it's how you play the game."

2.7 Resocializing Society to Mitigate Injustice Rather than Resocializing the Individual

Durkheim asserted, "Crime is an integral part of all healthy societies." If society itself is the origin of conflict, is it rational to discuss the resocialization of criminals, aiding their reintegration into a society that is fundamentally flawed and inherently conflictual? The resocialization of offenders is only justifiable within the framework of a fair society with an equitable social and legal system. Otherwise, what is its purpose? Should we not prioritize the resocialization of society itself? Why invest in the socialization of a young man if, upon release from prison, he returns to a dysfunctional home in impoverished conditions, unemployed, and surrounded by delinquent peers? Rather than focusing on the resocialization of criminals, I advocate for the resocialization of society to reduce injustice, diminish social inequalities, and create structures less conducive to crime. Furthermore, we must ensure that society does not dissocialize criminals.

The efficacy of the treatment will not solely, or even predominantly, hinge on the enforcement of incarceration or punitive measures, but rather on an extra-penitentiary element: the nature of the society we cultivate. An inmate may exemplify exemplary behavior within the confines of prison, where systems exist to encourage and commend such conduct. However, what transpires when those systems are dismantled, when the individual reenters society and is liberated from the constraints of prison walls and regulations? As one author astutely observed, "It is exceedingly challenging to prepare individuals for freedom in environments devoid of freedom."[10]

---

10 José Antonio Choclán Montalvo, *Individualización judicial de la pena. Función de la culpabilidad y la prevención en la determinación de la sanción penal*, Madrid, Colex, 1997, pp. 95–99, addresses the criminal science debate on incarceration as a tool of social adjustment and reeducation: "a) it is hard to 'readjust' individuals who were never well-adjusted in the first place, due to difficulties in their socio-psychological learning process; b) there is some doubt as to whether the idea of resocialization is predicated on the society that actually exists or an ideal model of society; c) treatment is not necessary when the individual can be socialized by means other than the enforcement of a sentence; d) the real conditions in which prison sentences are served primarily focus on mitigating the detrimental effects of the loss of freedom rather than on reeducating those who, prior to sentencing, were in need of certain treatment and helping them adjust to society."

2.8 The Refinement of Criminal Law

The progression of criminology has demonstrated that the refinement of criminal law does not entail the elimination of punishment, as one might presume, but rather its enhancement and sophistication. Similarly, psychological trauma cannot be evaded but can be surmounted, not through denial but by recognizing its presence and addressing its ramifications. Criminals will persist, and penalties for their offenses will remain. The efficacy of this discipline should not be gauged by its quantitative application, dictated by external factors such as crime rates, but rather by the qualitative aspects of criminal punishment, specifically the clarity and substance of penalties and the extent to which their objectives align with the higher principle of justice. Punishment should be personalized, emphasizing special prevention rather than merely being humanized or individualized.[11]

2.9 Addressing a Multifaceted Interdisciplinary Issue

In my view, akin to numerous academic disciplines, there is no singular correct answer regarding the foundations and objectives of criminal punishment. The authority to impose punishment encompasses multiple legitimate purposes, as evidenced by the case law of the Spanish Constitutional Court that examines this issue within our constitution. The principle of retribution – understood not in an antiquated metaphysical context, but as a foundational premise and constraint of *ius puniendi* – should be integrated with the objectives of both general and special deterrence. Furthermore, even the ostensibly laudable aim of resocialization must be subject to certain limitations to prevent therapeutic abuse.

The pivotal term here is "dialectic." Instead of focusing solely in one direction, we must broaden our perspective and acknowledge that we are confronted with a multifaceted issue necessitating a correspondingly intricate solution. Additionally, the responses and conciliatory solutions offered by various schools of thought should not be delineated in a fragmented manner, but rather as opposing forces engaged in continuous dialectical interaction. This interplay of contradictions will yield a synthesis that is dynamic, provisional, and perpetually receptive to novel viewpoints and methodologies.

---

11 Raymond Saleilles (1855–1912), *L'individualisation de la peine*, Paris, F. Alcan, 1898, 3rd. ed. 1927, introduction by Gabriel Tarde; *The Individualization of Punishment,* translation of the 2nd French edition by Rachel Szold Jastrow, introduction by Roscoe Pound, Boston, Little Brown, 1911.

CHAPTER 4

Guilt and Punishment in Some of the Greatest Works of World Literature of All Time

In this chapter, before focusing on the main theme of this work (the analysis of guilt and punishment in the life and work of Cervantes, Dostoyevsky, and Kafka), we will take a journey through time, examining how this topic has been treated in some of the greatest works of world literature of all time. This is not an in-depth study,[1] but simply a brief overview of how these issues are addressed in the literary creations analyzed.

1 *The Oresteia* by Aeschylus

The plot of *The Oresteia* by Aeschylus[2] may basically be summarized by stating that it concerns a story of war and vengeance – the Trojan War, to avenge the seduction of Helen by Paris. In a celebrated episode, Agamemnon sacrifices Iphigenia,[3] an innocent victim, to appease the wrath of the gods, followed by the subsequent killing of Agamemnon and the vengeance taken by his son Orestes, murdering his mother, Clytemnestra, for which he is judged and pardoned. Until the judgment, it is taken for granted that Clytemnestra's murder by Orestes, though justifiable and inevitable, must be punished in the same

1 For an in-depth analysis of all these works, see María José Falcón y Tella, *Derecho y Literatura, op. cit.*, pp. 61–203. English translation, *Law and Literature, op. cit.*, pp. 52–222.

2 Aeschylus (525 B.C.–456 B.C), *La Orestiada,* translation into Spanish by Álvaro del Amo, Madrid, Instituto Nacional de las Artes Escénicas y de la Música, 1990. Maria Aristodemou, "Seduction of Mimesis: Theater as Woman and the Play of Difference and Excess in Aeschylus's *Oresteia,*" in *Cardozo Studies in Law and Literature,* vol. 11, issue 1, summer 1999, pp. 1–34.

3 P. Pether, "Trouble with Iphigenia: Feminist Critiques of Feminist Crime Fiction and the Case against Sara Paretsky," in *Australian Journal of Law and Society,* 9, 1993, pp. 3–18. See also: Thomas Pfau, "The Pragmatics of Genre: Moral Theory and Lyric Authorship in Hegel and Wordsworth," in *Cardozo Arts & Entertainment Law Journal,* 10, 1992, pp. 397–422. Judith Resnik, "Singular and Aggregate Voices: Audiences and Authority in Law & Literature and in Law & Feminism," in Michael Freeman – Andrew Lewis (eds.), *Law and Literature. Current Legal Issues,* volume 2, London-New York, Oxford University Press, 1999, pp. 687–728. Judith Resnik – Carolyn Heilbrun, "Convergences: Law, Literature and Feminism," in *Yale Law Journal,* 99, 1990, pp. 1913–1953.

manner as Agamemnon must pay for the death of his daughter, for which reason he was forced, in turn, to end the Trojan War.[4]

If one had to summarize the complex intrigues of *The Oresteia* in a single phrase, one might say that it tells of the difficulties of the law of retribution and, as a counterpoint, of the experience of human justice understanding how to integrate the dimension of forgiveness. As regards the theme of retribution, three additional concepts must be noted: that it is applied to both the guilty party and their descendants without distinction; that it may arise out of the violation, not necessarily intentional, of implicit prohibitions or of taboos that are obscure to a greater or lesser degree; and that it is enforced both through acts of justice and by way of natural disasters (as with the storm that undermines the Greek fleet on its return from Troy).

The question of responsibility (will, guilt) is presented as a counterpoint to justice through vengeance. Without a minimal level of imputation and personal responsibility, it is argued that it is impossible to imagine any judgment. But the central question, in truth, is to know whether one answers in the first person for one's own behavior in Aeschylus' universe. The answer is linked to this image of archaic vengeance, barely distinct from collective responsibility. *Agamemnon* considers responsibility for two crimes: the sacrifice of Iphigenia by Agamemnon and the death of the latter at the hands of Clytemnestra and her lover. The first of these responsibilities is presented in genuinely problematic terms. Agamemnon has undoubtedly acted deliberately, weighing up the consequences of his acts, as is reflected in verses 206 to 217, which hide nothing of the leader of the Greek expedition's process of inner debate.[5]

Clytemnestra's adultery and entry into public life cross the boundaries for someone of her sex. But she does not show any feelings of guilt or regret for her transgressions. She responds to the continuing accusations of the Chorus by stating that Agamemnon has killed her sister.

4 Richard A. Posner, *Derecho y Literatura,* Valladolid, Cuatro y el Gato, Colegio de Abogados de Valladolid, 2004, pp. 60–61. Sophie Klimis, "Amour, droit et harmonie cosmique dans la trilogie des Danaïdes d'Eschyle," in François Ost – Laurent van Eynde – Philippe Gérard – Michel van de Kerchove (dirs.), *Lettres et lois. Le droit au miroir de la littérature,* Brussels, Publications des Facultés Universitaires Saint-Louis, 2001, pp. 11–38.

5 François Ost, *Raconter la loi. Aux sources de l'imaginaire juridique,* Paris, Odile Jacob, 2004, pp. 91–151, esp. pp. 91–104.

2 *Antigone* by Sophocles

In Classical Greece, in Sophocles' *Antigone*,[6] Antigone embodies the ideal of a justice identified with piety, founded upon a sacred, eternal, and immutable order. Opposite to this, Creon represents a new type of order, of justice, one of a legal-political nature. The resulting conflict between the two is inevitable. Both embody extreme poles and therefore the situation has a fatal dénouement, proper to Greek tragedy. The application of one of the two laws presupposes the transgression of the other, making obedience to both impossible. Creon has broken the unwritten law of the gods, the *nomoi agrafoi*.[7] Antigone has broken the *nomos* of the city. Both, though in different ways, have gone against justice, and both, therefore, must pay.[8]

Antigone was moved by her conscience. Her act was deliberate and intentional. Further, appealing to the judgment of the entire community, she explains her conduct to the Chorus. Antigone does not act secretly, but rather the burial of her brother was open and public. When the soldiers left to guard the body of Antigone's brother discover her intention of burying him, she does not deny her intent, nor does she do so when questioned by Creon, to his great astonishment. Hence, Creon judges Antigone to be guilty of a double crime: first, disobeying his orders; second, the temerity of doing so openly.[9] On the other hand, Antigone does not act violently, neither does she violate the rights of other citizens. Finally, Antigone accepts her death sentence. Hers is not a revolutionary or subversive act, rather she accepts the system.[10]

---

6 Sophocles (496 B.C.–406 B.C.), *Antígona*, in Colección Clásicos Inolvidables, 2nd ed., Buenos Aires, El Ateneo, 1950. There is another Spanish version by Francisco Miguel Del Rincón Sánchez, Madrid, Escolar y Mayo, 2013.

7 See, James Boyd White, *The Legal Imagination, op. cit.* Joseph P. Tomain, *Creon's Ghost: Law, Justice, and the Humanities*, Oxford, Oxford University Press, 2009.

8 Giovanni Cosi, *Saggio sulla disobbedienza civile. Storia e critica del dissenso in democrazia*, Milan, Giuffrè, 1984, pp. 118–124.

9 Joseph Betz, "Can Civil Disobedience Be Justified?," in *Social Theory and Practice*, I, 2, fall 1970, pp. 13–30, esp. pp. 16–17.

10 Lewis H. Van Dusen, Jr., "Civil Disobedience, Destroyer of Democracy," in *American Bar Association Journal*, 55, February 1969, pp. 123–126, esp. pp. 123–124.

3 *Electra* by Euripides

Euripides' *Electra*[11] tells the story of how Electra and her brother, Orestes, murder their mother, Clytemnestra, in solidarity with their father, Agamemnon.

This story has held interest for legal theorists, psychoanalysts and feminists, with respect to the link between blood debts and justice. As is narrated in Euripides' *Electra*, Aeschylus' *The Oresteia* and in Sophocles' *Electra*, the story follows Agamemnon's children, Electra and Orestes, completing their vengeance upon their mother, Clytemnestra, and her lover, Aegisthus, with Electra condemned to exile and Orestes being acquitted at trial in an Athens court. The Furies, who would otherwise have pursued Orestes until his death, are dispersed by Apollo. The fact that the circle of vengeance ends with a legal trial reveals the story as a triumph of justice as a legal procedure over ancient ideas of blood vengeance, which is represented by the final dispersion of the Furies.

Electra is a story in which the primitive and anarchic world of blood vengeance – that is, the feminine aspect – is replaced by the development of a more civilized side, that of public justice and legality, which represents the masculine.

In Euripides' *Electra*, the young avengers Electra and her brother Orestes often speak of the duty to pay a debt, as do the Chorus and other characters. Unlike Hamlet, Electra does not agonize over the guilt of having to carry out vengeance. Apollo said that Clytemnestra and Aegisthus must pay for their crimes, and the siblings take strong action to ensure that this happens.

Feeling that perhaps Orestes is not the brave warrior she has imagined him to be, Electra pushes him to act as a man, using manipulative arguments like those that the ghost of Hamlet's father would later make in Shakespeare's *Hamlet* to provoke and convince Hamlet. It is undoubtedly the blind will of Electra that ensures vengeance is taken. She is probably the dominant child of a dominant mother. In contrast, the Orestes of Euripides is doubtful and pensive, and not the enthusiastic avenger that Electra would have wished for. He is full of doubts and vacillations regarding the morality of killing his own mother, despite his orders from Apollo. As with Hamlet, Orestes thinks that the voice he hears that drives him toward vengeance must be that of a demon. And his ultimate assent and action are more out of a form of resignation to his cruel destiny than out of a belief that the action Electra implores is a good one.

---

11 Euripides (484/480 B.C.–406 B.C.), *Electra*, edition and introduction by P. J. Finglas, Cambridge, Cambridge University Press, 2007.

For him, vengeance is bitter – not sweet. There is a contrast between the dominant Electra and the doubtful Orestes.

4 The Judgment of Solomon in *the Bible*

The judgment of Solomon in the First Book of Kings, part of the Pentateuch, faced with the pleas of two women who claim to be the true mothers of a recently born infant, is considered wise. Positivism would have provided a solution such as remitting the child to a public institution until the identity of the real mother was discovered. But the wisdom of Solomon is not limited to a mechanical application of the law. Rather, displaying great imagination, he completely avoids a procedure involving expert evidence, which would have delayed the resolution of the situation to the detriment of the truly innocent party: the baby, separated from its mother until its true lineage was determined. Solomon seeks something more profound: to do justice, that is, to comply with the law, but to avoid the unnecessary suffering of the child and the true mother. He hence proposes the surprising solution of "splitting the child in two and giving half to each woman." But knowing that no true mother would permit the death of her child, preferring to lose it forever, upon hearing the selfish motives of the false mother: "it shall be neither mine nor yours – divide it!", he finds the correct solution, giving the child to the first mother. This is an example of a just solution and gave rise to the classical expression "Solomonic justice."[12]

5 *Doctor Faustus* by Christopher Marlowe

A famed piece of Elizabethan drama relating to contracts is the pact made with the devil in the renowned *Doctor Faustus*, by Christopher Marlowe.[13]

---

12 *Pentateuco, Primer Libro de los Reyes*, chap. XXIX ff. Pedro Talavera, *Derecho y Literatura*, Prologue by Adela Cortina, Granada, Editorial Comares, 2006, pp. 40–41. *Id., Law and Literature: A Still-Thriving Relationship*, María José Falcón y Tella (ed.), Prologue by Javier De Lucas, translation into English by Deirdre B. Jerry, Leiden-Boston, Brill-Nijhoff, 2025. Robert A. Ferguson, "On the Judicial Opinion as a Literary Genre," in *Yale Journal of Law and Humanities*, 2, 1990, pp. 201–219. *Id.*, "Untold Stories in the Law," in Peter Brooks – Paul Gewirtz (eds.), *Law's Stories*, New Haven, Yale University Press, 1996, pp. 84–98.

13 Christopher Marlowe (1564–1593), *Doctor Faustus: The A-Text*, Ed. David Ormerod – Christopher Wortham, Nedlands, University of Western Australia Press, 1989. Also edited by Linda Cookson, with an essay by Jan Kott, Harlow, Essex, Longman, 1984. And edited by Roma Gill, New York, Hill and Wang, 1966.

Faustus, a doctor of theology, conjures Mephistopheles[14] and, following a brief negotiation, signs a pact in blood, selling his own soul in exchange for various benefits. This pact may be interpreted as a metaphor for the man who prefers the material to the spiritual, losing his soul as a result. In contrast to the orthodox Christian view that the soul belongs to God, Faustus believes that his soul belongs only to him, and that he can therefore trade it in exchange for benefits.

Faustus' intent may be compared to Icarus, who flew so close to the sun that his wings of wax melted, and he was killed by the ensuing fall. Similarly, Lucifer, the demon, was first an angel, before later rebelling against God and being condemned to spend eternity in hell. Yet it is not pride that leads Faustus to his destruction, but his thirst for knowledge. In the first scene, Faustus seeks to obtain all knowledge, which does not exist in logic, medicine, law or theology, but only in magic.

Faustus' decision to sell his soul to the devil is not taken lightly and, moreover, when it is announced to Faustus that he will die, at the beginning he seeks (unsuccessfully) to renegotiate the contract. Finally, being a man of honor and, in his own fashion, a hero, he makes no attempt to break the pact when the time comes to comply with his obligations. He replaces the sanctity of God with the sanctity of the agreement. But he cannot conceive of God as a merciful God; rather, merely, as a just one.

6 William Shakespeare

6.1 *The Merchant of Venice*

In *The Merchant of Venice,* by William Shakespeare,[15] much has been written on the quality of the mercy shown by Portia toward Shylock. On one hand, she requests that Shylock be merciful, while on the other, she later acts with tremendous cruelty toward him. Portia should have been content with preventing Shylock spilling Antonio's blood. Was it necessary to appropriate all his

14 Wolfgang Holdheim, "Ways of Mephistopheles," in *Cardozo Studies in Law and Literature*, vol. 1, issue 2, fall 1989, pp. 211 ff.

15 William Shakespeare (1564–1616), *The Merchant of Venice*, Ed. M. Mahood, Cambridge, Cambridge University Press, 1987. *El mercader de Venecia,* Foreword by Vicente Molina Foix, Madrid, Alianza Editorial, 2010. There is also an ed. and trans. by the Instituto Shakespeare, supervised by Manuel Ángel Conejero Dionis-Bayer, Madrid, Cátedra, 2007.

property and threaten him with death, in addition to forcing him to convert to another religion?

Another theme is omnipresent in Shakespeare's work – see *Hamlet, King Lear,*[16] *Othello,*[17] and *Julius Caesar* – and is also found in *The Merchant of Venice*: that of vengeance through the law. This is a work of vengeance but using the law. Shylock does not take the law into his own hands and carry out an act of private vengeance against Antonio through private violence.

6.2 *Hamlet*

Hamlet, then, is a play about vengeance.[18] Was this Shakespeare's position regarding vengeance? This question suffers from three errors: it projects the values of a work of literature onto its author; it expects literature to be edifying or didactical; and it forgets that on the topic of vengeance, the question of its morality depends on the circumstances. Shakespeare's works reveal a considerable ambivalence concerning vengeance, with *Hamlet* fitting among works such as *Titus Andronicus, Julius Caesar, King Lear,* and *Macbeth,* which view it uncritically, and *The Merchant of Venice* and *Romeo and Juliet,* which clearly reject it.[19]

And the fact is that the most important work of literature about vengeance since Greek Antiquity – *The Oresteia,* for example – is the great *Hamlet.* Shakespeare's work urges caution in our responses to passion-driven vengeance. For Hamlet to be able to cause the death of his uncle with moral propriety, he must not do it in the heat of the moment. But Hamlet's justified doubts over the identity of the ghost's message force him – as they do the observer of the

---

16 William Shakespeare, *King Lear,* translation into Spanish by Luis Astrana Marín, Madrid, Imagine Ediciones, 2002. *El Rey Lear,* Foreword by G. K. Hunter, trans. by Javier Montes, Madrid, Gredos, 2011. Also edited by the Instituto Shakespeare, under the supervisión of Manuel Ángel Conejero Dionis-Bayer, Madrid, Cátedra, 2008. There is also a trans. with Foreword, by Enrique Moreno Castillo, Barcelona, DVD Ediciones, 2001.

17 See, James Boyd White, *The Legal Imagination...,* 1985 edition, *op. cit.,* pp. 109–205.

18 William Shakespeare, *Hamlet,* Ed. Philip Edwards, Cambridge, Cambridge University Press, 1985. There is a bilingual English Spanish edition by Luis Astrana Marín, Madrid, Imagine Ediciones, 2002. There is also a trans. and ed. by the Instituto Shakespeare, supervised by Manuel Ángel Conejero Dionis-Bayer, Madrid, Cátedra, 2011.

19 Richard A. Posner, *Law and Literature. A Misunderstood Relation,* Cambridge, Massachusetts, Harvard University Press, 1988. There is a translation into French by Christine Hivet and Philippe Jouary, *Droit et Literature,* Paris, PUF, 1996, pp. 76–92. *Id., Law and Literature,* Cambridge, Massachusetts, Harvard University Press, 1998. 3rd. ed. 2009. There is also a translation into Spanish by Pilar Salamanca and Marina Muresán, *Ley y Literatura,* Valladolid, Cuatro y el Gato, Colegio de Abogados de Valladolid, 2004.

play – to constantly reflect upon the task that falls to him, contradicting the impulses of his blood.

Hamlet shows the special moral status of pre-meditation as opposed to passion in the heat of the moment. Had Hamlet killed Claudius when the opportunity arose, in scene III, during the oration, in which Claudius orates without being aware of the presence of Hamlet on stage, the audience would understand it to be murder. In contrast, the death of Claudius occurs at the end of the play, when Hamlet has seen his mother poisoned in error. Shakespeare does not allow Hamlet to kill Claudius until he is faced with an irresistible provocation in front of his own eyes, which any audience would understand as making the act of vengeance necessary.

One scene in *Hamlet* refers to the tyrant Claudius' guilty conscience, in a manner that recalls the protagonist of *Crime and Punishment,* Dostoyevsky's celebrated novel, a work that we shall analyze later. Hamlet has the idea of performing a play, "something like the murder of my father," before Claudius, to see whether the king's guilty conscience would betray him. This technique, not applicable to emotionally cold psychopaths, was used with great skill as a useful tool for extracting confessions by Earl Rogers, a famed criminal attorney in California during the early 1900s. Following Hamlet's suggestion, Rogers attempted, through his crossfire of questions in court cross-examinations, a form of hypnosis of witnesses who lied, which would transport them to the time and place of the crime and force them to issue contradictory statements that betrayed the truth.

7 *Faust* by Johann Wolfgang Von Goethe

Marlowe's *Doctor Faustus* ends tragically, with Faust, an inveterate sinner and convinced of the unyielding nature of his error, as were Cain and Judas, closed to any opportunity for regret, in the hands of the devil who tortures him such that he suffers the torments of hell for all eternity. However, on the contrary, Goethe's *Faust*[20] is the object of a divine grace that absolves him, because "he has always struggled."

20 Johann Wolfgang von Goethe (1749–1832), *Fausto*, bilingual ed. by Helena Cortés Gabaudan, Madrid, Universidad Autónoma de Madrid, 2010. Also trans. by Miguel Salmerón, Madrid, Espasa Calpe, 2009. And in Barcelona, Océano, cop., prologue by Francisco Ayala. And in Madrid, Santillana, 1999, trans. and notes by Emilio Tadeo Blanco. And with Prologue by El Duque de Alba, Madrid, Espasa Calpe, 1998.

8 *Michael Kohlhaas* by Heinrich Von Kleist

Heinrich von Kleist was a German poet of the Romantic School. Amongst his many works, we find the plays *Hermann's Battle* and *The Prince of Homburg*, both of which had a great impact in their time. However, he is most famous for his celebrated novel *Michael Kohlhaas*.[21]

In Kohlhaas, we find a conflict of duties like that in Sophocles' *Antigone*, that is, a conflict between the duty to disobey the unjust law and the duty to respect it, though unjust, because it is in force. Von Kleist's Kohlhaas, like any literary character, is an ideal type, not directly transferable to reality. We deal with a limit case to be observed in theory, *in vitro*, as in a laboratory. What most stands out in this work is its showing, via the hero's oscillation, just how slippery the limits between revolt – in favor of the law – and revolution – against it – might be.

The "revolutionary" will thus once more become a wholesome rebel "defender of rights," accepting – as in civil disobedience – the penalty imposed by legitimate authority. Kohlhaas will receive justice – by the sword as he is noble. As for von Tronka, like Creon in *Antigone*, we assume his ruin is imminent.[22]

Kohlhaas embodies the wonder of the pathetic hero, the threat of law as opposed to freedom, a tragic dimension of heroism. As against arbitrary law, he emphasizes and radicalizes his posture using violence. Wishing to reform the law and drive the community, he begins by fomenting disorder.

9 *The Count of Monte Cristo* by Alexandre Dumas

In *The Count of Monte Cristo*,[23] Alexandre Dumas recounts how the protagonist, Dantès, seeks vengeance as the consummation of a kind of "personal justice." The Count's perspective is understandable through the empathy that his own personal history arouses; he has been the victim of sly tricks and

---

21 Heinrich von Kleist (1777–1811), *Michael Kohlhaas*, Barcelona, Pomaire, 1980. J. Hillis Miller, "Laying down the Law in Literature: The Example of Kleist," in *Derecho Natural*, 1985, pp. 1491–1514.

22 Giovanni Cosi, *Saggio sulla disobbedienza civile…*, *op. cit.*, pp. 167–175.

23 Alexandre Dumas (1802–1870), *El Conde de Montecristo*, translation into Spanish by Gregorio Cantera Chamorro, Buenos Aires, Losada, 2005. Also in Madrid, El País, 2004. And in Madrid, Debate, 2001. And in Barcelona, Folio, 2000. And in Barcelona, SAV, 2000. And in Madrid, Alhambra, 1932. There is also a translation into Spanish by Belén Jáuregui, Buenos Aires, Gradifco, 2007.

machinations by some of his most beloved friends. Dumas directly addresses the theme of the meaning of reparation for a crime in relation to the deepest wishes of the victim.

Beyond the narrative of the drama and the different intrigues that unfold within it, the basis of the work concerns profound themes such as loyalty, vengeance and the service of God. The protagonist is essentially obsessed with the search for justice, becoming the guardian of those who supported him and an avenging angel, a kind of executioner of God's justice, for those who betrayed him. But when innocent people are harmed by this vengeful enterprise, Dantès realizes that he cannot take punishment and vengeance into his own hands and that only God can carry out justice, and he ceases his attempts at vengeance.

10 *Wuthering Heights* by Emily Brontë

Wuthering Heights[24] is a literary work that portrays sexist values in a text written by a woman. There is a version with the same title, published under the pseudonym Ellis Bell, which is known for its violence and the presence of evil. Emily Brontë's version is more of a story of doomed love.

Since 1847, the year in which Brontë's novel was published, critics have described their astonishment at the ability of the author to address the theme of evil. Though her personal life was only somewhat unhappy, she shows a great ability to analyze the depths of evil. The text concerns the human capacity to cause violence, which takes a great variety of forms: legal, physical, sexual, emotional, social, and financial. The indirect narration of the author does not imply any open condemnation or intention to judge or punish those who commit such violence. Unlike those who consider that literature must have a moralizing and edifying purpose, the author of *Wuthering Heights* neither judges nor sermonizes. There is no evidence of repentance or reconciliation on the part of the villains in this book.

---

24 Emily Brontë (1818–1848), *Wuthering Heights*, Harmondsworth, Penguin, 1965. There is an edition by Paz Kindelán, translation into Spanish by Rosa Castillo, *Cumbres borrascosas*, Madrid, Cátedra, 2011. There is also a translation into Spanish by Carmen Martín Gaite, Barcelona, Alba Editorial, 2010. Also in Madrid, Siruela, 2007, with preface by Alejandro Gándara, translation into Spanish and notes by Cristina Sánchez-Andrade.

11 *Billy Budd, Sailor* by Herman Melville

In America, where individual rights, ever since independence was gained, have been considered natural, Herman Melville, in *Billy Budd, Sailor,*[25] written toward the end of his life, asserted the duty of authority to set aside those rights for "reasons of state."

Billy is a young, innocent sailor, incapable of any evil whatever. As opposed to him, there is John Claggart, the Master-at Arms. Both figures are perhaps drawn from Melville's innumerable, true-life years of navigation. The work is an, apparently, simplistic tale of the confrontation between good and evil, innocence and maleficence, ingenuity and warped. However, had the tale remained on that level, it would have been nothing but a Far West-style yarn of the goodies and the baddies, where the goodies always win in the end.

This is not the case. In this confrontation, Billy is falsely accused of plotting a mutiny. A third major character, who gives depth to the novel, is Captain Vere (the name is nothing accidental), who acts as an exceptional witness to the clash. Vere watches stupefied and impotent this duel between good and evil, this struggle without quarter which is carried on within every human being. When Captain Vere encourages Billy to defend himself, Billy loses all power of argument and releases his anger by dealing a blow to his accuser, the Satanic Claggart, who falls dead. Knowing the characters and the circumstances of those involved, the Court Martial, convened to judge the deed, holds that "Budd aimed at neither mutiny nor at homicide" and is reluctant to condemn him.

Captain Vere also considers Billy innocent but insists that "in the clash between military duty and moral scruple… the moral conscience must bow down before the power of command." Therefore, he sees himself obliged to court martial Billy and to execute him. Otherwise, the rest of the crew might think that an act of mutiny had gone without punishment and themselves also be led to mutiny. When Billy Budd is hanged, he cries out: "God save Captain

---

25 Herman Melville (1819–1891), *Billy Budd, Sailor*, Ed. Harold Beaver, Harmondsworth, Penguin, 1967. There is a translation into Spanish with notes, by José María Valverde, Madrid, Fascículos Planeta, 1984. *Billy Budd, marinero*, Madrid, El Mundo and Revista, Unidad Editorial, 1998. Also in Madrid, Compañía Europea de Comunicación e Información, 1991, translation by Julia Lavid. Also in Barcelona, Salvat; Madrid, Alianza, 1971. Cf. also, James Boyd White, *The Legal Imagination…*, 1985 ed., *op. cit.*, chapter 1, B, 2, c, p. 60. Richard H. Weisberg, *Law, Literature, and History. A Fateful Rendezvous with the Shoah*, in *International Studies in Law and Literature*, vol. 2, María José Falcón y Tella (ed.), Leiden-Boston, Brill-Nijhoff, 2025, pp. 156–165.

Vere!," and, from the sailors comes an echo of sympathy: "God save Captain Vere!"[26]

Order and authority are maintained even at the cost of the sacrifice of the innocent. Remorse and grief will not leave Vere for the rest of his days, and he will die with Billy's name upon his lips. Captain Vere, in *Billy Budd, Sailor*, is the portrait of the tormented man who is not alone, who lives in a greater or smaller community, on a ship or in the world, and who, like the civil disobedient, faces the dilemma of respecting the unjust law or, obeying justice, must disobey the law.

As with Pontius Pilate,[27] we are dealing with the dilemma of the man who would wash his hands, who acts unjustly regarding the individual with the mere end in view of observing the established order. It is a foretaste of the dilemma which U.S. society would confront in the 1960s and which had already been acutely intuited by Melville.[28]

One might affirm that Billy is Rousseau's "noble savage," Nietzsche's "master," while Vere, as well as Claggart, are consumed by resentment. Billy's execution is a great injustice. One may argue that the court martial was irregular as Claggart was not performing the duties of his position when Billy struck him. But the truth is that he was, because preventing mutiny was the official's main security duty. Rather than abandoning his position, he was abusing it in accusing Billy.

The death penalty appears excessive for conduct such as that of Billy Budd, but it must not be forgotten that in the 18th century a seaman who caused the death of an official could be executed. However, under English law, Vere should have waited until legal action had been taken against Billy and should have asked the Admiral Commander in this respect. The speed with which Billy is judged would only be justified if the conduct could have given rise to mutiny, although striking a superior officer during a time of war was a mutiny.

26 Michael Hancher, "Billy Budd Famous Last Words," *Symposium*, in *Cardozo Studies in Law and Literature*, vol. 1, issue 1, spring 1989, pp. 97 ff.

27 See the second tale ("Ius et Agape: The Trial of Jesus, or Impossible Justice") of François Ost, *Legal Tales. Once upon a Time, the Law*, in the series *International Studies in Law and Literature*, vol. 4, María José Falcón y Tella (ed. and foreword), Leiden-Boston, Brill Nijhoff, 2025, pp. 20–38.

28 Juan José Coy Ferrer, "Melville, Herman," in *GER*, 15, pp. 507–509. Ernest van den Haag, *Political Violence and Civil Disobedience*, New York, Harper & Row, 1972, pp. 11–13. Thomas Brook, *Cross-Examinations of Law and Literature: Cooper, Hawthorne, Stowe, and Melville*, Cambridge-New York, Cambridge University Press, 1987. Susan Weiner, *Law in Art. Melville's Major Fiction and Nineteenth-Century American Law*, Frankfurt am Main, Peter Lang, 1992.

The truth is that the fact that Billy was judged on the boat was a literary requirement for the development of the work, instead of moving the action to a later time when Vere would not play any role. It was an artistic requirement for the sake of the plot. Art sometimes goes against the due process of law.

Billy has a primal rage, but not bitterness or a spirit of vengeance – he has the natural animal instincts of a man of nature. He does not stop considering the consequences of acting as he does on a boat in a time of war. Billy is associated with Adam before fall. He is also related with the lamb of Christ, because he forgives Vere. Vere's paternal attitude toward Billy is comparable to God's sacrifice of Christ to save humanity. Claggart, on the other hand, is linked to the serpent, to the devil, rather than to God.

The contrast between Billy and Vere is the contrast between the natural and the civilized man. This is seen in Billy's lack of education as opposed to the well-read Vere.

The captain's dilemma is between obedience to positive law and obedience to natural law. In the end, positive law triumphs over natural law, according to which Claggart's death would have been just. But Vere does not only refer to the letter of the law. He also considers public order, the risk of mutiny. That is, there is a certain invocation of utilitarianism: the sacrifice of an innocent to safeguard the common good, the killing of one person for the benefit of society, the cutting out of the cancerous organ to save the body.[29]

12 *The Strange Case of Dr. Jekyll and Mr. Hyde* by Robert Louis Stevenson

In *The Strange Case of Dr. Jekyll and Mr. Hyde* (1886),[30] a doctor attempts a scientific experiment that would allow him to separate good from evil in a human being. Among other consequences, the experiment causes the murder of a Member of Parliament. The novel raises the question of the protagonist's criminal and moral responsibility in the commission of the crime. To solve the

29 Richard A. Posner, *Law and Literature, op. cit.*, pp. 165–171.

30 Robert Louis Stevenson (1850–1894), *The Works of Robert Louis Stevenson*, Swanston Edition, London, Chatto and Windus, in association with Cassell and Company Limited, William Heinemann and Longmans Green and Company, 1911–1912. Vol. V: *Strange Case of Dr. Jekyll and Mr. Hyde*. Vol. VI: *Treasure Island. Id., Dr. Jekyll y Mr. Hyde*, transl. into Spanish by Carmen Criado, Madrid, Alianza, 2004.

crimes, the narration contains the figure of a lawyer, who seeks to decipher the enigmas included in a mysterious testament.[31]

This novel is one of the most widely studied from the perspectives of numerous fields of knowledge, including psychology, criminology, psychiatry, medicine and moral philosophy. It reflects features of Victorian society such as its rigid moralism. Every bourgeois, such as Jekyll, hid a troglodyte such as Hyde.

The novel addresses various legal issues – for example, the theme of "duality" between the good side of a person (represented by Dr. Jekyll) and the evil side (embodied by Mr. Hyde). This duality gives rise to the following legal doubt: Is the doctor legally and morally responsible for the crimes that Hyde commits? The novel reflects how complicated it is to identify the doctor's criminal responsibility with respect to his "alter ego," Mr. Hyde.

The theme of the profound duplicity of life is at the core of this work. Jekyll's existence is an unending source of moral fears and rebukes, while the existence of Hyde is entirely free and without moral binds. There is no fear in Hyde's personality, while Jekyll is all fear. This is the consequence of separating the good and the evil of a single person. The experiment that is recounted is none other than a projection of the idea that happiness cannot be achieved by doing good, but by committing evil. This is the moral concept behind Orthodox Calvinism, as opposed to Hutchinsonian morality, according to which virtue is synonymous with happiness. From this perspective, the only way in which Jekyll can feel free of his obligations is to carry out his fantasies and become Hyde.

Nothing frightens Dr. Jekyll so much as confronting his internal darkness and shadows – those that all humans have within them. The novel reflects the conflict that arises when people do not know how to reconcile the internal inclinations that emerge from these shadows. To attain a harmonious life, we must walk alongside our dark sides, not hide from them. The shadows tend to cover all those things of which we do not feel proud, what we keep in dark rooms. As Socrates would say, one must know oneself.

If, on the contrary, we split the poles, the good and the bad, we will see the schizophrenic disintegration of the person. Because Jekyll's thirst for knowl-

31 Colin Manlowe, "Closer than an Eye: The interconnection of Stevenson's Doctor Jekyll and Mr. Hyde," in *Studies in Scottish Literature*, XXIII, Columbia, South Carolina, University of South Carolina, 1988. Jean-Pierre Naugrette, "The Strange Case of Dr. Jekyll and Mr. Hyde: pour une relecture ecossaise," in *Cahiers Victoriens et Edouardiens*, Montpellier, Université Paul Valéry, 54, October 2001. Edwards Owen Dudley, "Stevenson, Jekyll, Hyde and all the Deacon Brodies," in *FOLIO*, National Library of Scotland, issue 1, fall 2000. Christine Persak, "Spencer's Doctrines and Mr. Hyde: Moral Evolution in Stevenson's 'Strange Case'," in *The Victorian Newsletter*, University of Kentucky, 86, fall 1994.

edge, in wishing to separate the dark and light sides of humanity, leads him to pursue something which is impossible even for the most renowned scientists. The case is the same as that of Faust, who agrees to a pact with the devil motivated by his thirst for knowledge. The result is the death of no less than three people – Carew, Lanyon, and Jekyll himself – and a chain of criminal and unjust acts.

But Stevenson's attitude toward these facts is certainly not a moralistic one. He avoids moral judgments, covering the complexity of the human condition without moralizing, without puritanism and without referring to Victorian moral categories. The novel's chronicle is no more than the description that Dr. Jekyll's experiment does not have a future, because "Jekyll suffers both from the good and from the bad."

The novel *Dr. Jekyll and Mr. Hyde* admits various interpretations or readings. It is a story of suspense and intrigue; it is also an analysis of split-personality psychosis; and it is also a discourse on the dual morality of man, on the battle between good and evil, between the angel and the devil, between Cain and Abel.[32]

13 *1984* by George Orwell

George Orwell's celebrated novel *1984*,[33] a political work of dystopian fiction – along with Aldous Huxley's *Brave New World* (1932), and Ray Bradbury's *Fahrenheit 451* (1953) – and one of the most influential books of the 20th century, was published in 1949. During the process of writing the book, Orwell was already seriously ill with tuberculosis. He tells of the terrors of modern times, partly bearing witness to the horrors that had already happened and partly anticipating those still to come, all of which have fortunately yet come to pass.[34]

32 Albert Fina Sanglas, *Justicia y Literatura*, prologue by Eugeni Gay Montalvo, Barcelona, Bosch, 1993, pp. 110–112.

33 George Orwell (1903–1950), *1984*, epilogue by Thomas Pynchon, transl. by Miguel Temprano García, Barcelona, Penguin Random House Grupo Editorial, 2014. Also in Barcelona, Destino, 2012. Introduction by Fernando Galván, Reading guide by Francisco Alonso. *Id.*, *Animal Farm*, Barcelona, Destino, 2010, Spanish trans., *Rebelión en la granja*, by Rafael Abella. Also in Barcelona, Unidad Editorial, 1999, Foreword by Juan Pedro Aparicio.

34 See, George Orwell, "Lear, Tolstoy, and the Fool," in Sonia Orwell – Ian Angus (eds.), *The Collected Essays, Journalism and Letters of George Orwell*, 4, 1968. And in the same work, *Id.*, "Politics vs. Literature: An Examination of *Gulliver's Travels*." See also, François Ost

Disillusioned over his task of hiding the truth, Winston attempts to evade the vigilance of Big Brother and falls in love with a young rebel, also disillusioned with the Party, and called Julia. Both embody resistance and dissidence to society. To resist, they join an insurgent group led by Emmanuel Goldstein, author of *The Book*, a character who appears to be a reference to Trotsky, Stalin's nemesis, and who is just another member of the State's control apparatus. They are captured and tortured, and in room 101 Winston is forced to concede something that is evidently false: that 2 + 2 = 5. When the protagonists finally meet each other again, their love has been extinguished and replaced with love for Big Brother.

The work ends on a bitter note, when the rebel Winston, destroyed by torture and fear, ends up capitulating – not merely externally, but with an internal conviction, as expressed in the final words of the novel: "… but it was all right, everything was all right, the struggle was finished. He had won the victory over himself. He loved Big Brother."[35]

14 *The Firm* by John Grisham

The prolific John Grisham and his legal thrillers offer broad and not always superficial portrayals of legal practice (law in action, rather than law in books) in the world of the common law. His novel *The Firm* (1991)[36] is a genuine treatment of legal sociology, which describes in detailed fashion the way in which large law firms, lacking moral principles and scruples and desperate for financial profit, use all kinds of influences and pressure, legal ruses and tricks, to deprive the law of all its meaning, purpose and justice.

The Firm can be seen as a kind of allegory of the "a-professional professional," and of the categorical distinction between good and bad people, with lawyers who earn more than they deserve and whose ethical practices are more than questionable. It can also be read as a simple page-turner, offering pure entertainment and relaxation and without great literary pretensions.[37]

(with S. Van Drooghenbroecke), "George Orwell à la Cour de Cassation (note sous Cass. Fr. 9 October 2001)," in *Journal des Tribunaux*, 2002, pp. 1–57.

35 Alfredo Montoya Melgar, *El trabajo en la Literatura y el Arte*, Madrid, Civitas, 1995, pp. 131–133.

36 John Grisham (1955–), *The Firm,* translation into Spanish, *La tapadera,* by Enric Tremps, Barcelona, Planeta, 1993.

37 Richard A. Posner, *Law and Literature, op. cit.*, pp. 37–40.

CHAPTER 5

Miguel de Cervantes Saavedra

1 Significant Aspects of His Life[1]

The author of *Don Quixote*, who also composed significant works such as the *Exemplary Novels* (1613), featuring notable narratives like "Rinconete and Cortadillo," "The Glass Graduate" (alternatively rendered as "Doctor Glass-Case" and "The Glass Lawyer"), and "The Illustrious Scullery-Maid," among others, as well as *The Travails of Persiles and Segismunda* (1617), was born in Alcalá de Henares in 1547. The city is currently the site of the writer's birthplace-museum and annually confers the esteemed Cervantes Prize, the Spanish counterpart to the Nobel Prize in Literature. Our author succumbed to diabetes in Madrid in 1616.[2] The institute dedicated to promoting the practice and study of the Spanish language globally is named after him: Instituto Cervantes.[3]

Cervantes subsequently traveled to Madrid, where, it is suggested, he may have been a Jesuit student under an instructor enamored with Erasmus of Rotterdam,[4] the author of *In Praise of Folly* – the identical idea, depicted as folly or madness, that recurs in *Don Quixote*.

Cervantes did not originate from aristocratic lineage. His father was a "barber surgeon," a prevalent occupation rather than a prestigious vocation during that era. The sole relatively renowned member of the family was his grandfather, Juan de Cervantes, an attorney for the Royal Exchequer of the Inquisition in Córdoba, who later served as a prosecutor and royal counsel in cases related to the city's revenue. Subsequently, he was designated as deputy magistrate in

1 See our work, *El Derecho en Cervantes y Shakespeare*, Foreword by Carla Faralli, Madrid – Barcelona – Buenos Aires – Sâo Paulo, Marcial Pons, 2021. There is a translation into English by Deirdre B. Jerry, *The Law in Cervantes and Shakespeare*, Leiden-Boston, Brill-Nijhoff, 2021. Reviewed by Christina G. Waldman, What's New on SirBacon.org, pdf.

2 Jacques De Bruyne, "Introducción a la lectura del mejor libro de todos los tiempos," in Various Authors, *Tras las huellas de Don Quijote. Actas de la Jornada dedicada a* Don Quijote de la Mancha, Antwerp, Lessius Hogeschool, December 9, 2005, edition and translation by Lieve Behiels, Ministerio de Educación y Ciencia de España – Lessius Hogeschool (Associatie K. U. Leuven), 2007, pp. 9–22, quote on pp. 10 and 11.

3 Bruno Aguilera Barchet, "El Derecho en el *Quijote*. Notas para una inmersión jurídica en la España del Siglo de Oro," in *Anuario de Historia del Derecho Español*, 76, 2006, pp. 173–214, quote on p. 180.

4 José Moreno Ruffinelli, "El *Quijote* y el Derecho (I)," in *ABC Color*, October 2, 2005, p. 3.

HTTPS://DOI.ORG/10.1163/9789004766006-006

Alcalá de Henares and served as Acting Lord Mayor of Córdoba. Juan maintained a close bond of duty and camaraderie with Diego Hurtado de Mendoza, Duke of El Infantado.[5]

Cervantes's life, from a legal standpoint, was far from monotonous,[6] characterized by numerous lawsuits, frequent court appearances, and intermittent incarcerations. Despite maintaining an unwavering belief in the necessity of

5 Gonzalo Quintero Olivares, "La imagen de la justicia en el *Quijote*, en Cervantes y en su tiempo," in *Revista del Colegio de Abogados de Tarragona*, pp. 3–4: "With regard to his grandfather, I think there are just three pertinent facts we should remember: he always had a fair amount of money and did not leave his son (Rodrigo, Miguel's father), a poor barber but a medical surgeon; the family, including Miguel, knew what a judge was and what it meant for a public servant to be the mirror of honesty or corruption, something that would find its way into *Don Quixote*; and, finally, he did not want to spend his entire life in the same city and was constantly changing residences and professions, just as his grandson would."

6 José Manuel Pérez-Prendes Muñoz-Arraco (1933–2017), "Cervantes y los juristas. (Esbozo de una guía historiográfica)," in *Foro, Nueva Época*, Facultad de Derecho, Universidad Complutense de Madrid, 2, 2005, pp. 47–130. A summary of this work, without notes, is due to appear in the *Enciclopedia cervantina*, published by the Centro de Estudios Cervantinos in Alcalá de Henares. In his text (pp. 61–65), Professor Pérez-Prendes supplies many biographical details on Cervantes: "at age twenty-two he was already a fugitive from law enforcement officers [...] as he wished to elude the customary barbarous sentence of mutilation and banishment for a reported crime of grievous bodily harm" for which a warrant was issued for "his capture and arrest to carry out the sentence, handed down in absentia, which ordered 'that his right hand be severed' [...] At age forty he resurfaced, making an unglamorous living as a royal officer charged with military procurement and tax collection duties [...] It is well known that most of this period of his life was spent traveling roads and frequenting inns, he met speculators like the banker whose bankruptcy landed him in a Seville prison in 1597 [...] not to mention his ignominious excommunication by the Archdiocese of Seville [...] [later] the writer petitioned for an overseas post, whether as comptroller in the Kingdom of New Granada, or governor of Soconusco in Guatemala [...] The answer he received made it clear that the gates of the Americas were forever barred to him [...] [due to] the discrepancy between his own and his family's turbulent legal history and the type of character required, at least in theory, for such posts [...] as repeated situations had forced both him and his relatives to appear before the civil and criminal courts of the day [...] returning him time and again to a painful relationship with the law. The question of his innocence or guilt is a separate matter and does not eradicate the reality of murky proceedings resulting from the actions of his immoral grandfather Juan, or his insolvent, debt-ridden father Rodrigo, or his, shall we say, 'free and easy' Aunt María and daughter Isabel [...] [who] entered into temporary common-law unions (it would seem that they were a cut above mere mistresses) with men of certain status, priests, gentlemen, or merchants [...] Moreover, the rumor that he was descended from converted Jews, if true, would have placed him in a particularly labile group among those permitted to hold rights and obligations under the law [...] These circumstances of the great writer's life must have led him to view the law with more fear than hope of succor."

divine justice and the king as its embodiment, he vehemently opposed corruption and injustice, viewing them as detrimental afflictions of his era.

Cervantes's litigious disposition led him to encounter legal troubles from a young age. At the age of twenty-two, he was compelled to depart from Spain due to an unpleasant incident involving the injury of a royal master builder, Antonio de Segura, during a street altercation in Madrid. Cervantes was sentenced to ten years of banishment and the amputation of his right hand. To evade this, the youthful Cervantes absconded to Seville and subsequently to Italy. This experience elucidates the author's inclination to assert immunity from criminal law under the pretext of self-defense, attributing the following statement to Sancho Panza: "As of myself I am peaceful and no friend to mixing in strife and quarrels: it is true that as regards the defense of my own person I shall not give much heed to those laws, for laws human and divine allow each one to defend himself against any assailant whatever" (*Don Quixote* I, 8).

Nonetheless, Cervantes's disputes persisted; he was additionally accused of involvement in another altercation resulting in the death of a nobleman named Gaspar de Expeleta. Fortunately for the author of *Don Quixote*, the trial concluded with a verdict of not guilty.

Cervantes directly encountered the partiality of the judicial system in both the Segura case and the Expeleta issue.[7]

He took part in the Battle of Lepanto, incurring an injury to one hand; hence the renowned *moniker el manco de Lepanto*, the "one-armed man of Lepanto,"[8] he did not actually lose an arm. He was captured and detained in Algiers. Upon his return home after five years of captivity, he was accused by the Inquisition of conspiring with Muslims. Fortunately for him, the accusation was dismissed when it became apparent that he had been detained in Algiers involuntarily, where he attempted to escape on four distinct occasions and declined to convert to Islam to render his confinement more tolerable. All his attempts to escape were unsuccessful, and he ultimately attained his freedom through the intervention of a Dominican priest, who paid the ransom of five hundred ducats required for his release. This ransom arrived promptly, as his kidnappers intended to transport him to Turkey as a slave, where an unpredictable destiny loomed.[9]

---

7 Bruno Aguilera Barchet, "El Derecho en el *Quijote*. Notas para una inmersión jurídica en la España del Siglo de Oro," *cit.*, pp. 193–194.

8 Benito Juárez Carrasco, in *El Quijote Virtual. Revista anual Escuela no. 189*, Montevideo, p. 4.

9 José Moreno Ruffinelli, "El *Quijote* y el Derecho (I)," *cit.*, p. 4.

Besides being captured by the Turks, he was imprisoned twice and excommunicated on two occasions. Sixteen years after his return from Algiers, he was incarcerated in the Royal Prison in Seville for seven months due to his inability to provide an adequate explanation for the funds he had acquired as a tax collector, his profession at that time.[10] He subsequently returned to incarceration, this time in Valladolid.[11] Consequently, he possessed an intimate familiarity with the prisons of his era, depicting them in the preface to *Don Quixote* as places "where every misery is lodged and every doleful sound makes its dwelling." Although Cervantes had indeed experienced the harshness of justice, it was not for violent offenses or property crimes, akin to the galley slaves in *Don Quixote*, but predominantly for indebtedness.

Indeed, Don Miguel habitually accrued debts. Cervantes's financial misfortunes were deeply rooted, as monetary issues pervaded his family history. They commenced with his tragic father, who was incarcerated for failing to repay a loan; all his possessions were confiscated, necessitating his appeal to his father, the attorney Juan de Cervantes, for assistance. Furthermore, his female relatives became entangled in legal disputes seeking restitution for the termination of engagements.[12]

This elucidates how Cervantes attained considerable legal knowledge without formal study. This knowledge is definitely evident in *Don Quixote*, and this work intends to examine it. It is essential to elucidate that *Don Quixote* is a fictitious narrative, not a legal document.

Cervantes's notable connection to the legal realm is evident from a brief analysis of his life and oeuvre, which are permeated with hearings, trials, judgments, sentencing, and various legal references. This is partially elucidated by his familial background; as noted, his grandpa, Juan de Cervantes, was a prominent lawyer in Córdoba, and Miguel resided in his household until his grand-

10 Bruno Aguilera Barchet, "El Derecho en el *Quijote*. Notas para una inmersión jurídica en la España del Siglo de Oro," *cit.*, p. 197.

11 See Daria Galateria, *Scritti galeotti: letterati in carcere*, Rome, Rai Eri, 2000.

12 "Cervantes had ample opportunity to observe numerous conflicts and lawsuits and was personally involved in various legal proceedings. His tempestuous life as a soldier, agent of the king, tax collector, and procurement officer made him familiar with a variety of institutions and allowed him to become well versed in the language of the law; it also gave him a profound knowledge of the society and government of his day. We know that he was educated in the humanities, Latin, and literature, but there is no evidence that he ever studied law, 'except perhaps to complement other studies considered essential at the time'." Francisco Javier Blázquez Ruiz, "El sentido de la dignidad. Libertad, justicia y utopía según D. Quijote," in José Francisco Alenza García (ed.), *Cervantes y el Derecho. Ideas cervantinas para el aprendizaje del Derecho,* Colección Facultad Ciencias Jurídicas UPNA, no. 2, Cizur Menor (Navarre), Thomson Reuters Aranzadi, 2016, p. 76.

father's demise in 1556, when the writer was nine years old. The protagonist of *Don Quixote* is fundamentally motivated by a search for justice and freedom in his numerous adventures.

It has been proposed that the author of *Don Quixote* may have pursued legal studies at the University of Salamanca; nevertheless, his name is absent from the enrollment records of that institution. Cervantes's understanding of the law can be attributed to his practice of studying legal materials.[13]

One ponders Cervantes' perception of his own legal acumen. Although his work has no explicit references, we can draw some assumptions from the character of Don Quixote, who serves as a partially autobiographical figure. Cervantes stated, "For me alone was Don Quixote born, and I for him; it was his to act, mine to write; we two together make but one" (*Don Quixote* II, 74). This suggests that, since Cervantes regarded Don Quixote as a "jurisperito," he likely perceived himself similarly. The term jurisperito denotes an individual possessing practical, rather than technical, legal knowledge, while jurispericia, or "legal expertise," represents a colloquial variant of a lawyer's proficiency, considered inferior to "jurisprudence." Consequently, a jurisperito is characterized by a limited and superficial understanding of a nation's laws. Don Quixote was evidently not a jurisconsult; at most, he may be characterized as a jurisperito.[14] Sancho Panza could not even aspire to this inferior rank, and his success as a judge in the Island of Barataria was solely attributable to his own ingenuity, as his legal knowledge was utterly nonexistent.[15]

Cervantes undoubtedly lacked a genuine jurist's understanding of the law, as seen in the absence of references to the extensive Spanish legislation of his

---

13 Rafael Álvarez Vigaray, *El Derecho civil en las obras de Cervantes*, Granada, Comares, 1987, pp. 42–43. David Eisemberg, "La biblioteca de Cervantes," in Riquer, *Studia in honores prof. M. de Riquer,* 4 vols., Barcelona, 1987, II, pp. 271–328.

14 Germán José María Barreiro González, "El Derecho en la Literatura. ¿Cervantes iurisperito?," in *Gacetilla Colegial, Colegio de Graduados Sociales de León,* 79, 2004. *Id.*, "Don Quijote. Caballero andante jurisperito," in *Revista del Consejo General de Graduados Sociales de España,* 4, 2005. *Id.*, "Cervantes y Don Quijote Jurisperitos," in *Anales de Derecho: Colección Huarte de San Juan,* 6, 2005, pp. 13–38. *Id.*, "Cervantes y Don Quijote Jurisperitos (Una visión literaria del Derecho en Don Quijote de la Mancha)," in *Anales de Derecho, Universidad Pública de Navarra,* 6, 2005. *Id.*, "El Derecho como recurso literario en el *Quijote*: Cervantes y el ingenioso caballero jurisperito," in *Homenaje a Don Miguel de Cervantes Saavedra con motivo del IV Centenario del nacimiento de Don Quijote, Anuario da Facultade de Dereito,* 2005. *Id.*, "Ius quijotescum (El Derecho como recurso literario en el *Quijote*: Cervantes y el Ingenioso Caballero Jurisperitos)," in *Anuario da Facultade de Dereito da Universidade da Coruña,* 9, 2005.

15 Rafael Álvarez Vigaray, *El Derecho civil en las obras de Cervantes, op. cit.*, pp. 43–47.

era in *Don Quixote* or any of his other writings.[16] Cervantes similarly refrains from referencing the regulations pertaining to knights-errant or the testament of Don Quixote, nor does he acknowledge any prominent legal scholars of his era – such as the civil jurist Gregorio López or members of the Salamanca School like Francisco Suárez, Francisco de Vitoria, and Juan de Mariana – or the notable dispute between Fray Bartolomé de las Casas and Juan Ginés de Sepúlveda. Nonetheless, Avellaneda's spurious *Don Quixote* demonstrates an understanding of notable figures across various scientific disciplines.[17]

Cervantes maintained a significant connection to civil law due to his roles as a husband, father, testator, and executor of his brother Rodrigo's will; to commercial law, as he often utilized financial instruments such as letters of credit, payment orders, and promissory notes in his professional endeavors and dubious personal transactions; and to labor law, stemming from his interactions with various employers throughout his tumultuous career. Therefore, while lacking any legal education and without being a jurist, he acquired substantial knowledge through intensive reading, as demonstrated by the over three hundred volumes in his personal library.[18]

There is a distinct distinction between the lives of Cervantes and Shakespeare. The former dedicated his life to traveling, engaging in warfare, undertaking many occupations, and experiencing multiple incarcerations and releases, whilst his English counterpart never traveled beyond London.[19] Both *Don Quixote* and *Hamlet* employ the idea of lunacy as a literary trope. It is noteworthy that Sigmund Freud, the pioneer of psychoanalysis, acquired proficiency in Spanish to read Cervantes's work in its original language.

---

16 Francisco Manuel García Costa, "El Derecho constitucional en el *Quijote*," in *Anales de Derecho*, Universidad de Murcia, 23, 2005, pp. 187–202. This article is a transcript of the lecture titled "El *Quijote* y los fundamentos del Derecho," delivered at Cajamurcia Aula de Cultura on October 25, 2005, as part of the international course "La modernidad del *Quijote*," p. 192: "As we know, in 1605 the *Nueva Recopilación* [New Code of Laws] enacted by Philip II in 1567 was still in force, a code which upheld the *Fuero Juzgo* (654), *Fuero Real* (1254), *Espéculo* (1256), *Siete Partidas* (1265), *Fuero Viejo* (1356), *Ordenamiento de Alcalá* (1348), and the Royal Ordinances of Castile (1404), according to the order of precedence established in 1505 by the Laws of Toro. Yet in *Don Quixote* we find no reference to the myriad and heterogeneous Spanish laws that existed at the time."

17 Francisco Manuel García Costa, "El Derecho constitucional en el *Quijote*," *cit.*, pp. 193–194.

18 Xabier Añoveros Trías de Bes, "El Derecho y la justicia en la obra de Cervantes," in *Digestum Legal* and at http://digestum.es/el-derecho-y-la-justicia-en-la-obra-de-cervantes/, pp. 9 and 10.

19 Manuel Richard González – Iñaki Riaño Brun, "Jueces y Administración de Justicia en el *Quijote*," in José Francisco Alenza García (ed.), *Cervantes y el Derecho. Ideas cervantinas para el aprendizaje del Derecho, op.cit.*, pp. 255–256 and 265.

Don Quixote arguably elevates its author, Miguel de Cervantes, to the status of a literary character, a fictional hero in whom the distinction between life and writing is challenging to discern. Nevertheless, "The most revered author in history passed away in complete destitution, unaware that his writing would create an unparalleled legacy for humanity. Due to the benevolence of the Third Order of St. Francis, he was interred in the convent of the Discalced Trinitarian nuns. Recently, the globe was astonished by reports regarding the 'discovery' of his remains."[20]

2 Cervantes and the Law

Legal issues are prominently and frequently featured in the works of Miguel de Cervantes.[21] The concepts of fairness in contrast to legality and the idea of

20 Edwin Arteaga Padilla, "Editorial. Hacia una quijotización del Derecho Penal," in *Justicia*, 30, December 2016, pp. 9–12, quote on p. 9.

21 José Manuel Pérez-Prendes Muñoz-Arraco, "Cervantes y los juristas...," *cit.*, pp. 48ff.: Legal expressions were one of his most habitual ways of writing, just as they later would be for Leopoldo Alas, aka "Clarín." (On this topic, see José Manuel Pérez-Prendes Muñoz-Arraco, *Leopoldo Alas "Clarín" y el espíritu de las leyes*, Oviedo, 2002. Ignacio Torres Muro, "Clarín, jurista," in María José Falcón y Tella – Juan Antonio Martínez Muñoz (eds.), *Estudios Jurídicos Multidisciplinares. José Iturmendi Morales, Maestro Complutense. Homenaje*, Valencia, Tirant lo Blanch, 2020, pp. 1015–1026. There is a translation into English by Deirdre B. Jerry, in María José Falcón y Tella and Juan Antonio Martínez Muñoz (eds.), *Challenges to Legal Theory. Essays in Honor of Jose Iturmendi Morales*, Leiden-Boston, Brill-Nijhoff, 2021.) Cervantes was familiar with the law in general and had a special interest in certain legal issues. For example, he used the term "generales de la ley" (generalities of the law) in reference to grounds for exemption or disqualification from trial proceedings; notarial phrases like "libre y sin cautelas" (free and unencumbered); trial terminology such as "traslado a la parte" (make known to the party); concepts like civil death, the loss of a person's legal capacity; the aphorism "mejora de tercio y quinto" (improving the third and fifth part), when a testator increases the share of one of his legitimate heirs; and the "dote" (endowment) mentioned by Sancho Panza, as well as the bridal dowry. We also find Roman maxims like "summum ius, summa iniuria" and "nulla est redemptia," indicating a final judgment that cannot be overturned, and others such as "con pie derecho" (on the right foot) or "por el hábito de San Pedro" (by St. Peter's habit). This list is by no means exhaustive; p. 55: "A series of laws on specific matters gradually dislodged, first the *Ordenamiento de Montalvo* and later Philip's *Recopilación*, and Cervantes shows that he was not ignorant of this new legislation. This is evident in his more or less explicit yet always obvious references to norms enacted in his lifetime, such as the exceptions to the sumptuary laws (Q., II, 14); the legal regulation of the use of weapons (Q., II, 34, 38) or carriages (Q., II, 36); laws on gambling (Q., II, 49), the attire of pilgrims (Q., II, 54), etc. He even knew of the Cortes' petitions to pass other new laws, as apparently did occur with the act proposed in

freedom are persistent themes. He frequently references human dignity and what is currently termed fundamental rights and freedoms. His work also addresses marriage and familial relationships, as well as labor connections, providing significant essential insights on the governance and organization of republics and nations.[22]

The prevalence of legal themes in Cervantes's oeuvre is so significant that he was formerly thought to be a jurist. Currently, that argument has been rejected in favor of the assertion that his legal knowledge was predominantly a result of his own humanistic self-education. Miguel de Cervantes, in contrast to Quevedo, Góngora, and Calderón, did not acquire a university degree in any discipline; rather, possibly due to his fervor for reading and a life immersed in practical experiences, he chooses to cultivate himself as a man of considerable erudition. Additionally, it is essential to consider the extensive life experiences gained from his diverse vocations, such as secretary or chamberlain to a cardinal, professional soldier, tax collector, and procurement officer for the Spanish Armada. An additional significant factor – common with Shakespeare – was his engagement with the court system on multiple occasions for both personal and familial reasons.[23]

3 Analyzed Work: *Don Quixote*

3.1 General Considerations

In 2002, the Nobel Prize Committee conducted a survey of one hundred distinguished authors, requesting them to choose the one hundred most signifi-

Valladolid in 1555 on begging, which Sancho applied as governor (Q., II, 51), or the 1592–1598 laws of Madrid on Moriscos (Q., II, 54), etc."

22 José Manuel Pérez-Prendes Muñoz-Arraco, "Cervantes y los juristas…," *cit.*, pp. 59 ff.: Cervantes favored a greater emphasis on ius commune. His opinion of the value of a legal education varied depending on the quality of each university. Throughout *Don Quixote*, Cervantes snubs the smaller schools and praises the most renowned, such as the universities of Salamanca, Alcalá and Paris. In this respect, he "speaks satirically of the curate's alma mater and has Samson Carrasco boast of having graduated from Salamanca […] he is not above making disparaging remarks when those who speak are legal professionals: 'I know, as everyone knows, that the gownsman's weapon is the same as a woman's, the tongue.'"

23 José Francisco Alenza García, "Estudio Preliminar," in the compilation *Cervantes y el Derecho…*, *op. cit.*, pp. 39–40.

cant works of world literature.[24] At the pinnacle of the list, akin to a phoenix emerging from its ashes, was *The Ingenious Gentleman Don Quixote of La Mancha*.[25]

Miguel de Cervantes, the author of *Don Quixote* (the surname Saavedra was appended for publishing purposes),[26] had already reached the age of 57 when the first part of his esteemed novel was published. It emerged after precisely twenty years of official literary silence, as no works of his had been published since *Galatea*, despite his having written, but not printed, six of his *Exemplary Novels* and numerous comedies, most of which remained unperformed.[27]

The initial volume of *Don Quixote* was released in 1605 in Madrid, lacking the acknowledgment it warranted, as it was not regarded as a significant artistic endeavor during the apex of the Spanish Golden Age, which was characterized by prominent authors such as Lope de Vega, Fernando de Rojas, and

---

24 José Ricardo Pardo Gato, "El Derecho en la época del *Quijote*," published on February 10, 2009, at https://aranzadiycivitas.wordpress.com72009/02/10/el-derecho-en-la-epoca-del-quijote/, pp. 1ff.: On the occasion of the recent centennial, the Instituto de Estudios Jurídicos Internacionales Conde de Aranda organized an international seminar at the Vicálvaro Campus (March 15–17, 2005) led by the institute's director, Bruno Aguilera Barchet, who gave a keynote address titled "El *Quijote* como fuente jurídica." Other lecturers included Escudero López, who spoke on "El *Quijote* y la Inquisición," Gilardeau on "Le Quichotte ou les prodromes de l'Ecole Moderne du Droit Naturel," and Ruiz Rodríguez on "La enseñanza del Derecho en las universidades castellanas en tiempos del *Quijote*."

25 Miguel de Cervantes Saavedra (1547–1616), *Don Quijote de La Mancha* (1605–1615), edited by John Jay Allen and illustrated by Jean Mosnier, Madrid, Cátedra, 2015. There is also an edition by Florencio Sevilla Arroyo and Antonio Rey Hazas, Alcalá de Henares, Centro de Estudios Cervantinos, 1993; Madrid, 2005. Other noteworthy editions are those of Diego Clemencín of 1833–1839 (whose notes were incorporated in the 1966 Madrid edition published by Ediciones Castilla and for which the *Índice* by Carlos F. Bradford, Madrid, 1885, reprinted in 2005, is quite useful); Francisco Rodríguez Marín (Madrid, 1906–1917, 1927–1928, and 1947–1949); Vicente Gaos (Madrid, 1987); Francisco Rico (Barcelona, Crítica, 2001); Instituto Cervantes (2 vols., Madrid, 2004); and the Fourth Centennial edition (Real Academia Española and Asociación de Academias de la Lengua Española, 2004). On the editions of this work, see the catalogue of the exhibition *El* Quijote, *biografía de un libro* (Madrid, Biblioteca Nacional, 2005) and the essential *Catálogos*, 179, 180, and 184 by Luis Bardón, Madrid, 2005. All English quotations in this book are taken from the translation by John Ormsby (1885), *The Ingenious Gentleman Don Quixote of La Mancha*, New York/Boston, Thomas Y. Crowell and Co., 1906.

26 Luis Vásquez Coronel, "Don Quijote constitucionalista, adalid de la libertad," published on June 12, 2017, at http://legis.pe/don-quijote-constitucionalista-adalid-libertad/, p. 2 of 7.

27 Juan Luis Alborg (1914–2010), *Historia de la Literatura española*, 2nd ed. with an index of names and works, vol. II, *Época barroca*, Madrid, Gredos, 1970, pp. 127–195, quote on p. 127.

Francisco de Quevedo, among others. As time progressed, the effort garnered the attention of not only the Spanish-speaking community but also of humanity at large.[28]

In 1615, Cervantes produced the second part of his magnum opus, also printed by Juan de la Cuesta. The impetus for this second installment was the 1614 publishing of an apocryphal version attributed to Alonso Fernández de Avellaneda, released in Tarragona.[29] This is thought to be a pseudonym that obscured the author's true identity, "potentially Jerónimo de Pasamonte, a comrade of Cervantes, who was offended by his derogatory portrayal in the first part of *Don Quixote* and conceived the 'vindictive' plan to exploit the initial volume's success by publishing a sequel, which, fortunately, has been recorded in history without undermining the integrity of Cervantes's work."[30]

Don Quixote is a seminal work in the Spanish language and one of the preeminent achievements in global literature. It is an enduring product, "the flaws of which are graciously disregarded due to its profound insights. It serves as an unending resource and reference for psychology, psychiatry, history, philosophy, politics, sociology, law, and various other disciplines."[31]

Excluding the Bible, no other work has been published and translated as extensively.[32] Indeed, one of the initial languages into which Cervantes' novel was translated was Italian. In 1622, Lorenzo Franciosini translated the initial

---

28 Edwin Arteaga Padilla, "Editorial. Hacia una quijotización del Derecho Penal," *cit.*, p. 9: "For some, *Don Quixote* is a lesson about the grandeur and misery of the human condition. For others it is a treatise on psychiatry; others, on the contrary, regard it as a study of split personality [...] In my limited understanding, *Don Quixote* is an X-ray of Cervantes, that is, an autobiography [...] The author becomes one with his work [...] Not even Cervantes himself is more famous than *Don Quixote*. The main character of the work took on a life of his own, overshadowing the author [...] This is uncommon, for not even *Hamlet* is fused with Shakespeare."

29 Alonso Fernández de Avellaneda, *Nuevas andanzas del ingenioso hidalgo Don Quijote de la Mancha: (El "Quijote" apócrifo)*, edited, revised, and annotated by Mercedes M. Villalta, with a preface by Emiliano M. Aguilera, Barcelona, Iberia, Diamante, 1961. Another more recent edition is that of F. García Salinero, Madrid, Clásicos Castalia, 1971; reprinted in 1999. Jean Sarraïlh, "Lesage, adaptateur d'Avellaneda," in *Bulletin Hispanique*, Faculté des Lettres de Bordeaux, LXVI, July–December 1964, pp. 359–362.

30 Gonzalo Quintero Olivares, "La imagen de la justicia en el Quijote, en Cervantes y en su tiempo," cit., pp. 9–10.

31 Edwin Arteaga Padilla, "Editorial. Hacia una quijotización del Derecho Penal," *cit.*, p. 10.

32 "Today the novel has conquered the entire world and is perhaps, together with the Bible, the Koran, and the complete works of Lenin, the book that has been translated into the greatest number of languages, for example its first English translation by Thomas Shelton in 1612. Since its first edition, a total of more than 500 editions in Spanish and over 1,500 in nearly 50 languages, including Gaelic, Javanese, and Tibetan, have been published." http://www.rinconcastellano.com/renacimiento/quijote_idiomas.html#.

part, while the second was published precisely one and a half centuries prior to Beccaria's work. Upon analyzing the works of Cervantes and Beccaria, it becomes evident that certain requests of the Italian author were intricately integrated into the narrative of the Spanish writer's novel years prior.[33]

The novel has established Cervantes as the preeminent writer in the Spanish language, comparable to Shakespeare in English, Dante in Italian, and Homer in Greek.[34] The genuine aesthetic merit of *Don Quixote* lies in its ability to confront us with greatness. The protagonist of *Don Quixote* has achieved legendary status. Madariaga observes that this pertains to *Don Quixote, Hamlet, La Celestina* or *The Tragicomedy of Calisto and Melibea, Don Juan Tenorio*, and *Faust*. Each embodies freedom, dignity, love, and paradise, respectively.[35]

---

33 Edwin Arteaga Padilla, "Editorial. Hacia una quijotización del Derecho Penal," cit., p. 10. On p. 12, he writes that "Sancho did not act as a judge who is the 'mouthpiece of the law', as Beccaria said," but rather played a creative role by exercising careful deliberation.

34 Manuel Jofré, "*Don Quijote* como novela moderna y la conjunción de géneros altos y bajos. *Don Quixote* as a modern novel and the mixture of high and low genres," Universidad de Chile, Facultad de Filosofía y Humanidades, http://www.scielo.cl/scielo.php?script=sci_arttext8pid=S07-18220120060001000003, p. 1; p. 3: In the novel *Don Quixote* we find a "conjunction of old discursive and literary genres, such as the biography (of the problematic hero) but, above all, it is an adventure novel;" p. 4: "Cervantes's revolutionary artistic act consisted in combining a series of high, sublime, erudite, canonical genres with another set of low, popular, oral, and marginal genres.

The high genres with intertextual influence – as model, parody, or critique – are the epic, lyrical poetry, rhetorical tradition, Aristotelian poetics, Renaissance theater, and different novel styles. Only in one of these high genres, such as the novel, can we distinguish the following subgenres present in Cervantes's work: pastoral, sentimental, chivalrous, picaresque, and Byzantine/baroque."

P. 5: "On the other hand, the low genres that came to roost in *Don Quixote* are folk tales, romances, the guile that is the guiding spirit of the picaresque, popular proverbs and sayings, folklore, comedy, Socratic dialog, and Menippean satire."

P. 6: "There is a set of traits that characterize the modern novel, all of which are found in Cervantes's novel. The conflict between the hero and the world is central [...] The modern novel might easily be understood as the sum of obstacles the hero must overcome to attain his objective."

P. 10: *Don Quixote* is a "multi-vocal" work, alternating between the cultured, learned voice of Don Quixote and the rustic, down-to-earth voice of Sancho. To this we must add a third voice, that of the narrator, and the voices of the different characters who appear in the various adventures.

35 Salvador de Madariaga (1886–1978), *Guía del lector del* Quijote, Madrid, 1926, and Madrid, Espasa Calpe, 2005.

The novel elucidates the chivalric ideal while adopting a satirical stance against it.[36]

Numerous authors, including Franz Kafka, Jorge Luis Borges, Milan Kundera, Benito Pérez Galdós, and Thomas Mann in his *Voyage with Don Quixote*, have articulated their interpretations of *Don Quixote*. In Spain, the Generation of '98 consistently scrutinized the work: Unamuno in his *Vida de Don Quijote y Sancho*,[37] Ortega y Gasset in *Meditaciones del Quijote*,[38] Azorín in *Castilla*,[39] and Salvador de Madariaga in *Guía del lector del Quijote*. The knight and his squire epitomize the Spanish psyche, which Unamuno termed "the tragic sense of life."[40] Manzoni, Dickens, Fielding, Sterne, Goethe, Flaubert, Stendhal, Melville, Mark Twain, and the Russians Gogol, Tolstoy, and Dostoyevsky[41] are all esteemed lovers and disciples of Cervantes.[42] Dostoyevsky referenced *Don Quixote* over thirty times in his oeuvre, asserting that "only one such book is bestowed upon humanity every few centuries." The Russian author's most significant insights regarding Cervantes's work are manifested in *The Idiot*, particularly through the character of Prince Myshkin, and in *Devils* (also known as *Demons* or *The Possessed*).

36 Néstor De Buen, "Derecho y Justicia en Cervantes: burla burlando," in *Revista de Derecho Privado*, IV, 11, May–August 2005, pp. 3–17. Laurent De Sutter, "The Quixote Principle, or Cervantes as a Critique of Law," in *Law & Literature*, vol. 26, issue 1, 2014, pp. 117–126.

37 Miguel de Unamuno (1864–1936), "Sobre la lectura e interpretación del *Quijote*," in *La España moderna* (April 1905), reprinted in *Obras Completas*, Madrid, 1958. *Id.*, *Vida de Don Quijote y Sancho*, Madrid, Espasa-Calpe, 1964 and 1971. Also with introduction by Ricardo Gullón, in Alianza Editorial, 1987 (comprising the paper "El sepulcro de Don Quijote"). Also in Madrid, Cátedra, edited by Alberto Navarro, 1988 (1905). Felipe González Vicén, "La figura de Don Quijote y el donquijotismo en el pensamiento de Miguel de Unamuno," in *Romanische Forschungen*, Hamburg, 57, 2/3, 1943.

38 José Ortega y Gasset (1883–1955), *Meditaciones sobre el* Quijote, in his *Obras Completas*, vol. I, Madrid, Alianza Editorial/Revista de Occidente, 1983 and 2014 (1914). Also in Madrid, Cátedra, 2001. And *Meditaciones del* Quijote *con un apéndice inédito*, Madrid, Alianza, 1981.

39 Also Azorín (José Martínez Ruiz) (1873–1967), "Cervantes y América," in *Con permiso de los cervantistas*, Madrid, Biblioteca Nueva, 1948. Also in Alicante, Biblioteca Virtual Miguel de Cervantes, 2004.

40 Fernando Benzo Mestre, *Las ideas jurídicas de Don Quijote*, Discurso pronunciado en la toma de posesión como académico numerario de la Real Academia de Doctores el día 4 de febrero de 2005. Contestación del Académico Excmo. Sr. Dr. D. Jesús López Medel, p. 40.

41 Tamara Djermanovic, "Dostoyevski y Don Quijote: poética y estética de una ilusión," in *Anales Cervantinos*, XLVII, 2015. Arturo Serrano-Plaja, *Realismo "mágico" en Cervantes: "Don Quijote" visto desde "Tom Sawyer" y "El idiota,"* Madrid, Gredos, 1967.

42 Juan Luis Alborg, *Historia de la Literatura española*, 2nd edition with an index of names and works, vol. II, *Época barroca*, *op. cit.*, p. 187.

Numerous renowned painters, such as Salvador Dalí (in his *Retrat de Don Quixot*) and Pablo Picasso, paid tribute to the Gentleman of La Mancha in their creations. His influence is seen in the works of Sorolla and Goya. *Don Quixote* has similarly influenced several cultural forms, including music, as demonstrated in the compositions of Henry Purcell, G. P. Telemann, Jules Massenet, Manuel de Falla, Cristóbal Halffter, and even Broadway productions such as *The Man of La Mancha* (1965).

Julio Calvet Botella articulated a prevalent perspective, stating, "*Don Quixote* is our inaugural and most comprehensive novel [...] In Spain, Cervantes possessed the exceptional insight to definitively shape the novel genre, which during the seventeenth century was still oscillating between forms akin to the epic and the fable chronicle."[43] He further contextualized the work by noting, "Don Quixote's existence spanned from 1556 to 1615, coinciding with the reigns of Philip II and Philip III in the Spanish monarchy [...] a remarkable epoch in Spanish history." Regarding the Spanish Church during *Don Quixote*'s era, it was also the institution of eminent saints: Teresa de Cepeda, Saint Teresa of Ávila, and Juan de Yepes, Saint John of the Cross.

Everyday discourse in Spanish incorporates terms such as *quijotesco, quijotil, quijotesca, quijótico, quijotada, quijotería,* and *quijotismo*, which reflect the quintessential notion of confronting an illusory peril or attempting to modify that which is immutable. "Quixotism is a fundamental aspect of human existence, a dialectical process wherein our perceptions of reality and our ambitions, both simplistic and grandiose, progressively adjust to the vicissitudes of life, never achieving complete success. Quixotism is characterized by the creation of illusions about reality, or, as Sancho humorously articulated, harboring windmills in one's mind (I, 7). From this perspective, *Don Quixote* itself would be the inaugural *quijotada*."[44]

43 Julio Calvet Botella, "Don Quijote y la justicia o la justicia en Don Quijote," lecture, in Biblioteca Virtual Miguel de Cervantes, http://www.cervantesvirtual.com/obra-visor/don-quijote-y-la-justicia-o-la-justica-en-don-quijote-conferencia-0/html/00921af6-82b2-11df-acc7-002185ce6064_3.html, p. 1.

44 Jesús Ruiz Fernández, "El *Quijote* y el fenómeno del quijotismo," in *Revista de Humanidades*, 20, January–December 2013, p. 2: "It is often said that *Don Quixote* is a critique of idealism, of our illusions which, like birds, soar above the grey ordinariness of life [...] neither Alonso Quixano nor Don Quixote are mad. They are rather worse off: they are dead. As both force their reasoning upon things, rather than allowing those things to improve them, they never move forward; they do not live." Pp. 3–4: "Quixotism is the same as utopia [...] If we build things up too much in our minds, we will eventually collide with our illusions [...] But *Don Quixote* has one ingredient that is missing from the popular concept of utopia: the necessity of illusions in life [...] In *Don Quixote*, sordid reality is no less absurd than the world of chivalry. It is almost like a new allegory of the

The Ingenious Gentleman of La Mancha was conceived in a prison. The specifics are somewhat ambiguous, although it appears that Cervantes commenced writing his timeless work while incarcerated in Argamasilla de Alba.[45]

In his analysis, the author juxtaposes Don Quixote with Leonardo's *Mona Lisa*, noting that "her enigmatic smile persistently defies the scrutiny of even the most astute art critics; within that smile, they perceive, or believe they perceive, an expression of a particular sentiment shaped by their individual temperament and mindset." Furthermore, he asserts that "figures such as Prometheus, Don Juan, and Hamlet have become essential components of the human spirit, coexisting with it and destined to endure only until its demise. Don Quixote, the Knight of the Rueful Countenance, ethereal like El Greco's figures,[46] is one of humanity's enduring journeying companions. Its contents are inexhaustible, as it evades capture with the same finesse as a shadow pursuing us."[47]

María Dolores Borrell Merlín stated that "Cervantes composed a work in dialogue, as dialogue – masterfully employed by Plato and subsequently Cicero – facilitates a richness of registers and enables the reader to empathize with the characters, rendering them vibrant."[48]

Don Quixote is split into two volumes. The book is extensive, comprising 52 chapters in the first part and 74 in the second, with a total of 669 recognized characters, including 607 males and 62 females. Analyzing the characteristics

---

cave, a new formulation of Platonic dualism. One might say that the cave of Montesinos is *Don Quixote* in a nutshell [...] It seems as though Cervantes took pleasure in revealing the meanness of reality, the accursed ugliness of that vale of tears, in this evil world of ours, where hardly anything is untainted by a blend of wickedness, skullduggery, and slyness [...] Nabokov called *Don Quixote* an encyclopedia of cruelty [...] Don Quixote's death is crucial to comprehending the work, shedding a new light that lets us see it in its entirety. For that light reveals how life cannot exist without illusions [...] The loss of illusions due to the accumulation of disappointments over the course of a lifetime is the ultimate cause of death."

45 José Moreno Ruffinelli, "El *Quijote* y el Derecho (I)," *cit.*, p. 4.

46 José María Callejas Berdonés, *Persona y ética en el* Quijote, research project supervised by Professor Ana María Layra, Madrid, May 13, 2003, Universidad Complutense de Madrid, p. 13.

47 Mario Alario di Filippo, "'El Quijote' en América," lecture delivered to the Colombian Academy of Language in Bogotá on August 6, 1975, on the occasion of his induction as a fellow; available at http://cvc.cervantes.es/literatura/quijote-america/colombia/alario.htm. Also in "La justicia en el *Quijote*," in *Universitas*, 49, 1975, pp. 19–30, quote on the first and second pages of the article.

48 María Dolores Borrell Merlín, "La justicia y la paz en el *Quijote*," in *Cuadernos de Estudios Manchegos*, 29, 2005.

of certain animals, such as Don Quixote's steed Rocinante and Sancho's donkey, is indeed intriguing.

The inaugural book was published in 1605, during the era of prominent intellectuals such as Erasmus of Rotterdam, Luis Vives, and Machiavelli, alongside renowned works like Thomas More's *Utopia*. The initial title of the first part was *El ingenioso hidalgo Don Quijote de la Mancha,* and, as already mentioned, it was published in Madrid by Juan de la Cuesta.

The second part was released by the same printer a decade later, in 1615, titled *Segunda Parte de El Ingenioso caballero Don Quijote de la Mancha*. Notably, in this context, the term *hidalgo*, denoting a member of the Spanish gentry, was supplanted by *caballero*, signifying "knight" or "gentleman." This substitution likely aimed to prevent any ambiguity with the apocryphal *Quijote de Avellaneda*, which purported to be a continuation of the first part of *Don Quixote* and was attributed to an individual using the pseudonym Alonso Fernández de Avellaneda. In the subsequent section, various characters have perused the initial text and provide their critical assessments in a clever literary exercise.

Don Quixote is referred to as the "Knight of the Rueful Countenance" or "Knight of the Faith," a designation attributed to Miguel de Unamuno.

The primary theme of *Don Quixote* is the feasibility of discovering the ideal inside reality. This theme is closely connected to another: freedom. Cervantes was imprisoned in Algiers, where he attempted multiple escapes and endeavored to preserve Europe from the Ottoman Empire. Can we transform the world, or does the world transform us? What is more rational or less irrational? Do heroes genuinely exist? We encounter the notion that "things are not as they appear," highlighting the issue of lunacy and the disparity between appearances and truth. The theme of love is evident, chiefly represented by the figure of Dulcinea del Toboso and several secondary relationships, alongside the notion of jealousy.[49] Political idealism is also evident in the concept of utopia, illustrated in instances such as Sancho's administration of the Island of Barataria and Don Quixote's fantasies in the cave of Montesinos. The concept of justice is examined via the experiences of the young Andrés, the galley slaves, and various other narratives.

Cervantes's oeuvre is distinguished by its parody and satire of the fantastical, social critique, and psychological reality. It may be seen as a comedy, the

49 Roberto González Echevarría, *Amor y ley en Cervantes*, translated by Isabel Ferrer Marrades, Madrid, Gredos, 2008. English version, *Love and the Law in Cervantes*, New Haven-London, Yale University Press, 2005. Peter Goodrich, "Erotic Melancholia: Law, Literature, and Love," in *Law & Literature*, vol. 14, issue 1, spring 2002, pp. 103–129.

inaugural contemporary novel, and the first polyphonic narrative on multiple levels. This work serves as a conduit between the medieval and Renaissance eras and the early modern period. Like a cathedral, diverse genres cohabit happily within it: chivalric romance,[50] as well as picaresque, pastoral, romantic, and sentimental literature, culminating in the emergence of the modern novel.

In contrast to traditional knights-errant like Amadis of Gual, Palmerin of England, Tirant lo Blanc, or Lancelot, who typically triumphed over their foes, Don Quixote is inherently unsuccessful. His victories are only contingent upon his opponent's horse faltering or his adversary being disarmed at a pivotal moment in combat.[51]

Upon its premiere in 1605, *Don Quixote* was superficially regarded as a "humorous" work. Over the ages, researchers have thoroughly examined the novel, deriving numerous interpretations and analyses from various perspectives: literary, philological, philosophical, religious, social, political, and, in this instance, legal.[52]

---

50 "In the chivalric romance, there is a hero at the center of the plot. He has numerous adventures and emerges victorious from them. He fights injustice and social abuse, monsters, sorceresses, enchanters, and bandits, and frees princesses and other people in difficulties. He is assisted by a loyal squire, whom he rewards handsomely for his services. Moreover, the knight renders service to a chosen lady whom he worships and performs great deeds to win her heart. But the enchanter is also a character who frequently appears in books of chivalry: good and evil magicians influence the life and madness of Don Quixote. There is another common theme that cannot be omitted: the hero's return to his place of birth, where he receives a hero's welcome. Cervantes's reference to the classic chivalric romances is direct." Hans-Werner am Zehnhoff, "*Don Quijote* y la parodia," in Various Authors, *Tras las huellas de Don Quijote. Actas de la Jornada dedicada a* Don Quijote de la Mancha, *op. cit.*, p. 60.

51 Jacques De Bruyne, "Introducción a la lectura del mejor libro de todos los tiempos," in Various Authors, *Tras las huellas de Don Quijote. Actas de la Jornada dedicada a* Don Quijote de la Mancha, *op. cit.*, p. 14. "Don Quixote is a utopian thinker, an idealist. He is defeated but not humiliated; conquered but not convinced. Don Quixote is not driven by a mere longing for adventure, or lust for glory, or a desire to imitate the knights-errant he so admired [...] In Don Quixote we always find a zeal for noble and just causes." "Don Quixote places above civil law the ethical code which commands, 'Do good to all alike'." Fernando Benzo Mestre, *Las ideas jurídicas de Don Quijote, op. cit.*, pp. 8–10.

52 María A. González Encinar, "Prologue," in Various Authors, *Tras las huellas de Don Quijote. Actas de la Jornada dedicada a* Don Quijote de la Mancha, *op. cit.*, pp. 1–4, quote on pp. 2 and 3.

During the 16th and 17th centuries, crime lacked a definitive and explicit definition, as it was sometimes conflated with ideas such as malice, offense, hurt, or sin.[53]

The novel addresses criminal law in multiple contexts.[54] For instance, a distinction is made between "capital punishment" and "other slow forms that effectively constitute civil death indefinitely," referencing "gambling houses," which underscores Cervantes's unequivocally negative perspective on the activities occurring within them. Sancho asserts, "Either I am not good for much, or I'll get rid of these gambling houses, for it strikes me they are very mischievous."[55] Additionally, Governor Sancho is resolute in his intention to rid his island of "all idle good-for-nothing vagabonds [...] who have neither profession nor property."

Furthermore, there are several references to mitigating circumstances in a legal or literary-legal context. One of these is "lovesickness," a euphemism for emotional turmoil characterized by mental and psychological repercussions stemming from romantic betrayal and disillusionment, chiefly jealousy.

Another manifestation of madness is exemplified by Don Quixote, an elderly man by contemporary standards, irritable and irascible, emotionally unstable, a highly original and imaginative megalomaniac afflicted by a mental disorder that commenced when his alter ego, Alonso Quixano, succumbed to feverish fantasies and resolved to become a knight-errant. The story presents

53 Xabier Añoveros Trías de Bes, "El Derecho y la justicia en la obra de Cervantes," in *Digestum Legal* and at http://digestum.es/el-derecho-y-la-justicia-en-la-obra-de-cervantes/, p. 1.

54 On this subject, see Luis Arroyo Zapatero, "Delitos y penas en el *Quijote*," *blog.uclm.es*, 1993. Enrique De Benito y La Llave, "La criminología del 'Quijote'," in *Lecciones Universitarias del* Quijote, III, Universidad de Zaragoza, 1905. Quintiliano Saldaña (1878–1938), "La criminología de el *Quijote* (notas para su estudio)," in *Revue Hispanique*, 68, 1926, pp. 552–581. *Id.*, "Picardía y criminología españolas en Cervantes," in *Filosofía y Letras*, 1, 4, 1916, Madrid, Universidad Central; and in "La criminología de el *Quijote*," in *Revue Hispanique*, 68, 1926. Rafael Salillas (1854–1923), "La criminalidad y la penalidad en el 'Quijote,'" in *El Ateneo de Madrid en el III Centenario de la Publicación de "El Ingenioso Hidalgo Don Quijote de la Mancha," Conferencias*, Madrid, Imprenta de Bernardo Rodríguez, 1905, pp. 85–118. Sergio Vela Treviño – Sergio Vela Martínez, "Don Quijote y el Derecho penal," at the round table on "El concepto del Derecho en el *Quijote*," held during the assembly at Guanajuato, *Actas*, VI, 1994. Juan Diego Vila, "Delincuencia e imaginario femenino en el *Quijote* de 1605: Don Quijote, Ginés de Pasamonte y los galeotes," in Edith M. Villarino *et al.* (eds.), *La cultura hispánica y Occidente. Actas del IV Congreso Argentino de Hispanistas*, 1995.

55 Rafael Álvarez Vigaray, *El Derecho civil en las obras de Cervantes*, *op. cit.*, pp. 141–142.

numerous examples of the protagonist's psychological instability, which in certain situations is regarded as a condition that exonerates him from responsibility.

Cervantes critically and sarcastically reveals the great severity and harshness of sentences and punishments during his era. The author's perspective on prostitution and pandering is quite intriguing.

The previous action was permitted during his era. Sex trade was not overtly persecuted, and the Inquisition did not regard it as a grave sin, although circumstances altered following the Council of Trent. This elucidates why Governor Sancho regarded the case of the cattle-dealer and the prostitute as a transaction for services performed rather than a criminal offense.

This aligns with Don Quixote's positive perception of the profession of pimp (but not sorcerer) as an amusing and tranquil vocation, attempting to mitigate its criminal implications by proposing that it be regulated, inspected, and overseen by authorities, thereby incorporating it into the roster of legally recognized professions.

Contrary to the prevailing inquisitorial sentiment of the age, Cervantes challenges the legitimacy of torture as a legally permissible and customary method for obtaining evidence, especially through coercing a prisoner into confessing his crime.

Cervantes meticulously examines and delineates the individuals in his work, focusing on their physical, anatomical, and psychological characteristics, foreshadowing the emergence of criminal anthropology. Centuries later, Garofalo developed his thesis of the "criminal man" (*l'uomo delinquente*), asserting that specific individuals were inclined to criminality due to their physical characteristics, thereby perpetuating the historical debate on the innate goodness or evil of human beings. Thomas Hobbes endorsed the notion that humanity is intrinsically malevolent, but Jean-Jacques Rousseau advocated for the other perspective.

An examination of the casuistry in *Don Quixote* reveals numerous instances pertaining to criminal law. For example, numerous individuals perceive an instance of abuse in the narrative of a farmer who is discovered whipping a youngster for losing his sheep. Historically, it was prevalent for a master to administer corporal punishment to his subordinates, and not long ago, this practice was also standard inside the educational system, particularly in prestigious English public schools.

Other scholars categorize the innkeeper's exploitation of the "girls of the district" as a manifestation of human trafficking.

Some perceive an element of sexism in Sancho Panza's characterization of Aldonza Lorenzo as a "brave lass, and a right and stout one" with a somewhat "goaty" or masculine scent.[56]

Miguel de Cervantes's absence of formal legal education did not inhibit him from incorporating specific legal terminology from the *Ancien Régime* in his magnum opus, such as *mero et mixto imperio*, the royal authority conferred by ancient Roman emperors to their vassals, encompassing the power to penalize offenders (*mero imperio*) and to adjudicate civil matters (*mixto imperio*). Cervantes humorously employs the phrase to denote complete and unequivocal dominion over an object, namely that of Sancho over a pot.[57]

3.2 Aggravating and Mitigating Factors in the Narrative

Añoveros Trías de Bes identifies several circumstances that alter criminal liability in *Don Quixote*: premeditation or treachery (an aggravating factor evident in Chapter 3 when Don Quixote was dubbed a knight at the inn, where he refers to the carriers and the landlord as "knaves and traitors"), self-defense (a mitigating factor in the windmill episode), insanity (grounds for exemption), operating under cover of darkness (an aggravating factor, as demonstrated when the bandit Gines de Pasamonte steals Sancho's donkey at night in the Sierra Morena), obedience to superior orders (a mitigating factor applicable to Sancho, who, as a subordinate, cannot be deemed accountable), recidivism (an aggravating factor illustrated by Gines de Pasamonte's narrative in the episode involving the galley slaves), and temporary insanity (grounds for exemption, central to Cardenio's tale in Chapter 24).[58]

3.3 Distinct Offenses Referenced in the Novel

The novel mentions a number of specific crimes, aside from those committed by Don Quixote:[59] adultery; pandering, the offense of the fourth galley slave interrogated by the knight; murder, specifically that of Vicente Torrellas by his lover Claudia and the crime of Roque Guinart, both narrated in Chapter 60 of

56 Pedro García Martín, foreword to the compilation *Cervantes y el Derecho. Ideas cervantinas para el aprendizaje del Derecho*, Cizur Menor (Navarre), Thomson Reuters Aranzadi, 2016, p. 28.

57 Bruno Aguilera Barchet, "El Derecho en el *Quijote*. Notas para una inmersión jurídica en la España del Siglo de Oro," *cit.* pp. 192–193.

58 Xabier Añoveros Trías de Bes, "El Derecho y la justicia en la obra de Cervantes," in *Digestum Legal* and at http://digestum.es/el-derecho-y-la-justicia-en-la-obra-de-cervantes/.

59 *Ibid.*

the second part; bribery; criminal damage to property, such as the assaults on the windmills, the wine skins, and Master Pedro's puppet-theater, or the burning of books from Alonso Quixano's library by the curate, the barber, the housekeeper, and the niece; disorderly conduct, which Sancho attempts to ban by making proclamations on his island; sorcery, which was a frequent accusation in Cervantes's time and part of the reason why the fourth slave was sent to the galleys; larceny and theft, illustrated when the adventurers found a valise with gold crowns in the Sierra Morena which Don Quixote wanted to return to its owner but Sancho prevailed upon him to keep, when Gines de Pasamonte stole Sancho's ass, when Roque Guinart's band robbed the travelers, and the "spoils" taken in Chapter 8 ("Sancho Panza, when he saw the friar on the ground, dismounting briskly from his ass, rushed towards him and began to strip off his gown. At that instant the friars' muleteers came up and asked what he was stripping him for. Sancho answered them that this fell to him lawfully as spoil of the battle which his lord Don Quixote had won"); slander; gambling, of which Sancho says, as mentioned before, "I am not good for much, or I'll get rid of these gambling houses," though one of the notaries with him advises against it, saying that "as the vice of gambling has become common, it is better that men should play in houses of repute," for their powerful owners would be difficult to overcome, and it is better to control than to outlaw gambling; personal injury, for instance in Don Quixote's altercation with the Toledo traders on their way to buy silk (Chapter 4), the sad passage in which he attacks the friars of St. Benedict, the skirmish that Don Quixote and Sancho had with a group of Yanguesan carriers, and the knight's famous assault on a herd of sheep and rams which he mistook for armies, to mention but a few of the cases when Don Quixote injured others or was injured himself; perversion of the course of justice (Don Quixote calls Sancho a "perverter of the squirely rules of knight-errantry" during an argument about the wages Sancho is owed, and the same crime is mentioned in the sentences handed down to the galley slaves and the aforementioned instances of "arbitrary law"); and prostitution, the world's oldest profession, which though formally prohibited is viewed with a degree of tolerance, as denoted by the fact that the prostitutes, whom Don Quixote takes for lovely maidens, assist him in his dubbing ceremony, and by the likeable character of Maritornes, who combines sexual services with her employment as a maid-of-all-work at the inn of Juan Palomeque the Left-handed.

3.4 *Don Quixote*'s Perspective on Criminals

Don Quixote's perspective on criminal justice, rooted in kindness, charity, mercy, and compassion, prompts him to perceive delinquents as victims rather than offenders, thereby rendering the punishment of criminal behavior as unjustified, a notion clearly illustrated by his liberation of the galley slaves. Don Quixote perceives delinquents as casualties of an inequitable society and a corrupt judicial system. It is important to remember that throughout Don Quixote's era, torture was a commonplace method for eliciting confessions, although even the most innocent individuals would concede to guilt under such coercion. Moreover, the defendants possessed minimal financial resources and infrequently managed to present an effective case. Even now, justice remains susceptible to arbitrariness and partiality.[60]

Delinquents are frequently portrayed in a more favorable manner than conventional, law-abiding individuals. Cervantes's work reveals[61] that criminals were often assigned nicknames or sobriquets reflecting their moral characteristics and particularly their physical attributes, including natural or accidental deformities, or other distinctive features that aided in their identification, which were also documented in their criminal records to enhance their capture. In *Don Quixote*, it is noted that Gines de Pasamonte is strabismic, the innkeeper Juan Palomeque is sinistral (hence his moniker), Maritornes is exceedingly unattractive, Sancho possesses a protuberant abdomen, Altisidora has halitosis, Aldonza emits an unpleasant odor, and the duchess suffers from suppurating lesions on her thighs. All these elements serve as distinguishing features, like Odysseus's scar discussed by Auerbach.[62]

Cervantes mostly focuses on offenses related to women and love, such as adultery. Additionally, he discusses various transgressions, including cattle rustling (*Don Quixote* I, 22), attempted sorcery (I, 22), coin counterfeiting (II, 3), and offenses such as the rape of a minor, sexual abuse, and child abandon-

60 Francisco Javier Nistal, "La percepción del delincuente, por Don Quijote de La Mancha. Su posible traslado a la sociedad actual," at https://cj-worldnews.com/index.php/criminologia-30/historia-de-la-criminologia/item/1738-la-percepci/C3/B3n-del-delincuente-por-don-quijote-de-la-mancha.

61 See Constancio Bernaldo de Qirós (1873–1959), "Figuras delincuentes en el *Quijote*," in *Anales de la Universidad de Santo Domingo*, 12, 1947. Ignacio Rodríguez Guerrero, *Tipos delincuentes del* Quijote, 2 vols., foreword by Carlos López Narváez, Quito, Ed. Casa de la Cultura Ecuatoriana, 1966, and Medellín, Bedout, 1974. Julio Garet Mas, "Sobre *Tipos delincuentes del* Quijote" (Quito, 1966), in *Revista Nacional*, 228–229, Montevideo, April–September 1966, vol. XI, pp. 317–319.

62 Roberto González Echevarría, "El amor y el Derecho en Cervantes. Love and the law in Cervantes," *cit.*, esp. pp. 16–17.

ment, perpetrated through false promises of marriage (I, 22 and 24), bribery (II, 41), and banditry (II, 40).[63]

One year prior to Cervantes' birth, the distinguished legal scholar Francisco de Vitoria passed away in Salamanca. Other prominent figures of the 16th-century academic tradition included Diego Covarrubias and Antonio Gómez, a professor at the University of Salamanca. Cervantes likely lacked familiarity with their beliefs regarding crime and prisoner treatment, as his schooling did not encompass such topics; however, he acquired insights from his experiences on the streets and in jails, where he spent more time than in academic settings. His tenure as a soldier in Italy was enlightening, as the country was a nexus of innovative ideas during that period. Cervantes was progressive, championing the humanitarian principles articulated by Beccaria and Howard in the 17th century, perceiving the prisoner as a human rather than an object. He likely also remembered Saint Augustine's renowned admonition: "love the sinner and hate the sin."[64]

Don Quixote's conception of punishment is future-oriented, aimed at the offender's rehabilitation and reeducation – *punitur ut ne peccetur* – rather than retrospective, focused on retribution and "an eye for an eye" – *punitur quia peccatum est.* Cervantes anticipated contemporary "deterrents" in contrast to the conventional concept of "penalties." He asserted, "Punishment which is not followed by pardon nor is allayed in the end by forgiveness is not punishment, but hateful gloating and exultation in hurting another." Don Quixote states, "My intentions are always directed to worthy ends, to do good to all and evil to none." "For Cervantes, the crux of social interactions was the imperative for individuals to abstain from transgressing the values of fellow community members. As Don Quixote advised Sancho to console him after relinquishing his governorship, the paramount concern is a tranquil conscience, which is forfeited when one unjustly assaults others." "He perceived criminality as one of life's myriad adversities, a natural occurrence, yet he did not examine it with the detached scrutiny of an academic, nor did he disdain it as a base issue to be hidden away."

---

63 José Manuel Pérez-Prendes Muñoz-Arraco, "Cervantes y los juristas...," *cit.*, pp. 129–130.

64 Luis Garrido, *La criminología en la obra de Cervantes*, speech on the occasion of his induction into the Mexican Academy of Language, June 11, 1956, Mexico, 1956, pp. 273 and 275. P. 276: "In the Cervantine world we sense a desire to mitigate severity, teaching us to treat prisoners not in a cruel but a Christian way. It also shows us that the loss of freedom entails suffering, so it behooves us to examine whether or not that loss is truly warranted and, if it is, ensure that prisoners are not mistreated by their warders, for 'it is not fitting that honest men should be the instruments of punishment to others, they being therein no way concerned'."

Durkheim may be referenced here. He underscores the distinction between psychology and sociology about punishment. From a psychological perspective, punishment may be a pathological phenomenon. Nonetheless, for Durkheimian sociology, it constitutes a typical, *normal* social phenomena.[65] This presents a notion of normality that deviates from conventional understanding. In sociology, normality is defined by its prevalence in specific types of societies at a particular stage of their development. Crimes, a phenomenon ubiquitous across all civilizations and eras, do not diminish with civilization but rather escalate alongside it. Therefore, from a sociological perspective, it can be stated that crime is a normal occurrence in every community. There exists only one constraint regarding the perception of crime as normal. Crime should not disrupt social equilibrium, which, according to Durkheim, is essential for societal health. The concept of social equilibrium, deemed vital, is fundamentally supported by flexibility: a system must possess adequate flexibility to allow for a certain degree of illegality. When the incidence of crime is minimal, society faces no significant threats and remains stable. Moreover, aberrant behavior is characterized by its personal and original nature, which may render it a creative or heroic act. For heroism and creativity to thrive in society, a requisite level of freedom must exist, necessitating a departure from established norms. The antithesis of liberty is crime. The optimal scenario would be a balance between compliance and regulation on one side, and dissent and innovation on the other. It is advisable to maintain the *status quo*, preserving equilibrium without deviation or excess.

Likewise, Durkheim differentiates between the Moral and the Sociological aspects of crime, in addition to its classification as a normal social reality and a *positive* social fact. Psychology may interpret crime as a manifestation of pathology, and moralists may regard it as deserving condemnation; however, Sociology posits that, provided no social imbalance arises – meaning crime remains within acceptable limits – criminality serves a constructive social function, reflecting societal health as an expression of freedom and creativity, albeit in a negative form. Durkheim's thesis reformulates the theological dilemma of good and evil in sociological terms, positing that the existence of good is contingent upon the possibility of evil. The rationale is straightforward: both

65 Hans Haferkamp, *Kriminalität ist normal – Zur gesellschaftlichen Produktion abweichenden Handelns*, Stuttgart, Ferdinand Enke Verlag, 1972. Cf. by the same author "Zur Notwendigkeit handlungstheoretischer Analysen der Kriminalität und der Kriminalisierung," in Arbeitskreis Junger Kriminologen (ed.), *Kritische Kriminologie,* 1974. Bernhard Haffe, "Hat emanzipierende Sozialtherapie noch eine Chance?," in *Seminar: Abweichendes Verhalten. III.* Ed. by Lüdersen and Sack, *Die Gesellschaft Reaktion auf Kriminalität,* Frankfurt am Main, 1977.

good and evil presuppose freedom. In the absence of freedom, individuals are incapable of committing evil, yet they are equally unable to perform good deeds. They represent two facets of the same entity. In addition to its indirect societal benefit, crime can, in specific instances, serve a direct purpose: it may facilitate social change and foreshadow future moral standards. This was true for Socrates. He was avant-garde, advocating for freedom of thought, even incurring a death sentence in accordance with Athenian law. Similarly, Jesus Christ, who was executed on the cross and deemed a common criminal by contemporary laws, disseminated the message of brotherly love for future generations.[66]

Don Quixote is a book that not only scrutinizes penalties but also investigates the individual who enforces them, the judge or arbiter of justice. Regarding this matter, Sancho asserts, "Judges are only flesh and blood, and must give to Nature what she naturally demands of them." In essence, "A judge must possess psychological insight and penetrate the depths of individuals' souls."[67]

3.5 The Episode of the Galley Slaves

Sancho's governance of justice as the ruler of his island exemplifies a singular instance of judicial proceedings. These instances often recur in other sections of the novel, with Don Quixote serving as an arbiter in the story involving the galley slaves and the case of the affluent farmer Juan Haldudo, who had abused his servant, the young shepherd Andres, delivering a punishment akin to a "labor law."

The narrative of the galley slaves[68] evokes multiple instances from Dante's *Inferno*, wherein the pilgrim interrogates the condemned regarding the

---

66 Gregorio Robles Morchón, *Crimen y castigo (Ensayo sobre Durkheim)*, Madrid, Civitas, 2001, pp. 73–83.

67 Luis Garrido, *La criminología en la obra de Cervantes*, Induction speech at the Mexican Academy of Language on June 11, 1956, Mexico, 1956, pp. 282–283 and 285–286. Francisco Javier Nistal, "La percepción del delincuente, por Don Quijote de la Mancha," *cit.*

68 On this subject, see Mair J. Bernardete, "Los galeotes (I, 22, 23, 25, 29): el criminal y la sociedad," in *Revista Hispánica Moderna (Columbia University Hispanic Studies)*, 31, 1965. Jean Canavaggio, "Burlas y veras en la aventura de los galeotes. Nueva reflexión sobre un episodio del *Quijote*," in *Anales Cervantinos*, 18, 1979–1980. Miguel García Posada, "El episodio quijotesco de los galeotes, ambigüedad lingüística y significación," in *Hispanic Review*, 2, 1981. José F. Martín, "Diálogo y poder en la liberación de los galeotes," in *Cervantes*, 11, 1991. Ángela Pérez García, "La aventura de los galeotes," in the compilation edited by María Ángeles Varela Olea and Juan Luis Hernández Mirón, *Huellas de Don Quijote: la presencia cultural de Cervantes*, Madrid, Universidad San Pablo CEU, 2005. Agustín Redondo, "De las terceras al alcahuete del episodio de los galeotes en el *Quijote* (I, 22). Algunos rasgos de la parodia cervantina," a work from 1989 reprinted several

essence of their transgressions to comprehend their torments. The identical device is employed in other theatrical productions, including Cervantes's own interlude, *The Judge of the Divorce Court*.[69]

Chapter 22 of the first part recounts the confrontation between Don Quixote and his loyal companion Sancho and a group of galley slaves. Don Quixote resolves to assist them and liberate them, disregarding Sancho Panza's prudent cautions against such actions. Upon hearing the narratives of the galley slaves,[70] Don Quixote demands their emancipation and assaults the guards when they decline. He successfully liberates the galley slaves with their assistance and instructs them to proceed to the city of El Toboso to exhibit themselves before his mistress, Dulcinea. The men decline, provoking an angry reaction from Don Quixote, who then faces abuse, stones, and theft from those he has just liberated.[71]

---

times, for instance, in *Actas del X Congreso de la Asociación Internacional de Hispanistas, I*. Theo Reichenberger – Kurt Reichenberger, "El alcahuete condenado: un detalle enigmático en el episodio de los galeotes," in the compilation edited by Kurt Reichenberger – Darío Fernández Morera, *Cervantes y su mundo*, vol. I, 2004. José Rosell Villasevil, "Los galeotes, espejo de Cervantes vapuleado," in *Toletum: Boletín de la Real Academia de Bellas Artes y Ciencias Históricas de Toledo*, 43, 2000.

69 Roberto González Echevarría, "El amor y el Derecho en Cervantes. Love and the law in Cervantes," cit., pp. 11–31, quote on p. 20.

70 *Don Quixote* tells the various stories of the men being taken to the galleys. The first galley slave says his offense was "that I loved a washerwoman's basket of clean linen so well, and held it so close in my embrace, that if the arm of the law had not forced it from me, I should never have let it go of my own will to this moment." The prisoner adds that, as he was caught in the act, "there was no occasion for torture."

The second galley slave speaks of "singing under suffering," a graphic description of his confession under torture. Here Cervantes seems to comment on the unreliable nature of confessions extracted by torture as a means of obtaining a fair criminal trial.

The third galley slave raises an important point regarding the corruption of the criminal system when he says that his crime was not having ten ducats, with which he would have "greased the notary's pen and freshened up the attorney's wit."

The fourth galley slave was condemned as a pimp and a sorcerer.

The fifth slave explains that his crime consisting in having sexual relations with four women, two of them his first cousins, by which he had several children. He also alludes to judicial corruption, saying that if he had had influence and money his fate would have been different.

The sixth and last galley slave is presented to Don Quixote as a famous prisoner, Gines de Pasamonte, whose crimes are not specified, only his ten-year sentence. Manuel Richard González, "Jueces y administración de justicia en el *Quijote*," in Various Authors, *Cervantes y el Derecho…, op. cit.*, pp. 266–269.

71 Albert Fina Sanglas, *Justicia y Literatura*, foreword by Eugeni Gay Montalvo, Barcelona, Bosch, 1993, pp. 17–24.

In this episode, Don Quixote's actions serve as a remarkable and unequivocal defense of due process in criminal proceedings and the notion of legal certainty, often neglected during that era.[72]

In Cervantes's Spain, torture was frequently employed to elicit confessions utilized as evidence in judicial trials, especially before the Tribunal of the Holy Inquisition. This differs from the contemporary concept of due process, which is founded on the principle that a defendant is presumed innocent until proven guilty, with the burden of proof resting on the party making the allegation, specifically the accuser. The accused is presumed innocent until contrary evidence is shown, therefore bearing no burden of proof. However, these regulations were not applicable in the criminal justice system of Cervantes's era. The trials were succinct and investigative. The defendant was a passive participant, anticipating to admit guilt, while the judge functioned as both investigator and inquisitor. In numerous instances, the defendant was unaware of the specific charges against him or the identity of his accuser.

During that period, torture was employed as an investigative method in criminal trials. Crime was seen as a sin for which the offender must seek atonement. Judicial authorities acted *ex officio* and resisted *favor libertatis*; hence, the accused was deprived of his liberty throughout the procedure, which was handled in secrecy and allowed no dissent from the prisoner. Torture was considered an acceptable method for obtaining confessions to be utilized as evidence against the accused. Methods of torture, like garrucha, are referenced briefly in *Don Quixote*. The text alludes to the brutality of torment: "For sudden pain is soon over, but that which is protracted by tortures is ever slaying without ending life" (*Don Quixote* I, 27). Nonetheless, it is important to acknowledge that the Castilian or "Christian" judicial system, despite its shortcomings, was superior to that of the "Moors," under which Cervantes endured captivity in Algiers.[73]

In the incident about the galley slaves, all the captives share a commonality: their sentences are disproportionate to their offenses. As each individual recounts his narrative, we observe other deficiencies within the criminal justice system of that era, including torture, corruption, the criminalization of poverty, and the harsh behavior of the guards. During Cervantes's era, penalties were grossly disproportionate.

Conversely, Don Quixote represents the essence of "humanism." "When equity may and should be brought into play, press not the utmost rigor of

---

72 Manuel Richard González, "Jueces y administración de justicia en el *Quijote*," in Various Authors, *Cervantes y el Derecho…*, *op. cit.*, p. 270.

73 *Ibid.*, pp. 259–265.

the law against the guilty, for the reputation of the stern judge stands not higher than that of the compassionate" (*Don Quixote* II, 42). Due to the unfavorable outcome of this interaction for our protagonist, most scholars have regarded it as a setback for idealism and a failure of perfect justice.

Historically, during the era of Don Quixote in the 16th century, imprisonment was not considered a formal sentence; the concept of prison as an autonomous punishment emerged only in the late 18th century. Although individuals who perpetrated crimes have been incarcerated since ancient times, such confinement was not regarded as a formal sentence. The initial endeavors of this nature were the English workhouses. Nonetheless, there were prior instances involving women, who were initially sentenced to the galleys, which were not exclusively for men, and then transferred to houses of correction. Galleys were primarily intended for the incarceration of immoral rather than criminal women. Their objective was to expunge these women – vagrants, criminals, prostitutes, and the like – from society to avert the dissemination of their moral corruption for religious and ethical purposes. Being dispatched to the galleys was a punitive action. Prison sentences, in the modern context, did not become prevalent until the late 19th and early 20th centuries.[74]

Cervantes astutely centered the episode of the galley slaves on a fundamental aspect of legal penalties, both historically and contemporaneously: the authority of the state to revoke individuals' intrinsic right to "freedom." While sentencing practices have progressed, the ethical quandaries remain unchanged: liberty, justice, the prerogative to punish, and the suitable modalities of punishment.

Due to their gallant act of liberating the galley slaves, Don Quixote and Sancho became fugitives from the law. Their offense constituted a "court case" as they had perpetrated a crime against the crown by liberating individuals condemned by the king's courts. In this regard, Don Quixote may be regarded as the inaugural heroic outlaw in the annals of Western literature. From that time until the conclusion of the first half, he would be chased by law enforcement authorities. Upon his detention by the officials of the Holy Brotherhood, he was entrusted to the curate and the barber due to his mental derangement, precluding any possibility of trial. They dispatched him home confined within a cage.[75]

74 Paz Francés Lecumberri, "De los pecados y las galeras en tiempos del *Quijote* hasta nuestros días," in José Francisco Alenza García (ed.), *Cervantes y el Derecho. Ideas cervantinas para el aprendizaje del Derecho.* Colección Facultad Ciencias Jurídicas UPNA, no. 2, Cizur Menor (Navarre), Thomson Reuters Aranzadi, 2016, pp. 179–198.

75 Roberto González Echevarría, "El amor y el Derecho en Cervantes. Love and the Law in Cervantes," *cit.*, pp. 10–31, quote on pp. 10–11.

CHAPTER 6

Fyodor Mikhailovich Dostoyevsky

1 Significant Aspects of His Life[1]

Dostoyevsky and his narrative[2] are related to Miguel de Cervantes, whom he admired,[3] or to Unamuno.[4] The Russian writer, whose life and work[5] still

1 *Vid.* María José Falcón y Tella, *Derecho y Literatura, op. cit.*, pp. 155–160. There is a translation into English, *Law and Literature, op. cit.*, pp. 166–172. *Id.*, "El progreso de la Humanidad: Dostoievski y Kafka," *cit.*, pp. 213–131.

2 Dostoyevsky's poetics and stylistics have been extensively studied by, among others, Natalia Arséntieva, "Tomar conciencia y expresarlo: 'el realismo en un sentido amplio' como método artístico de Dostoievski," in *Mundo Eslavo*, no. 5, 2006, pp. 251–252. *Id.*, "Dostoievski," in *Materiales e Investigación*, no. 20, Saint Petersburg, Nestor Historia, 2013. Mijaíl Mijaílovich Bajtín, *Problemas de la poética de Dostoievski*, translation by Tatiana Bubnova, Mexico, Fondo de Cultura Económica, 1986. Buenos Aires, FCE, 1993. *Id.*, *Dostoevskij: poetica e stilistica*, translation into Italian by G. Garritano, Turin, Einaudi, 1968.

3 On the subject, see, Tamara Djermanovic, "Dostoyevski y Don Quijote: poética y estética de una ilusión," in *Anales Cervantinos*, XLVII, 2015, pp. 9–24. Natalia Arséntieva, "Dostoievski: clave del 'Código Cervantes'," in Miguel Ángel Garrido Gallardo – Luis Alburquerque García (dirs.), *El* Quijote *y el pensamiento teórico literario*: *Actas del Congreso Internacional celebrado en Madrid los días del 20 al 24 de junio de 2005*, 2008, pp. 353–372. Arturo Serrano-Plaja, *Realismo "mágico" en Cervantes: "Don Quijote" visto desde "Tom Sawyer" y "El idiota,"* Madrid, Gredos, 1967. Joaquín Verdú de Gregorio, "Huellas de la inocencia en la creación artística (Cervantes-Dostoievski-Velázquez-Dreyer)," in *Miscelánea Comillas, Revista de Ciencias Humanas y Sociales*, vol. 65, issue 126, January-June 2007.

4 Jorge Serrano Martínez, "Influencia literaria de Dostoyevski en la obra de Unamuno," 2020. There is a translation into English, "On the Influence of Dostoyevsky in Unamuno's Work," in *Revista Científica Electrónica de Ciencias Gerenciales*, no. 45, year 15, 2020, pp. 35–42.

5 Abrahan Yarmolinsky, *Dostoievsky. La vida y la obra,* preliminary note by Aníbal Castelnuovo, Buenos Aires, Zamora, Colección Los Genios, no. 3, 1947. Serge Persky, *La vie et l'oeuvre de Dostoievski*, Paris, Payot, 1924. Orest Miller, "Materialen zur Lebensgeschichte Dostojewskis," in the *Dostojewski-Gesamtausgabe* by Piper & Co., vol. 11, Russian edition, 1882. Francisco Rodríguez Criado, *Mi querido Dostoievski*, Alpedrete (Madrid), Ediciones de La Discreta, 2012. J.-Wladimir Bienstock, *Les inédits de Dostoievski*, translation into French by J.-Wladimir Bienstock. Rafael Cansinos Assens, *Obras completas de Fiódor M. Dostoievski*, Madrid, Aguilar, 1961. Pilar Andrade Boué, "La figura del idiota de Dostoievski y sus reescrituras literarias y cinematográficas," in *Anuario de la Sociedad Española de Literatura General y Comparada*, 4, 2014, pp. 129–151. Edward Hallet Carr, *Dostievski, 1821–1881: lectura crítico-biográfica*, Barcelona, Laia, 1972. James P. Scanlan, *Dostoevsky, the Thinker*, Ithaca (New York), Cornell University Press, 2002. Segundo Serrano Poncela, *Dostoievski menor*, Madrid, Taurus, 1959. *Id.*, *Estudios sobre Dostoievski*, Caracas, Universidad Central de Venezuela, Ediciones de la Biblioteca, 1968. Nikolai Strachow, "Über Dostojew-

HTTPS://DOI.ORG/10.1163/9789004766006-007

highly relevant today,[6] had a great influence on European culture,[7] including Spain,[8] and has been widely studied.[9] He endured family hell without ever yielding to animosity, despite the pervasive hostility directed toward

skis Leben und literarische Tätigkeit von 1860–1881," in the *Dostojewski-Gesamtausgabe* by Piper & Co., vol. 12, Russian edition, 1882. Eduard Thurneysen, *Dostojewski*, Chr. Kaiser, 1921. There is a translation into English by Keith R. Crim, *Dostoevsky*, Richmond, Va., John Knox Press, 1964. Translation into French by P. Maury, *Dostoeivski ou les confins de l'homme*, Paris, Je Sers, 1934. Henri Troyat, *Dostoievski*, 1940, Barcelona, Salvat, 1986. Augusto Vidal, *Dostoievski*, Barcelona, Barral Editores, 1972. René Wellek, *Dostoevsky: A Collection of Critical Essays*, Englewood Cliffs, N. J., Prentice-Hall, 1962. Félix de Azúa, "Dostoievski," in Jordi Llovet (ed.), *Lecciones de Literatura Universal: siglos XII a XX*, 1995, pp. 635–644. Manuel Díaz Márquez, *Fiódor Mijáilovih Dostoievski. Existencia, sociedad y verdad*, PhD dissertation, supervised by Jesús de Garay Suárez Llanos, Universidad de Sevilla, 2011. Emil Lucka, *Dostojewski*, Deutsche Verlag-Anstalt, 1924. Werner Mahrholz, *Dostojewski. Ein Weg zum Menschen, zum Werk, zum Evangelium*, Berlin, Furche Verlag, 1922. Isabel Martínez Fernández, *Dostoievski*, Madrid, Ediciones del Orto, 1996. *Id.*, *Dostoievski: de la igualdad a la diferencia. Ensayo sobre la burocracia*, Madrid, Biblioteca Nueva, 2003.

6 Eva Requena, "Dostoievski. 200 años de actualidad," in *Alternativas económicas*, 98, 2022, pp. 62–63. Jean Steinmann, "Dostoievsky. Romancier de notre temps," in *La Vie intellectuelle*, year 15, no. 2, February 1947. Alexej Ugrinski – Frank S. Lambasa – Valija K. Ozolins (eds.), *Dostoievski and the Human Condition After a Century*, London, Praeger-Greenwood Press, 1986. Josef Matl, "Dostoievski y la crisis de nuestro tiempo," in *Revista de Estudios Políticos*, 57, 1951, pp. 35–54.

7 Javier Alcoriza Vento, *Dostoyevski y su influencia en la cultura europea*, Ed. Verbum, 2005. Catherine Dalipagic-Czimazia, *Dostoievski et l'Europe*, Dalipagic-Czimazia, 1993. Jorge Morillas Esteban, Review of Javier Alcoriza Vento, "Dostoyevski y su influencia en la cultura europea," in *Mundo Eslavo*, 2013, pp. 172–175. Tamara Djermanovic, *Dostoyevski entre Rusia y Occidente*, Barcelona, Herder, 2006. *Id.*, "Profecías de Dostoyevski," in *Claves de Razón Práctica*, 228, 2013, pp. 142–151.

8 Jorge Morillas Esteban, "F. M. Dostoievski en España," in *Mundo Eslavo*, no. 10, 2011, pp. 119–143. Noa María Carballa Rivas – José David Urchaga Litago, "La presencia de Fiódor Dostoyevski en los estudios científicos publicados en España," in *Tonos digital: Revista de estudios filológicos*, 34, 2018.

9 See, James Boyd White, *The Legal Imagination…*, *op. cit.* Hans Ehernberg, *Dostojewski. Volk und Mensch*, 1921. Paul Evdokimov, *Introducción a Dostoyevski* (*en torno a su ideología*), translation and foreword by Alberto Colao, Cartagena, Athenas Ediciones, Colección Diapasón, 1959. René Füllop-Miller, *Der unbekannte Dostojewski*, edited by René Füllop-Miller and F. Eckstein, 1926. *Id.*, *Dostoïevski, le intuitif, le croyant, le poète*, translated from English by Louise Servicen, Editions Albin Michel, 1954. Víctor Gallego Ballestero, "Introducción," in Fiódor Dostoyevsky, *Diario de un escritor*, translation, selection, introduction, and notes by Víctor Gallego Ballestero, Barcelona, Alba Editorial, 2010. André Gide, *Dostievski*, translation by Laura Claravall, Ediciones del subsuelo, 2016. *Dostoevsky*, 1923. André Glucksmann, *Dostoievsky en Manhattan*, Barcelona, Taurus, 2002. José Manuel Grossman, *Dostoïevski*, L'Aventurine, 2003. Michael Grusemann, *Dostojewski*, Munich, Rosl, 1921. Max Holzmann, *Dostojewski. Sein Leben und Werden*, Musarion Verlag, 1923. John Jones, *Dostoevsky*, Oxford, Clarendon Press, 1983. Oxford, Oxford University Press, 1985. Geir Kjetsaa, *Dostoyevski. La*

him.[10] Despite enduring a cruel alcoholic father, the son, rather than adopting a victim mentality, assumed responsibility, with his sole transgression being his desire for his disgraceful father's demise. In 1928, Sigmund Freud authored an article titled "Dostoyevsky and Patricide."[11] Dostoyevsky experienced epilepsy, a condition that influenced numerous narratives in his works.[12]

He was also aware of the torment[13] of being confined in the Peter and Paul Fortress, having secretly denounced the Tsar's absolutism and advocated for the abolition of serfdom.[14] Despite being shackled to his cell by his feet, as Cervantes,[15] he maintained his faith in life,[16] asserting that "life resides within us and not in the external world."[17]

Dostoyevsky underwent a simulated execution, in which he genuinely felt he would perish. At that moment, a thought occurred to him: if I survive, I will transform every minute into a century, and I will not squander or trivialize a single instant.[18]

---

vida de un escritor, Buenos Aires, Javier Vergara Editor, 1989. About Dostoyevsky's brother, see, Nina Hoffmann, *Th. M. Dostojewski. Eine biograpische Studie*, Hamburg, Hansebooks, 2022.

10 These are some of Dostoyevsky's demons, to whom he dedicated one of his works, which bears that title. See, in this regard Richard Peaver, "Foreword," in Dostoyevsky, *Demons*, Vintage Books, 1995, pp. vii-xxiii. Ludmila Saraskina, *Fiodor Dostoïevski. Une victoire sur les démons,* translation from Russian by Bruno Bisson, Lausanne, L'Age d'Homme, 2008.

11 Freud's study of parricide in Dostoyevsky is particularly interesting. Sigmund Freud (1856–1939), "Dostojewski und die Vatertötung," in *Die Urgestalt der Brüder Karamazov,* Piper-Verlag, 1928. *Id., Obras completas*, translation from German by Luis López Ballesteros y de Torres, Madrid, Biblioteca Nueva, D. L., 1983. *Id.*, "Dostoyevsky y el parricidio," in *Obras Completas*, Buenos Aires, Amorrortu Editores, 2001, vol. CLVI. Louis Breger, *Dotoevsky: The Author as Psychoanalyst*, New York, New York University Press, 1989. Jolan Neufeld, *Dostojewski. Skizze zu seiner Psychoanalyse*, Vero Verlag, 1919.

12 Iván Iniesta López, *Enfermedad en la literatura de Dostoyevski*, PhD dissertation, supervised by Luis Enrique Montiel Llorente, Universidad Complutense de Madrid, 2005.

13 Hans Ehernberg, *Gogol et Dostoïevski ou la descente aux enfers*, Paris, Corlevour, 2011.

14 Rubén Gutiérrez, "La representación de las doctrinas anarquistas en la novela 'Los demonios' de Dostoyevski. De la utopía revolucionaria a la ideología nihilista," in *Humanitas. Revista de Teoría, Crítica y Estudios Literarios*, vol. 2, no. 3, July-December 2022, pp. 171–195. Hermann Herzfeld, "Dostojewski und die russische Staatsidee," in *Universitas*, year 1, issue 3/4, June-July 1946.

15 Venceslao Ivanov, *Freedom and the Tragic Life: A Study in Dostoevsky*, New York, Noonday Press, 1960.

16 Rafael Narbona, "Dostoievski, el hombre que no perdió la esperanza," in *Nueva Revista*, 2022.

17 Predrag Cicovacki, *Dostoevsky and the Affirmation of Life*, New Jersey, Transaction Publishers, 2014.

18 Haydée Kohan, "La repetición en la vida y la obra de Fiódor Mijailovich Dostoyevski," in *Revista de Psicoanálisis*, vol. 52, no. 1, pp. 189–214.

He endured the existence of a conscripted soldier in a fusilier unit in the remote regions of Siberia, where he encountered a destitute woman, the mother of a child, whom he subsequently married.

This beleaguered individual, frequently beset by financial hardships and indebtedness, afflicted by life's adversities, encountered all those marginalized by society during his odyssey of despair and extended sojourn through the world's shadows: beggars, anarchists, prostitutes, religious zealots, patricides, murderers, and wayward souls.[19]

Dostoyevsky regarded his worry[20] for the future of humanity[21] as the principal focus of his literary works. His novels meticulously examine the human condition, featuring recurring themes like poverty, love, greed, and self-purifi-

---

19 Jacques Vergès, *Justicia y Literatura,* Barcelona, Ediciones Península, 2013. Spanish translation from *Justice et littérature,* Paris, Presses Universitaires de France, 2011, by Loles Oliván, pp. 85–87. Michael Christopher Domínguez, "Los Demonios de Fyódor Dostosyevski," in *Letras Libres,* September 2002. Serge Gutwirth, "Une petite réflexion sur l'importance de la flibusterie épistémologique des littéraires. Dostoïevski, la criminologie, les sciences, le droit et la littérature," in François Ost – Laurent van Eynde – Philippe Gérard – Michel van de Kerchove (dirs.), *Lettres et lois. Le droit au miroir de la littérature,* Brussels, Publications des Facultés Universitaires Saint-Louis, 2001, pp. 305–342. Gentil Faria, "Dostoevsky, the Law, and the Underground Man," in *Mundo Eslavo,* no. 16, issue dedicated to the 150th anniversary of the publication of the work *Crime and Punishment,* 2017, pp. 46–54. Catalina Elena Dobre, "Apuntes del subsuelo. La crítica del orden establecido en Fiódor Dostoievski," in *Revista de Filosofía,* vol. 54, no. 153, 2022, pp. 16–45.

20 Enrique Tierno Galván, "Un tema de Dostoyevski: La preocupación," in *Monteagudo: Revista de Literatura Española, Hispanoamericana y Teoría de la Literatura,* no. 1, 1953, pp. 11–17. *Id.*, "Concepción del mundo e ideas políticas en la obra de Dostoyevski," in *Revista de Estudios Políticos,* no. 70, 1953, pp. 83–106.

21 Vasily Leonidovich Komarovic, "Die Weltanschauung Dostojevskijs in der russischen Forschung 1914–1924," in *Zeitschrift für slavische Philologie,* vol. III, 1926, pp. 217–228. *Id.*, "Neue Probleme der Dostojevskij-Forschung, 1925–1930," in *Zeitschrift für slavische Philologie,* vol. X, 1933, p. 402; vol. XI, 1934, p. 193. F. Lieb, "Das Problem des Menschen bei Dostojewskij," in *Orient und Occident,* III, 1930. Susana Navarro Adam, *Narrativa de transgresión: Nabokov – Dostoievski: Intertextualidad en Lolita,* PhD dissertation supervised by María de los Llanos Kasheeva, José Luis Falcó Gens, and Santiago Renard Álvarez, Valencia, Universidad de Valencia, 2014. Also see, Joseph Frank, *Dostoevsky: The Seeds of Revolt 1821–1849,* Princeton, Princeton University Press, 1976. Translation into Spanish, *Dostoievski: las semillas de la rebelión, 1821–1849,* Mexico, Fondo de Cultura Económica, 1984. *Id., Dostoevsky: The Stir of Liberation 1860–1865,* Princeton, Princeton University Press, 1986. Spanish translation by Juan José Utrilla, *Dostoievski: la secuela de la liberación,* 1860–1865, Mexico, FCE, 1993. *Id., Dostoevsky: The Mantle of the Prophet 1871–1881,* Princeton, Princeton University Press, 2002. *Id., Dostoevsky: The Miracolous Years 1865–1871,* Princeton, Princeton University Press, 1995. Spanish translation by Mónica Utrilla, *Dostoievski: los años milagrosos, 1865–1871,* Mexico, FCE, 1997.

cation through suffering.[22] He employs psychological realism and addresses topics including psychology, philosophy, and ethics.

Stefan Zweig, the Austrian scholar and writer, regarded Dostoyevsky as "the preeminent connoisseur of the human soul throughout history."[23]

2 Analyzed Works

2.1 *Crime and Punishment*

Crime and Punishment[24] is a psychological book authored by Dostoyevsky. Initially released in twelve installments in the newspaper *The Russian Messenger* in 1866, it was subsequently published as a novel. It is regarded, alongside Tolstoy's *War and Peace*,[25] as one of the most impactful works of Russian literature,[26] particularly concerning the discussions between the protagonist, Raskolnikov, and the police detective. In *Twilight of the Idols*, Nietzsche extols

---

22 Robert Louis Jackson, *The Art of Dostoevsky: Deliriums & Nocturnes*, Princeton, Princeton University Press, 1981. *Id.*, *Dialogues with Dostoevsky. The Overwhelming Questions*, Stanford, Stanford University Press, 1993.

23 Stefan Zweig (1881–1942), *Tres maestros* (*Balzac-Dickens-Dostoievski*), Spanish translation by J. Fontcuberta, Barcelona, De Juventud, 1941. Barcelona, Acantilado, 2011. Hans Prager, *Die Weltanschauung Dostojewskis*, Foreword by Stefan Zweig, Hildesheim, Verlag Borgmeyer, 1923.

24 Fyodor Dostoyevsky, *Crime and Punishment* (1866), Novel in six parts with an epilogue, translated into English by Julius Katzer, Moscow, Raduga Publishers, 1985. Spanish translation, *Crimen y castigo*, Madrid, Ed. Fraile, 1981, p. 84. Also in Madrid, Alianza Editorial, 2013, and in Madrid, Gredos, 2011, with introduction by Vladimir Nabokov, and Augusto Vidal, translated by Augusto Vidal. There is also an edition and translation by Isabel Vicente, Madrid, Cátedra, 2007. Regarding this work, see: Harold Bloom (ed.), *Fyodor Dostoievsky's Crime and Punishment*, New York, Chelsea House Publisher's, 1988. Rubén Ayala, *Crimen y castigo. Fyodor Mikhailovich Dostoyevsky VI…* pdf. Jean Perrot, *Crime and châtiment de Dostoievski – analyse critique*, Paris, Hatier, 1970. Maéva Val Macé, *El Derecho en la literatura. Análisis filosófico de la obra Crimen y castigo*, Final Degree Project, supervised by María José Bernuz Beneitez, Zaragoza, Facultad de Derecho, Universidad de Zaragoza, 2017.

25 George Steiner, *Tolstoy or Dostoevsky: An Essay in Contrast*, London, Faber and Faber, 1989. Spanish translation by Agustí Bartra, *Tolstói o Dostoievski*, Madrid, Siruela, 2002. John Maxwell Coetzee, "Confession and Double Thoughts: Tolstoy, Rousseau and Dostoevsky," in *Comparative Literature*, 37, 3, summer 1985, pp. 193–232.

26 Olga Nóvikova, *Rusia y Occidente: N. Karamzin, P. Chaadáev, A. Jomiakov, Y. Kireevski, K. Leóntiev, F. Dostoievski, V. Soloviov, N. Berdiáiev, G. Fedótov, D. Lijachev*, Preliminary study and selection by Olga Nóvikova, translation and notes by Olga Nóvikova and J. Carlos Lechado, Madrid, Tecnos, 1997.

the merits of Dostoyevsky's oeuvre.[27] Raskolnikov[28] embodies Nietzsche's concept of the "superman." However, in contrast to existentialists, the Russian author upholds belief in God and the redemptive power of faith for humanity. Dostoyevsky's oeuvre seemingly influences Franz Kafka's *Metamorphosis*. Similar to Kafka, both authors experienced significant illnesses – epilepsy and tuberculosis, respectively – and endured challenging relationships with their dads.[29] Similar themes can also be identified in the works of Jean Paul Sartre, Albert Camus, Hermann Hesse, and others.[30] *Crime and Punishment* alludes to the Bible and the narratives of the New Testament, including the resurrection of Lazarus, which Dostoyevsky juxtaposes with Raskolnikov's conversion.

"The acclaim of *Crime and Punishment*, one of Dostoyevsky's most renowned novels, is often ascribed to its police-thriller narrative. The term may induce confusion, as it pertains to a criminal investigation conducted not by the police, but by a distinguished judge who uncovers the truth[31]

27 Charles Andler, "Nietzsche et Dostoievski," in *Mélanges offerts à Fernand Baldensperger*, vol. I. León Chestov, *La filosofía de la tragedia: Dostoievski y Nietzsche,* Buenos Aires, Emecé, 1949. William Hubben, *Dostoevsky, Kierkegaard, Nietzsche and Kafka: Four Prophets of Our Destiny*, New York, Collier Books, 1962. Jorge Morillas Esteban, "Bases filológicas para una comparación entre F. M. Dostoievski y F. Nietzsche," in *Estudios Nietzsche: Revista de la Sociedad Española de Estudios sobre Friedrich Nietzsche*, no. 11, 2011, pp. 163–187. Paolo Stellino, "El descubrimiento de Dostoievski por parte de Nietzsche," in *Contrastes. Revista Internacional de Filosofía*, vol. XIII, 2008. *Id., Nietzsche y Dostoievski. Psicología, resentimiento y moral*, PhD dissertation, supervised by Jesús Marcial Conill Sancho, Universitat de València, 2010. Walter Schubart, *Dostoyevski y Nietzsche: seguido de Ensayos sobre la relación spiritual entre Rusia y Europa*, Spanish translation by María Stock, foreword by Dalmacio Negro Pavón, CEU Ediciones, 2024. Lev Shestov (1866–1938), *Dostoievski y Nietzsche. Filosofía de la tragedia*, Spanish translation by D. J. Volgelman, Buenos Aires, Emecé Editores, S. A., 1949. There is also a translation by Alejandro Ariel González, Hermida Editores, 2022.

28 Dmitri Mereszhkowski, "Rodion Raskolnikoff," in the *Dostojewski-Gesamtausgabe*, by Piper & Co., vol. 1, 1920. *Id., L'âme de Dostoievski*, Paris, 1922.

29 Renato Poggioli, "Kafka and Dostoyevski," in A. Flires (ed.), *The Kafka Problem*, New York, Gordiam Press, 1975, pp. 69–83.

30 Nikolai Budánov, *Dostoievski y Turguénev. Tvorcheski dialog*, Leningrad, 1988.

31 The theme of truth and reason is central to Dostoyevsky's work. In this regard, see Reinhard Lauth, *"He visto la verdad." La Filosofía de Dostoievski en una exposición sistemática,* translation by Alberto Ciria, Seville, Thémata, 2014. David Montero Bosch, "El asalto a la razón de Dosotievski," in *Daimon. Revista Internacional de Filosofía*, no. 68, May-August 2016, pp. 115–129.

through a spectral analysis of Russian society rather than through conventional police methods such as strategies, threats, or coercive pressures."[32]

As previously mentioned, the theme of punishment is a prevalent motif and a common element in most world literature. Literature has effectively documented certain transcendental issues of philosophical discourse, particularly with the legitimacy of punishment, its forms and limitations, and the authority to administer it.[33] Selected works of Aeschylus, Euripides, Aristophanes, Thucydides, Dante, Shakespeare, Molière, Swift, Montaigne, Tolstoy, and Dostoyevsky exemplify the extensive discourse surrounding the issue throughout the literary canon across all eras and regions.[34]

The concept of *Crime and Punishment* likely originates from Dostoyevsky's imprisonment experiences. The work is partially a sociological fiction whereby money constitutes a fundamental topic. In this context, we consider the ideology of the youthful radicals, one of whom is the destitute protagonist of the novel, Raskolnikov. A nihilist in philosophical opposition to civilization, he

---

32 Jacques Vergès, *Justicia y Literatura…, op. cit.*, p. 85. Vittorio Frosini, "Letteratura e diritto penale," in *Rivista Internazionale di Filosofia del Diritto*, 2, 1993, pp. 281–287. Hal Gladfelder, *Criminality and Narrative in Eighteenth-Century England: Beyond the Law*, Baltimore, John Hopkins University Press, 2001. Peter J. Hutchings, *The Criminal Spectre in Law, Literature and Aesthetics: Incriminating Subjects*, London, Routledge, 2001. P. N. Meyer, "Convicts, Criminals, Prisoners, and Outlaws: A Course in Popular Storytelling," in *Journal of Law & Education*, 42, 1992, pp. 129–137. Jeffrey Miller, *The Structures of Law and Literature: Duty, Justice, and Evil in the Cultural Imagination*, Montreal, Ithaca, McGill-Queen's University Press, 2013.

33 Cornelia Vismann, "Rejouer les Crimes Theater vs. Video," in *Cardozo Studies in Law and Literature*, vol. 11, issue 2, winter 1999, pp. 161–178. Tomás Salvador Vives Anton – Juan Carlos Carbonell Mateu – José Luis González Cussac – Alberto Alonso Rimo – Margarita Roig Torres (dirs.), *Crímenes y castigos: miradas al Derecho penal a través del arte y la cultura*, Valencia, Tirant Lo Blanch, 2014.

34 Numerous studies have been written on Dostoyevsky's influence on or of other authors. On this subject, see: Miriam Díez Bosch – Josep Lluís Micó Sanz – Alba Sabaté Gauxachs, "Incomunicados: aislamiento espiritual en Dostoievski y su eco en la narrativa de Carson McCullers," in *Pensamiento. Revista de Investigación e Información Filosófica*, vol. 78, no. 297, January-April 2022. Joan B. Llinares Chover, "La crítica de F. Dostoievski a la antropología de N. Chernyshevski. Memorias del subsuelo como réplica a ¿Qué hacer?," in J. san Martín and T. Domingo Moratalla (eds.), *La imagen del ser humano. Historia, literatura y hermenéutica*, Madrid, Biblioteca Nueva, 2011, pp. 131–141. José Luis Álvarez Lopeztello, "Cioran y Dostoyevski. El despertar de la conciencia y la lasitud de estar despierto," in *Revista de la Sociedad Iberoamericana de Antropología Filosófica*, vol. 3, no. 2, 2021, pp. 123–140. Priscilla Meyer – Stephen Rudy, *Dostoevsky & Gogol: Texts and Criticism*, Ann Arbor, Ardis Publishers, 1979. Charles E. Passage, *Dostoievski the Adapter: a Study in Dostoievski's Use of the Tales of Hoffmann*, Baltimore, Maryland, H. G. Roebuck & Son, 1963. Nikolai Nikolaevich Vil'Mont, *Dostoievski y Shiller*, 1984.

oscillates between virtue and evil.[35] His pernicious idea that humanitarian objectives justified any means, even if malevolent, compelled him to commit murder. In prison, his intellectual pride, which led him to violate moral standards, enables him to see that happiness cannot be achieved through rational life planning; instead, it must be pursued through suffering. Other supporting characters, including Marmeladov, the prostitute Sonia, and Svidrigailov, are also masterfully depicted. The work adds a novel dimension to the suspense of a murder mystery. It integrates social, philosophical, and religious components. The novel achieved instant success. In the obscure realm of crime, a spiritual element illuminates Dostoyevsky's work.[36]

The religious dimension is not foreign to punishment in Dostoyevsky.[37] The concepts of the soul and psychological anguish, manifested through a guilty conscience, the process of atonement, tribulation, or the pain of the soul resulting from an offense – an act deemed sinful by the general populace – are all evident here. This moral anguish is illustrated by the literary figure of Raskolnikov, who psychologically torments himself due to his sense of self-betrayal as the perpetrator of his own crime.

---

35 Arthur Moeller van den Bruck, "Dostojewski, der Nihilismus und die Revolution," in the *Dostojewski-Gesamtausgabe* by Piper & Co., vol. 5, 1922. *Id.*, "Dostojewski als Dichter der Grossstadt," in the *Dostojewski-Gesamtausgabe* by Piper & Co., vol. 20, 1922. José Manuel Greco Haro, *Dostoyevski. Pánico al nihilismo*, tfg supervised by Jesús Francisco de Garay Suárez-Llanos, Universidad de Sevilla, 2024. Pdf.

36 Harold Bloom (ed.), *Fyodor Dostoievsky's Crime and Punishment*, New York, Chelsea House Publisher's, 1988.

37 Stanislas de Lestapis, "Le probléme de l'athéisme vu par Dostoievski," in *Études*, vol. 233, 1937. José Luis López Aranguren, *El cristianismo de Dostoievski*, Madrid, Librería Castrejón, 1969. Madrid, Taurus, 1970. Jacques Madaule, *Le Christianisme de Dostoievski*, 1939. Spanish translation, *El cristianismo de Dostoievsky*, Buenos Aires, Losada, 1952. Astolfo Ricardo Moreno Salamanca, "Dostoyevski en la Teología rusa del exilio y en la Teología católica del siglo XX," in *Cuadernos doctorales: Teología*, 73, 2023, pp. 79–158. Jorge Morillas Esteban, "La imagen de Cristo en Dostojewskij," in *Espíritu: Cuadernos del Instituto Filosófico de Balmesiana*, year 51, no. 126, 2002, pp. 287–295. Luigi Pareyson, *Dostoevskij: filosofia, romanzo de esperienza religiosa*, Turin, Einaudi, 1993. Spanish translation, *Dostoievski. Filosofía, novela y experiencia religiosa*, Madrid, Encuentros, 2008. Giovanni Cristaldi, *Dostoevskij o la scommessa della fede*, Milan, Vita e Pensiero, 1989. Romano Guardini, *Religiöse Gestalten in Dostojewskijs Werk: Studien über den Glauben*, Mainz, Mattias Grünewald, 1989. Romano Guardini – M. L. Rossi, *Il mondo religioso di Dostojevski*, Brescia, Mercelliana, 1968. Spanish translation, *El universo religioso de Dostoievski*, Buenos Aires, Emecé Editores, 1954.

Dostoyevsky's characters[38] differ fundamentally from those in the esteemed novels of Flaubert,[39] Dumas, or Balzac,[40] who represent the bourgeois class, characterized by their mundane concerns, infidelities, and trivial home rivalries. Dostoyevsky constructs his characters and situates them at the thresholds of human normalcy, on the borders of the precarious and the ecstasy.[41] The bulk appear malevolent and seemingly possessed by evil forces. Will these malevolent individuals, cast into the world, be redeemed? Dostoyevsky asserts that purification can only occur via pain. This discusses the notions of punishment as a means of expiation, serving as a purgative through which the individual undergoes moral improvement. The distressed Sonia implores Raskolnikov, the murderer: "Get down on your knees in the middle of the square, shout out your crime in all directions so that all the world might hear it, hug the Holy Earth which you have stained with innocent blood and kiss it." This embodies the notion of humiliation and acknowledgment of sin as prerequisites for redemption from malevolence.

Raskolnikov posited that individuals may be categorized as "ordinary" or "extraordinary." The former are obligated to adhere to the law and possess no authority to contravene it. The latter possess the right to violate the law and engage in criminal activities, contingent upon their decision to do so in the pursuit of a greater objective, thereby removing any impediments to their salvific goals by any means necessary. For these individuals, seen as demigods, the outcome legitimizes the methods employed, irrespective of their nature.

Through his transgression, Raskolnikov endeavored to position himself as a superior entity. He believed that his transgression was not a typical one motivated by selfish interests, such as the unjust misuse of funds or possessions, which might be perpetrated by any "ordinary" individual.

The synthesis of the message of *Crime and Punishment* is that "one cannot kill for ideals." The origin of crime is essentially ideological and punishment

---

38 Alí Víquez Jiménez, "Los hombres de Dostoievski," in *Revista de Filología y Lingüística de la Universidad de Costa Rica,* 35, 1, 2012, pp. 87–110.

39 Richard H. Weisberg, *Literature as Negativity: Ressentiment in Dostoyevski and Flaubert,* Univ. Microfilms Internat, Ann Arbor, Mich., 1982. *Id., The Failure of the Word: The Protagonist as Lawyer in Modern Fiction,* New Haven-London, Yale University Press, 1984. *Il fallimento della parola. Figure della legge nella narrativa moderna,* Il Mulino, 1990. *La "parole défaillante": l'homme du droit au coeur du roman modern (Dostoïevski, Flaubert, Camus, Melville),* Editions L'Epitoge, 2019.

40 J.-Wladimir Bienstock, "Dostoievski et Balzac," in *Mercure de France,* December 1, 1924. Supplement of the *Diario de La Marina,* June 12, 1927.

41 Juan Villoro, "Dostoievski: el aprendizaje del éxtasis," in *Revista de la Universidad de México,* no. 89, 2011, pp. 11–21.

psychological… On a philosophical level, freedom imposes itself as one of the central themes. What is at stake are the limits of freedom itself… The problem of freedom is when it is linked to the possibility of doing evil. First, this book can be read as a social and philosophical-moral critique of that part of youth which, seduced by nihilism and utilitarianism, propagated that all means are valid to change the state of things… This theory is not foreign to Raskolnikov, whose crime is motivated by the desire to alleviate social injustice, for he does not kill for money. It is extreme individualism (*me before the world*), the destructive and self-destructive spirit. But, although social motivation does accompany Dostoyevsky, it never determines action. For this writer, "it is character that determines destiny and not the other way around."[42]

"Am I a louse, like everyone else, or am I a man? Am I capable of transgression or not?" These are the reflections of the protagonist Raskolnikov. Raskolnikov proposes dividing humanity into "ordinary" people ("lice") and "extraordinary" people ("Napoleon, Muhammad, Newton, Kepler, Lycurgus, Solon"), who "dare to break the established rules," then assuming the contradiction that "what I killed was only a louse. A useless, disgusting, vile louse," but that "along with her, I killed myself, once and for all." He is a character trapped by "savage contradictions," the result of human ambiguity, another of Dostoyevsky's favorite themes. On the other hand, all the literary figures in *Crime and Punishment* are drawn with some excess: "the exaggerated baseness of Marmeladov, the extravagance of Raskolnikov, the willingness to sacrifice of Dunya, the mother and, above all, Sonia, the despair of Katerina, the insight of Porfiry Petrovich…." All of them are "individuals whose feelings and behavior always go beyond the limits of what is normal and, at times, even bearable." It is worth noting that the true heroine of the novel is the character of Sonia, who "not only symbolizes the ideal of sacrifice and love, but also refers to other values. She is clearly the bearer of the novel's evangelical message. Her sin is redeemed by the purity of her sacrifice." She is both a saint and a sinner, or in other words: "A 'great sinner' who has retained 'her purity of spirit'…, whose contradictions precisely make it possible for her and Raskolnikov *to be saved.*" *Crime and Punishment* is conceived as a "novel of resurrection, of redemption through the power of love."[43] This reminds us of the words of the 1991 Nobel Peace Prize winner, Aung San Suu Kyi of Burma, "an extraordinary example of the power of the powerless," as recognized by the Nobel Committee, when she said: "*Saints are precisely sinners who keep trying.*"

---

42 Tamara Djermanovic, *El universo de Dostoievski*, Barcelona, Acantilado, 2021, quotes on pp. 104, 112, 114–115, 117, 118, and 122.

43 *Ibid.*, quotes on pp, 104, 111, 113, 124–125, 126, 128, and 129.

"Concerned about the fate of humanity, Raskolnikov becomes a murderer. Although, according to his final confession, beyond altruism, his main motivation would have been diabolical pride."[44]

Marisa Mosto observes that "Raskolnikov, as indicated by his name (raskólnikov, schismatic), exists in isolation, distinct, and envious of his independence and autonomy. He too withdraws into his burrow and devises a strategy. He becomes ensnared in his thoughts. He employs meticulous reasoning, accentuated to the minutest particulars. It allows for no exceptions. He will illustrate his concept with a criminal act. God is nonexistent. Man is not subordinate to anything. This bestows upon him a power that transcends morality. To be human is to dare to wield that power."[45]

After the crime, Raskolnikov surrenders by delivering a formal confession to a legal authority, justifying his actions by asserting that he is not an ordinary criminal, but rather an extraordinary one. Raskolnikov realizes at this juncture that he is not the exceptional individual he presumed, but rather an ordinary guy who must atone for his criminal deeds. This individual, scarcely twenty-three years old, is ultimately sentenced to eight years of forced labor in Siberia.[46]

In the words of Marisa Mosto: "*Crime and Punishment* is the narrative of a man's spiritual elevation (and rebirth) through the experience of love that fosters empathy. His personal development is a reaction to affection, initially from Poletchka and subsequently from Sonia. The affection of Poletchka and Sonia was, in part, a manifestation of appreciation toward Raskolnikov. The affection of these ladies reflects his own dignity and his ability to remain connected to the broader human and cosmic family. It fundamentally alters his perception of self-worth and the worth of others, thereby reinstating his disrupted inner harmony and, consequently, the connections of brotherhood that link him to the planet and to others. Through this fraternity, he might connect with the filiation of a Father who, in the love of others, discloses Himself to him as Love. Affection reciprocates affection."[47]

---

44 *Ibid.*, quote on p. 113.

45 Marisa Mosto, "Empatía y compasión en la obra de Fiódor Dostoievski," in Martin Susnik, Cynthia Fox, Marisa Mosto, Marcos Jasminoy, and Alejandro Bertolini, *Manantial en el desierto. Ensayos multidisciplinares sobre empatía y compasión*, Offprint, Argentina, Ediciones El Rastro, 2016, p. 66.

46 Albert Fina Sanglas, *Justicia y Literatura*, foreword by Eugeni Gay Montalvo, Barcelona, Bosch, 1993, pp. 49–52.

47 Marisa Mosto, "Empatía y compasión en la obra de Fiódor Dostoievski," *cit.*, p. 72. Jorge Morillas Esteban, "La redención a través del amor: la Biblia en la vida y obra de Dostoievski," in *Mundo Eslavo*, no. 5, 2006, pp. 77–94. Lorena Rivera León, "Dostoievski: del héroe romántico al héroe de nuestro tiempo, o de la imposibilidad de ser Napoleón," in

2.2 *The Brothers Karamazov*

Most scholars regard *The Brothers Karamazov*,[48] Dostoyevsky's final novel, published in November 1880, as one of the author's masterpieces and a remarkable synthesis of his philosophical ideas. The work articulates his conviction that humanity must undergo transformation, depicting the societal conditions of the era and condemning the corruption engendered by wealth, avarice, unrestrained desire, and moral degradation. Writers and thinkers throughout, including Sigmund Freud, Franz Kafka, and Pope Benedict XVI, have lauded the novel as one of the greatest masterpieces in world literature. Serialized in *The Russian Messenger*, it was completed by late 1880, with Dostoyevsky passing away four months post-publication, so hindering the completion of the intended sequel.

The narrative develops over three dimensions. The initial narrative is the most cursory, recounting the murder of Fyodor Karamazov, wherein his three

---

La Torre del Virrey: Revista de Estudios Culturales, no. 15, 2014, pp. 49–58. *Id.*, "El eterno marido que no sabía amar: un parásito del deseo en la novelística de Dostoievski," in *Los retos de la filosofía en el siglo XXI*, vol. 2, 2015, pp. 21–33. *Id.*, *El amor en Dostoievski. Un estudio desde la antropología filosófica*, PhD dissertation, supervised by Faustino Oncina Coves and Joan B. Linares Chover, Universidad de Valencia, 2016. *Id.*, "Dostoievski: una lección de anatomía desde el subsuelo," in *Daimon. Revista Internacional de Filosofía*, no. 5 (supplement 5), 2016, pp. 867–875. *Id.*, "Entre Escila y Caribdis: razón y fe al hilo de 'Los demonios' de Dostoievski," in *Antropología filosófica y Literatura*, edited by Joan B. Llinares Chover, 2019, pp. 113–150. *Id.*, "Enfermedad y mal moral en el primer Dostoievski: el caso de Nétochka Nezvánova," in *Interessos filosòfics del present*, edited by Elena Nájera Pérez, Antonio de Murcia Conesa and Jorge Pulla González, 2019, pp. 323–333.

48 *Los hermanos Karamazov*, edited by Marina Ujánova, translated into Spanish by Augusto Vidal and José María Bravo, Madrid, Cátedra, 2011. Also in Barcelona, Planeta, 1988, with an introduction by Aquilino Duque, translation and notes by Augusto Vidal. Also in Barcelona, Bruguera, 9th ed., 1974. Alberto Aguilar, *Fedor Dostoiewski Los hermanos Karamazov*, pdf. Pablo Blanco Sarto, "Los Karamazov discuten. Dios y el mal en Dostoievski," in *Espíritu*, Notas, Textos y Documentos, LIII, 2004, pp. 77–85. Dmytro Cyzevskyj, "Schiller un di 'Brüder Karamazov'," in *Zeitschrift für slavische Philologie*, vol. VI, 1929, pp. 1–42. Serguéi Hessen, "Die Idee des Guten in den 'Brüdern Karamazov'," in *Der Russische Gedenke*, I, 1929. Boris de Schloezer, "Les Brouillons des Frères Karamasov," in *Mesures*, October 1935. Victor Terras, *A Karamazov Companion, Commentary on the Genesis, Language and Style of Dostoevsky Novel*, London, University of Wisconsin Press, 1981. Madison, The University of Wisconsin Press, 2002. *Id.*, *Reading Dostoevsky*, London, University of Wisconsin Press, 1998. Diane Thompson Oenning, *The Brothers Karamazov and the Poetics of Memory*, Cambridge, Cambridge University Press, 1991. Akim Wowitch Wolynski, *Das Reich der Karamasows*, Jazzybee Verlag, 1924. Tamara Ivancic, *La relación entre Rusia y Occidente en la obra de F. M. Dostoyevski. Apuntes del subsuelo. Los demonios y Los hermanos Karamazov*, PhD dissertation, supervised by Rafael Argullol Murgadas, Universitat Pompeu Fabra, 2004.

offspring exhibit varying degrees of culpability amidst familial discord and scandalous romantic entanglements. The most profound dimension illustrates the moral struggle and spiritual turmoil involving the three Karamazov brothers: Ivan, an atheist and skeptical intellectual, epitomizing rationality; Dmitri, passionate and hedonistic, representing corporeal pleasures; and Alexei, a novice monk, virtuous and embodying spirituality – the character to whom Dostoyevsky ascribes all virtues, seemingly inspired by his son Alyosha, who succumbed to epilepsy, a hereditary condition from his father, during the novel's composition. In this second, more profound dimension, Dostoyevsky elucidates his perspectives on philosophical matters, including doubt, freedom, and religion.[49]

Pavel Smerdyakov, the offspring of a mute lady from the streets, is an additional character. He is said to be the illegitimate offspring of Fyodor Karamazov. At the beginning of the story, Pavel is introduced as a servant of Fyodor Karamazov, characterized by a morose and unpleasant demeanor, who, in his youth, engaged in the cruel act of hanging and burying abandoned cats. Smerdyakov exhibits a chilly and aloof demeanor toward most individuals he encounters, although he harbors admiration for Ivan, who shares his atheistic beliefs. Pavel ultimately confesses to Ivan that he, rather than Dmitri, was responsible for Fyodor's death, but he maintains that his actions were justified.

The figure most akin to Fyodor is his son Dmitri, who possesses a profound desire for life's pleasures, recklessly dissipating substantial amounts of money like a libertine, following his youthful tenure as a soldier. At the outset of the narrative, he challenges his father on the inheritance and a woman who captivates them both. This positions him as the primary suspect in his father's demise.

---

49 For example, in the famous passage from this novel that recounts what is known as the Legend of the Grand Inquisitor. On this subject, see: Ana Isabel, *El gran inquisidor Fiodor Dostoievski*, Colombia, Ediciones La Cueva. Nicolás Berdiaev, *El espíritu de Dostoievski*, Buenos Aires, Carlos Lohlé, 1978. Spanish translation by Olga Trankova, Sebastián Montiel and Artur Mrwczynski-van Allen, Granada, Editorial Nuevo Inicio, 2008. *Id.*, *Sobre el Gran Inquisidor: Dostoievski y los siguientes*, Moscow, Joven Guardia, 1991. Antanas Maceina – Wladimir Szylkarski (Postface), *Der Grossinquisitor: Geschichtsphilosophische Deutung der Legende Dostojewskijs*, Heidelberg, Kerle, 1952. Vasili Rózanov, "La leyenda del gran inquisidor. F. M. Dostoievski," in Alexandr Nikoláyevich Nikolyukin (comp.), *Ensayos literarios. Sobre escritores y escritura*, Moscow, República, 1996. Eugenia Smokti, "La sed de crecer produce herejía: reflexiones sobre 'La leyenda del Gran Inquisidor' de F. M. Dostoievski," in *Revista de la Inquisición*, 10, 2001.

Fyodor had those three children from two distinct marriages, excluding Smerdyakov. He is opportunistic, imprudent, and cynical, exhibiting no interest in his children, who become estranged from him and one another.

In 1850, during his term of forced labor in Siberia for disseminating politically dangerous literature, Dostoyevsky saw the young Ilinsky, who had been convicted of patricide over an inheritance dispute. After a decade, Dostoyevsky learned that Ilinsky was innocent and had been wrongfully convicted, as the actual murderer had confessed to the crime. *The Brothers Karamazov*, particularly the physical and financial attributes of the character Dmitri, who bears a striking resemblance to Ilinsky, was evidently shaped by this encounter.[50]

Legally, Dmitri is not culpable for his father's death. Both Dmitri and Ivan are morally culpable: Dmitri for harboring the desire to kill his father and possessing the potential to act on it under suitable conditions, as well as for his villainous nature; and Ivan for having inadvertently incited Smerdyakov to commit the crime.

Amidst the hatred, passion, and grief that permeate the remainder of the narrative, the legal sequences serve as islands of human rationality. The preliminary inspection at the hotel when Dmitri is apprehended and the subsequent trial are analogous to the modern legal procedure. The primary reason for Dmitri's arrest is not bias against his erratic conduct; instead, the proof of his culpability is substantial. The trial is fundamentally equitable, while its verdict is flawed, and Dmitri's sentence of twenty years in Siberia is proportionate to a crime deemed patricide by the judges and jury.

There is a beautiful phrase in this novel: "I want to see with my own eyes how the doe lies next to the lion and how the stabbed man rises and embraces his murderer." As is usual in Dostoyevsky's mature work, there is a character who is above the passions that consume the other characters portrayed; "in *The Brothers Karamazov*, that role falls to Father Zosima... This old monk, who understands and forgives everything and everyone, rather than spreading the faith, tries to reconcile the destinies of others through love as a living force that is within everyone's reach."[51]

"On the other hand, when Dostoyevsky talks about his country and Russian identity, he always needs to make comparisons with Western Europe, as was customary among Russian intellectuals. In this regard, he states in the novel: 'They have the Hamlets; we, for now, only have the Karamazov. Can a Karamazov think Hamlet-like thoughts about what will happen next?' In other

---

50 Pedro Talavera, *Derecho y Literatura, op. cit.*, pp. 21–24.

51 Tamara Djermanovic, *El universo de Dostoievski, op. cit.*, pp. 210–211.

words, unlike Hamlet, a Karamazov, like a good Russian, acts without thinking, impulsively and fatally. He is incapable of weighing the consequences of his actions."[52]

"The relationship between two of the brothers Karamazov allows Dostoyevsky to describe in great depth the problem of the masses and power. Ivan thinks, while Smerdyakov does the dirty work. No revolution, war, or dictatorship in history would have been possible without the dynamics of this relationship. The masses come together, organize, and act based on ideas that are not their own and that they largely ignore or do not understand. But 'every idea finds its Smerdyakov to carry it out'; therein lies the tragedy of history."[53] This idea reminds us of Karl Popper and his book *The Open Society and Its Enemies*, which, despite being published in 1945, remains a key reference today in the defense of liberal democracies against totalitarianism.

Fyodor is the embodiment of the principle that "if God does not exist, everything is permitted." In the author's own words, the main theme of *The Brothers Karamazov* is the same question that had tormented him all his life: the existence of God. "All the characters debate the religious question, in a continuous *pro and con*. Even Alyosha says at one point: 'Perhaps I don't believe in God.' And the amoral Fyodor comments that he would accept faith if 'without God there were no cognac.' The passionate Dmitri acknowledges that 'God torments him,' and, regarding Ivan's atheism, it should be clarified that his faith in reason prevents him from understanding God… If Dostoyevsky shares anything of Ivan's arguments, it is the difficulty of accepting the idea of God in the face of the suffering of children." Dostoyevsky's religious conception contains what he considers to be the most authentic aspects of Western Christianity: the idea of "universal guilt," which is summed up in the phrase "every man is guilty before all and for all"; the serene and joyful acceptance of suffering and death; sincerity as the supreme value; the latent goodness inherent in all human beings; forgiveness; universal brotherhood; repentance; humility and silent love; faith in the simple people; pantheistic fusion with nature, etc. Dostoyevsky speaks to us of paradise and hell as feelings rather than places: "What is hell? I see it as the suffering of never being able to love again," says Zosima. As Dostoyevsky says through the mouth of Alyosha: "How beautiful life is when someone does something good and just!"[54]

The comparison between 19th-century Russian law and 20th-century American law depicted in *The Brothers Karamazov* contrasts with *Crime and*

---

52 *Ibid.*, quote on p. 215.

53 *Ibid.*, quote on p. 234.

54 *Ibid.*, quotes on pp. 237, 248, 250, 251, and 253.

Punishment. The former novel relies on an adversarial trial, whereas the latter embodies the inquisitorial method. *The Brothers Karamazov* is a comparatively less despondent and less obsessed work than *Crime and Punishment* and may be more aptly likened to *The Pickwick Papers*[55] than to Kafka's *The Trial*.

The Brothers Karamazov is a significant piece of Christian literature, arguably the most profound since the *Divine Comedy*.[56]

Lorenzo Zolezzi Ibárcena asserts: "*The Brothers Karamazov* represents Dostoyevsky's final work, thus serving as a synthesis of his philosophical ideas. The work explores several of the author's main concepts, including the notion that in issues of guilt, attitude supersedes action; that we are inherently culpable before others; that suffering serves as a purifying agent and a remedy for spiritual ascension; and the affirmation of free will. However, the work also narrates a criminal story. The author presents a death mystery, the perpetrator of which will be revealed in the conclusion. It also comprises a 25% segment dedicated to the examination of the case and the oral proceedings. The most intriguing feature is that an innocent individual is deemed guilty, a determination made because the law could not operate otherwise considering the facts. It is feasible to proclaim him not guilty; but this would necessitate the creation of an alternative paradigm for the criminal trial."[57] Richard H. Weisberg contends that the legal practitioners were promptly persuaded of Dmitri's culpability and then recounted a narrative aligned with their preconceived notions.[58]

Dostoyevsky's characters exhibit abrupt mood shifts; they are paradoxical, mutable, and erratic; they experience love and hatred nearly concurrently. In this regard, they contrast with the characters of authors such as Dickens, who are consistently either virtuous or malevolent throughout his narratives. Dostoyevsky's novels are polyphonic, replete with ideas and suspense. The protagonists of his works resemble ideologues, acting independently of the narrator. The novel encompasses several pivotal concepts: the advocacy for active love toward others; the aforementioned notion that attitude supersedes

55 Albert J. Guérard, *The triumph of the novel: Dickens, Dostoievski, Faulkner*, New York, Oxford University Press, 1976.

56 Richard A. Posner, *Law and Literature, op. cit.*, pp. 175–178.

57 Lorenzo Zolezzi Ibárcena, "El Derecho en Los hermanos Karamazov. The Law in The Brothers Karamazov," in *Derecho PUCP* (Pontificia Universidad Católica del Perú), 74, 2015, pp. 355–395.

58 Richard Weisberg – Jean-Pierre Barricelli, "Literature and the Law," in Joseph Gibaldi – Jean-Pierre Barricelli (eds.), *Interrelations of Literature*, New York, The Modern Language Association of America, 1982, pp. 150–175.

action, particularly evident in the guilt experienced by two Karamazov brothers – one as the actual murderer of their father, the other for his intense desire for the act; the concept of communal guilt, suggesting universal culpability that precludes judgment by others and advocates for leniency in assessments. However, in his later work, *Diary of a Writer*, the author expressed a contrasting view, arguing that juries can be excessively lenient and favoring conviction over acquittal, asserting that "punishment does not burden, but relieves," thus highlighting the theme of personal purification through suffering; and the affirmation of free will.

Marisa Mosto, as previously referenced, asserts: "The Karamazov family may encapsulate the myriad inclinations inherent in the human soul simultaneously: egocentric desire (Fyodor), corrosive skepticism (Ivan), tumultuous, unrestrained, and unconditional appreciation for life's beauty (Dmitri), destructive bitterness that intertwines in obscurity (Smerdyakov), and the quest for nobility and spiritual growth (Alyosha)." The reader identifies, if not with all, then with several characters concurrently. The human spirit is not a simple or homogeneous entity; it is, in fact, a genuine battleground.[59]

59 Marisa Mosto, "Empatía y compasión en la obra de Fiódor Dostoievski," *cit.*, p. 54.

CHAPTER 7

Franz Kafka

1 Significant Aspects of His Life

Franz Kafka was born in Prague on July 3, 1883, and died young at the age of forty-one from tuberculosis on June 3, 1924.[1]

1 Kafka has been the subject of numerous newspaper articles in Spain on the centenary of his death, in 2024, some of which, listed chronologically, are: José Andrés Rojo, "Canetti lee a Kafka," in *El País. Babelia*, July 11, 2023. Alfredo Asensi, "2024, el año más kafkiano: el autor de 'La metamorfosis' vuelve a la primera línea editorial," in *El Español. El Cultural*, December 31, 2023. Javier De Lucas, "Kafka en su centenario," in *infoLibre.es*, January 3, 2024. José María Guelbenzu, "'Señor Kfka', de Bohumil Hrabal: humor para sobrevivir al horror," in *El País. Babelia*, January 4, 2024. Preslava Boneva, "De Gabo a 'Gladiator 2' pasando por Kafka: lo más esperado de 2024," in *The Objective*, January 5, 2024. Mario de las Heras, "En el año de Kafka, ¿cuál es el verdadero significado de la palabra 'kafkiano'?," in *El Debate*, January 11, 2024. Anonymous, "Zenda recomienda: Diarios, de Franz Kafka," in *ZendaLibros.com*, January 13, 2024. Carlos Mayoral, "Prepárense para el año más kafkiano," in *Zenda XISemanal*, January 16, 2024. Álvaro de la Rica, "Una puerta para el centenario de Kafka," in *Las Terceras de ABC*, January 19, 2024. Antonio Lucas, "Franz Kafka, el triunfo de la angustia," in *El Mundo*, January 21, 2024. Martha Meier, "Releer a Kafka," in *Expreso*, January 21, 2024. Paula Corroto, "Milena Jesenká, la mujer que fue mucho más que el gran amor de Kafka (y de otras mujeres)," in *El Confidencial*, February 21, 2024. Marta Rebón, "Milena Jesenká, la sombra de la amante de Kafka entre la niebla del campo de exterminio de Ravensbrück," in *El Mundo*, El Libro de la Semana, February 26, 2024. Daniela Pasik, "¿De pronto te sentís un bicho? En 'La metamorfosis' Kafka mostró el efecto de los cambios sobre nosotros," in *Infobae*, February 26, 2024. Aída Ruescas, "¿Qué significa de algo es 'kafkiano'?," in *Infobae*, February 28, 2024. David Granda, "El universo kafkiano le sienta como un guante al siglo XXI," in *El País*. Cultura, February 28, 2024. Laura Galdeano, "Un año de homenajes para 'sacar a Kafka de lo kafkiano' y celebrar su carácter integrador," in *Libertad Digital*, 25 Aniversario, March 21, 2024. Gemma Marfany, "El sueño de Kafka," in *El Nacional.Cat*, April 13, 2024. César Antonio Molina, "'Tú eres la tarea. Aforismos', de Franz Kafka: inquietudes kafkianas," in *ABC Cultural*, April 16, 2024. Jaime Cedillo, "Los cuentos de Kafka, el corazón de su obra y la mejor puerta para entrar en su fascinante universo," in *El Español, El Cultural*, April 19, 2024. Rosa Marqués, "2024: el año kafkiano," in *Traveler*, April 22, 2024. Javier Ors, "Nada de cuentos con Franz Kafka," in *La Razón*. Cultura, April 27, 2024. EFE, "Una nueva traducción de 'El proceso' de Kafka incorpora un fragmento inédito en español," in *El Mundo*, May 2, 2024. Babelia, "Los libros del centenario de Franz Kafka," in *El País. Babelia*, May 4, 2024. José Andrés Rojo, "Diccionario Franz Kafka: el universo del escritor de la A a la Z," in *El País. Babelia*, May 4, 2024. Fernando García Ramírez, "Peculiaridades kafkianas," in *Letras Libres*, May 30, 2024. Enrique Krauze, "La elipse de Franz Kafka," in *Letras Libres*, June 1, 2024. Enrique Vila-Matas, "Los hijos de Kafka," in *Letras Libres*, June 1, 2024. Andrés Seoane, "En busca del Kafka desconocido: un escritor alegre, tierno, bromista…

 | HTTPS://DOI.ORG/10.1163/9789004766006-008

Against his will and subject to an iron paternal influence, he studied for a degree in law, which he found truly tortuous.[2] He achieved a doctorate and obtained a job at his uncle's Prague law firm. But he soon left to carry out legal practice in a civil court and later in another criminal court in the same city. Another uncle, the brother of the one previously mentioned, found him a job in an insurance company, an occupation from which he resigned because it did not leave him enough time for his real passion – writing. He finally obtained a more comfortable position, as a civil servant, also in Prague. Specifically, Kafka worked as an insurance inspector for workplace accidents, a position that he held for practically all his life whenever the tuberculosis from which he suffered allowed it. His working day ended at two in the afternoon, which allowed him time to write.

---

y hasta muy ligón," in *El Mundo*. La Lectura, June 3, 2024. Mauricio Montiel Figueiras, "Breve Diccionario Kafka," in *Letras Libres*, June 3, 2024. Rodrigo Cortés, "Kafka & Kafka," in *ABC Cultural*, June 6, 2024. Jaime G. Mora, "Kafka después del fuego: todas las novedades editoriales del centenario," in *ABC Cultural*, June 6, 2024. Mauricio Montiel Figueiras, "El tribunal invisible de Franz Kafka," in *El Universal*, June 9, 2024. José Quezada, "'Kafka es un experto en el poder': Reiner Stach," in *El Universal*, June 9, 2024. Juan Aparicio Belmonte, "Kafka, entomólogo," in *20 Minutos*, June 9, 2024. Daniel Capó, "Kafka en España," in *The Objective*, June 11, 2024. Rut de las Heras Bretín, "La tumba que nos acerca a Kafka," in *El País*, June 13, 2024. Fernando García Ramírez, "Kafka y el sueño de Sion," in *Letras Libres*, June 14, 2024. Julio César Londoño, "Kafka, la mirada, el estilo y la fractura," in *El Espectador*, June 15, 2024. Mario Alberto Carrera, "La poética intimista pero también social de F. Kafka," in *LaHora.gt*, June 17, 2024. Juan Manuel Godoy, "Salió a la venta una carta privada de Franz Kafka escrita en el año 1920," in *Infobae*, June 18, 2024. María Ovelar, "Las visiones de Kafka en su centenario: claves para entender el mundo," in *20 Minutos*, June 26, 2024. P. C., "La asombrosa lucidez de Kafka, Zweig y Roth para vaticinar el fascismo y la guerra," in *El Confidencial*, June 29, 2024. Esteban Ierardo, "Kafka en su laberinto," in *Perfil*, June 30, 2024. BBC News MUNDO, Redacción, "Orwelliano o kafkiano: qué significan realmente y cómo eran los escritores detrás de esos populares adjetivos," in *News Mundo*, June 30, 2024. Alexis Paiva Mack, "¿Qué significa el adjetivo 'kafkiano' y qué nos dice del célebre escritor de La metamorfosis?," in *La Tercera*, July 2, 2024. Daniel Gascón, "El secreto de la literatura es la letra K.," in *Letras Libres*, October 20, 2024. Pablo Cubí del Amo, "Franz Kafka, el escritor visionario: 'Sí, existe la felicidad perfecta: creer en lo indestructible que hay dentro de ti y no aspirar a ello'," in *Cuerpo Mente*, November 26, 2025.

2 Reza Banakar, "In Search of Heimat: A Note on Franz Kafka's Concept of Law," in *Law & Literature*, vol. 22, issue 3, fall 2010, pp. 463–491.

In a profile[3] of Kafka, we must mention his hometown, where he lived for most of his life, Prague,[4] that was part of the Austro-Hungarian Empire. He always wanted to leave, but his work kept him tied to his city. "Prague is in his literature, and his literature is Prague." *The Trial,* the work we are studying here, is the most Prague-centric of all his novels, although it is never mentioned by name. For example, it is generally accepted that the cathedral in the novel is St. Vitus Cathedral.[5] The language in which he wrote was German, the dominant language in the cultural environment of Prague.

He was the eldest of six siblings, of whom only three survived, including himself, with two others dying at an early age. His family was Jewish. His father was of humble origin, although he later rose socially as a result of his work.[6] His mother, on the other hand, came from a wealthy background. At the end of his life, Kafka settled with Dora Diamant,[7] in Berlin.

Kafka himself stated that his whole body of work came out of his conflict with his despotic father, to whom he dedicated the harsh and notorious *Letter*

3 Louis Begley, *El mundo formidable de Kafka. Ensayo biográfico,* trans. I. Villaro, Barcelona, Alba Editorial, 2009. Klaus Wagenbach, *Kafka,* Madrid, Alianza Editorial, 1981. *Id.*, "Franz Kafka: una biografía," in *Obras Completas de Franz Kafka,* vol. I, trans. J. Parra, Galaxia Gutenberg, Círculo de Lectores, 1999.

4 On Prague and Kafka, see: J. Insua (dir.), Marina Palà Selva (dir.), A. Cuenca (author), A. Ibañez (author), C. Gomis (author), L. Fronza (author), *La ciutat de K. Franz Kafka i Praga,* Barcelona, Instituts d'Edicions. Diputació de Barcelona. Centre de Cultura Contemporània de Barcelona, 1999. English ed., *The City of K: Franz Kafka and Prague*, Barcelona, Centre de Cultura Contemporània de Barcelona, 2002. Patrizia Runfola, *Praga en tiempos de Kafka,* Spanish translation by A. Becciu, Barcelona, Bruguera, 2006. Mark Anderson (ed.), *Reading Kafka. Prague, Politics and the fin the siècle,* New York, Schocken Books, 1989. Includes an "Introduction" by the author, and articles by Christoph Stölzl, "Kafka: Jew, Anti-Semite, Zionist," Gerhard Kurz, "Nietzsche, Freud and Kafka" (pp. 143 ff.), or Klaus Wagenbach, "Prague at the Turn of the Century."

5 Julio Picatoste Bobillo, *Kafka y el Derecho,* based on his inaugural speech at the Royal Galician Academy of Jurisprudence and Legislation on June 29, 2017, at a session held in the city of Vigo, Cizur Menor (Navarre), Thomson Reuters, Aranzadi, 2021, pp. 44–45. *Id.*, "La sombra de Kafka es alargada," in *Faro de Vigo*, September 11, 2016. *Id.*, "J. Kierkegaard y Kafka (I y II)," in *Faro de Vigo*, October 9 and 10, 2016. *Id.*, "Más Kafka," in *Faro de Vigo*, June 9, 2019.

6 Roberto Chacana Arancibia, *La familia de Kafka. Lealtad y sacrificio*, Pozuelo de Alarcón (Madrid), Plaza y Valdés, 2012. *Id., Kafka. La lucha por ascender.* Ediciones UACh, Colección Austral Universitaria de Ciencias Sociales, Artes y Humanidades, 2018.

7 Dora Diamant, "Mi vida con Franz Kafka. Recuerdos de Dora," in *Cuando Kafka vino hacia mi…Recordando a Franz Kafka,* ed. Hans-Gerd Koch, trans. Berta Vías Mahou, Barcelona, Acantilado, 2009.

to the Father. The panel in *The Trial*[8] has been described as a symbol of his father, of the bureaucratic or fascist State, of capitalism, and even of God.[9]

The Czech writer has been described, perhaps because of his literary work, as an "enigmatic, gloomy, sad, and paradoxical" man, despite the fact that many accounts from people who knew him – for example, his close friend and literary executor Max Brod – contradict this version and consider him to be someone who was funny, tender, kind, truthful, and full of life, authentic, honest, and a good friend to his friends, albeit quiet, shy, fearful, vulnerable, and lacking in self-confidence. This is, for instance, the testimony of Milena Jesenká,[10] Kafka's confidante, translator of his works into Czech, and with whom he maintained an intense correspondence. Kafka's physical appearance was that of a "thin and graceful" man.[11]

Kafka achieved universal posthumous fame. In the years following his death, his work spread throughout France and England, as well as Argentina, through the Losada publishing house – remember Jorge Luis Borges's translation of *The Metamorphosis*.[12] In Spain, his production was first received in the 1920s through the *Revista de Occidente* magazine, although it was not until the 1960s and 1970s that the Alianza publishing house began to distribute it more widely.[13] Today, Kafka is considered one of the most renowned writers of the 20th century,[14] studied as a precursor to the advent of totalitarianism by

---

8 Franz Kafka, *El Proceso*, edited and translated into Spanish by Isabel Hernández, Madrid, Cátedra, 2009.

9 Albert Fina Sanglas, *Justicia y Literatura, op. cit.*, pp. 30–32.

10 Freddy Timmermann, "Dolor, identidad y poder. Franz Kafka, Cartas a Milena," in *Revista Temas Sociológicos*, no. 8, 2002, pp. 208–236.

11 Julio Picatoste Bobillo, *Kafka y el Derecho, op. cit.*, pp. 35–38.

12 Jorge Luis Borges (1899–1986), "Prologue" to *Biblioteca personal Franz Kafka. América. Relatos breves*, Barcelona, 1988. *Id.*, *Las pesadillas y Franz Kafka, Textos recobrados (1931–1955)*, Buenos Aires, 1996. *Id.*, "Kafka y sus precursores," in *Obras Completas*, Buenos Aires, Emecé, 1974. Also in *Otras inquisiciones*, Destino, 2007.

13 Various Authors, *Kafka en las dos orillas: Antología de la recepción crítica española e hispanoamericana*, Selection, edition and introduction by Elisa Martínez Salazar and Julieta Yelin, Zaragoza, Prensas de la Universidad de Zaragoza, 2013. Elisa Martínez Salazar, "¿Hay que quemar a Kafka? La recepción española de Franz Kafka en su contexto internacional," in María Cecilia Trujillo Maza (ed.), *Lectores, ediciones y audiencia: la recepción en la literatura hispánica*, 2008, pp. 357–364. In América, see Jonathan Blackmore, "An Examination into the Influence of Franz Kafka on American Jurisprudence," in *The Journal of Jurisprudence*, 2009. Robert P. Burns, *Kafka's Law. "The trial" and American Criminal Justice*, Chicago, University of Chicago, 2014.

14 Radek Malý, *Franz Kafka. El hombre que trascendió su tiempo*, illustrations by Renáta Fucíková, trans. Núria Mirabet i Cucala, Barcelona, Libros del Zorro Rojo, 2019.

distinguished authors such as Hannah Arendt,[15] Walter Benjamin,[16] and Theodor W. Adorno.[17] The Kafka phenomenon, as we might call it, is truly extraordinary and unique, since at the time of his death he was known only to a small circle of writers and readers in Prague and Vienna. In fact, during his lifetime he only published a tiny fraction of his writings – no more than 350 pages – maybe because he was never completely satisfied with them, humbly describing them as "scribbles," which contributed to his reluctance to publish them, perhaps due to his high standards of perfectionism or perhaps due to a sense of modesty.

When he died, Kafka's work was like an "iceberg," only a small part of which was visible, with most of it remaining unpublished. And this would have continued if his last wish had been fulfilled: that all his writings be burned, as he asked Max Brod to do. Brod, on the other hand, was an acclaimed and prolific writer during his lifetime, but whose fame, unlike that of his friend, fell into oblivion after his death, and today he is known precisely for his connection with the figure of Kafka. Despite Max Brod's efforts, however, some of the Czech writer's manuscripts are lost and irretrievable forever.[18]

2 Kafka and the Law

Kafka had a connection with law, a frequent theme in his literature – some titles speak for themselves: *The Trial*,[19] *On the Question of Laws*,[20] *Before the*

15 Hannah Arendt (1906–1975), *Franz Kafka revalorado*, trans. J. Parra, in Franz Kafka, *Obras completas, vol. I: Novelas*, Galaxia Gutenberg-Círculo de Lectores, 1999, pp. 173–193.

16 Walter Benjamin (1892–1940), "Dos iluminaciones sobre Kafka," in *Imaginación y sociedad. Iluminaciones*, Madrid, Taurus, 1988, pp. 203–204. *Id.*, *Sobre Kafka. Textos, discusiones, apuntes, Eterna Cadencia*, ed. H. Schweppenhäuser, translation, prologue and notes by Mariana Dimópulus, Buenos Aires, 2014.

17 Theodor Ludwig Wiesengrund Adorno (1903–1969), "Apuntes sobre Kafka," in *Prismas. Crítica de la cultura y la sociedad*, trans. Manuel Sacristán, Barcelona, Ariel, 1962, pp. 260–292.

18 Julio Picatoste Bobillo, *Kafka y el Derecho, op. cit.*, pp. 48–53.

19 Franz Kafka, *The Trial* (1925), New York, Schocken Books, 1998. There is a translation into Spanish, *El proceso*, in *Obras completas de Franz Kafka*, I, ed. Jordi Llovet, trans. M. Sáenz, biographical essay by Klaus Wagenbach and prologue by Hannah Arendt, Barcelona, Galaxia Gutenberg-Círculo de Lectores, 1999. Also in Madrid, Nórdica Libros, 2008. Also edited and translated by Isabel Hernández, Madrid, Cátedra, 2009. And translated into Spanish by Emilio J. González García, Madrid, Akal, 2007.

20 Franz Kafka, *Sobre la cuestión de las leyes* (1915), in *La muralla china*, trans. into Spanish A. Pippig, A. Ruis Guiñázú and C. Gauger, Biblioteca Kafka de Alianza Editorial, 1999 edition (3rd reprint, 2008).

Law,[21] *In the Penal Colony*[22] ... –, [23] and also in his professional activity – in his work as an official at the Institute for Work Accident Insurance.[24] Law was also the degree he studied[25] – although he had initially considered the possibility of studying philosophy, as stated in his high school diploma, and he also began to study chemistry, a degree he abandoned very soon. But he never showed any passion or attraction for the subject of law, but rather, according to Max Brod, a genuine aversion to it. He wrote in his diary: "Everything that is not literature bores me and I hate it." He considered that the time his profession took up studying law was time stolen from his true vocation, that of a writer. Precisely what he liked about his professional work related to the world of law was that his working day ended at two in the afternoon, which allowed him to combine it with his literary aspirations.

Kafka's case is that of a man torn between his profession – law – and his vocation – literature – not hesitating to describe his craft of writing as "my job" or "my other job."[26] This double life, between his job as a civil servant and his passion for writing, undoubtedly hindered his psychological stability and balance, triggering an internal struggle between his super-ego and his ego. However, this did not make him an indolent or careless civil servant. On the contrary, he was zealous and scrupulous in the performance of his duties, earning general respect and affection and being highly valued in his work, which he performed in an exemplary manner.[27]

---

21 Enrique Barón Crespo, *Europa y el cristianismo. En torno a* Ante la Ley *de F. Kafka*, Barcelona, Anthropos, 2013. Justin Smolin, "Before the Law: An Introduction to Kafka," in *The Kafka Project*: http://www.kafka.org/essays/smolin.htm.

22 Franz Kafka, *In the Penal Colony* (1919), trans. into Spanish by Juan José del Solar and Manuela Sáenz, *En la colonia penitenciaria*, in *Obras completas III*, ed. and prologue by J. J. Llovet, Barcelona, Galaxia Gutenberg-Círculo de lectores, 2003. Fabio Caprio Leite de Castro, "El profetismo de la colonia penitenciaria de Kafka: aparato de justicia y Biopolítica," in *Franz Kafka: culpa, ley y soberanía*, Medellín, 2017. Juan Alfredo Obarrio Moreno, "La tortura judicial en Franz Kafka: En la colonia penitenciaria," in *Revista de la Inquisición, Intolerancia y Derechos Humanos*, 2019.

23 Julio Picatoste Bobillo, *Kafka y el Derecho, op. cit.*, pp. 69 ff.

24 Eberhard Eichenhofer, *Franz Kafka und die Sozialversicherung*, Stuttgart, R. Boorberg, 1997.

25 George Dargo, "Reclaiming Franz Kafka, Doctor of Jurisprudence," in *Spring Issue Brandeis L. J.*, 7, 2006.

26 Joachim Unseld, *Franz Kafka. Una vida de escritor*, Spanish translation by José María Mínguez, Barcelona, Anagrama, 2006. 1st ed. 1989.

27 Julio Picatoste Bobillo, *Kafka y el Derecho, op. cit.*, pp. 38–44.

A reader[28] of this work may wonder whether there is a connection between Kafka and law that allows us to write about it. The answer would undoubtedly be yes, because a large part of this author's work is a reflection on power, law, authority, and bureaucracy, as we will see in the following pages. Indeed, Kafka is one of the greatest experts on issues of power, as well as on legal matters, both of which are closely linked. It is no coincidence that those who want to wield power also want to control the sources of law. All of these are interrelated aspects or areas that are very present in the work of the Czech writer. It can be said that "Kafka stumbles upon the law everywhere."

However, it should be noted that when Kafka is interested in power, he does not do so from the point of view or perspective of those who possess it, but from the situation of those who suffer it, who feel subjugated, dominated, and objectified by it.[29] The individual is thus diluted into an anonymous, uniform mass lacking critical spirit, suffering the deviations of that power without the ability to react to them. As can be seen, this is one of the characteristic features of totalitarianism, in which there is a progressive concentration of power in a few hands. These are typical Kafkaesque nightmares, in which the individual feels marginalized and unable to influence decision-making in any way, even decisions that concern their personal sphere. In contrast to the rational and free man outlined by the Enlightenment, for Kafka, human beings are not free at all.[30]

3 Analyzed Work

3.1 General Considerations

Kafka's work is the product of the insecurity that affected his entire existence: fragile health, a complex character that made it hard for him to maintain stable emotional relationships, dissatisfaction with work, the disapproval of his father. This forged a personality strongly inclined toward pessimism, skepticism, and resignation, despite his brave battle against the tuberculosis that beset him and the need to write at night, stealing hours of sleep, which was of no help to him, particularly from the psychological point of view. Anguish is always present in Kafka's work. He describes the despondency of mankind in the face of the senselessness and absurdity of life. His output mixes this exis-

---

28 Marco Antonio de la Parra, "El lector de Kafka," in *Estudios Públicos*, no. 79, 2000, pp. 437–449.

29 Germán Martínez Cazares, *Kafka: el Derecho como amenaza*, Universidad Lasalle, 2005.

30 Julio Picatoste Bobillo, *Kafka y el Derecho, op. cit.*, pp. 17–21.

tential pain with irony and black humor, addressing issues such as religion, the Oedipal complex, power relationships, humiliation, and sexuality.[31]

Franz Kafka's writing has a sober[32] style,[33] devoid of metaphorical embellishments, poetic figures, and linguistic mannerisms, so as not to distract the reader from the substance of what he is telling, leading some interpreters to describe his style as objective and cold, with bureaucratic, clear, and neutral language, like that which we normally use in everyday life. The essence of Kafka's work "lies not in words, but in images, in a surreal world that belongs more to dreams than to wakefulness."[34]

In terms of his acknowledged intellectual influences, Kafka felt akin to Dostoyevsky, Von Kleist, Flaubert, and Kierkegaard. It is also easy to relate Kafka's conception of guilt "to the Hebrew idea of original sin, prior to any behavior or consciousness on the part of the subject… Man is, so to speak, *naturally guilty*. The guilt is not his as an individual, but as a member of the species… The result is that innocence does not exist… (This) demoralizes us on the question of whether the law thus configured achieves… security and certainty. The only thing that is really certain is punishment."[35]

3.2 *The Trial*

3.2.1 An Incomplete Novel and an Open Work

Kafka began writing *The Trial* in mid-August 1914, and continued writing it, as can be deduced from several entries in his diary,[36] until the end of Decem-

31 Nicolas della Fraille, "Le spectacle littéraire d'un droit aliéné et ses possibles lignes de fuite à travers deux textes de Kafka," in François Ost – Laurent van Eynde – Philippe Gérard – Michel van de Kerchove (dirs.), *Lettres et Lois. Le droit au miroir de la littérature, op. cit.*, pp. 187–217. Martha S. Robinson, "The Law of the State in Kafka's *The Trial*," in *American Legal Studies Association Forum*, 6, 1982, pp. 127–144. Elsbeth Schmidhäuser, "Die Verhaftung des Josef K. Zum Verständnis von Kafkas Roman 'Der Process'," in *Neue Juristische Wochenschrift*, 1991, pp. 1455–1460. George Steiner, "Introduction," in Franz Kafka, *The Trial*, New York, Knopf/Everyman's Library, 1992.

32 Heinz Politzer, *Franz Kafka. Parable and Paradox*, Cornell University Press, 1966. *Id.*, "Franz Kafka's Language," in *Modern Interpretations Franz Kafka's* The Trial, New York, 1987.

33 Santiago Martín Arnedo, "Ante la ley y la experiencia del sentido en F. Kafka," in *Álabe. Revista de Investigación sobre Lectura y Escritura*, no. 23, January-June 2021. *Id.*, "El estilo vertical en Franz Kafka," in *Revista de Filología Alemana*, vol. 31, 2023, pp. 65–77.

34 Julio Picatoste Bobillo, *Kafka y el Derecho, op. cit.*, pp. 45–47, quote on p. 56.

35 Lorenzo Silva, *El Derecho en la obra de Kafka. Una aproximación fragmentaria*, Breviarios del Rey Lear 12, 2008, pp. 37, and 89–93.

36 Franz Kafka, *Diarios (1910–1923)* (1948), edited by Max Brod, translated by Feliu Formosa, Barcelona, Tusquets, 2010. Guillermo Aguirre Martínez, "Gide, Kafka, Woolf. Iluminación

ber of the same year. On occasion, he refers to the work by its title. In January 1915, he stopped writing it and never returned to it. According to Borges' interpretation, Kafka did not finish several of his Works – specifically his three great novels: *Amerika, The Trial,* and *The Castle* – "because the most important thing was that they be endless." A year after the Czech writer's death, in 1925, Max Brod managed to get it published by the Berlin publishing house *Die Schmiede*. This makes it very difficult to know and say with certainty where Kafka ends and Brod begins. We cannot even say for sure that the order of the chapters arranged by Brod was the one initially planned by the author.[37]

According to Umberto Eco and Roland Barthes, *The Trial* can be considered a paradigm of what has come to be called an "open work."

3.2.2 Interpretations of the Work

There are multiple interpretations of Franz Kafka's work because it has infinite registers: religious, psychological, sociological, legal, philosophical, etc.[38] In this sense, it is a work that we could well describe as symbolic.

3.2.2.1 Metaphysical, Religious, or Theological Interpretation

Kafka's characters, for example, the troubled Josef K. in *The Trial*, are obsessed with the fruitless search for something supreme that will redeem their sins. According to this interpretation, the court that judges the protagonist is an allegory of divine justice. Nevertheless, there are renowned writers who have

de su vida y obra a través de los diarios," in *Tropelías. Revista de Teoría de la Literatura y Literatura Comparada*, vol. 18, no. 1, 2012, pp. 168–203.

37 Julio Picatoste Bobillo, *Kafka y el Derecho, op. cit.*, pp. 96–98.

38 Susan Sontag says: Kafka's work "has been subject to serial hijacking by no fewer than three armies of interpreters. Those who read Kafka as *social* allegory see in him clinical examples of the frustrations and senselessness of modern bureaucracy, and its ultimate expression in the totalitarian state. Those who read Kafka as *psychoanalytic* allegory see in him desperate revelations of Kafka's fear of his father, his castration anxieties, his sense of impotence, his dependence on dreams. Those who read Kafka as a *religious* allegory explain that K. attempts, in *The Castle*, to gain access to heaven; that Josef K., in *The Trial*, is judged by the inexorable and mysterious justice of God." Susan Sontag (1933–2004), *Contra la interpretación y otros ensayos,* translation by H. Vázquez Rial, revised by A. Major, Barcelona, Penguin Randome House, 2014 (reprinted 2019), pp. 19–20. Julio Picatoste Bobillo, *Kafka y el Derecho, op. cit.*, pp. 58–65.

refuted this approach, such as Elias Canetti, Jorge Luis Borges, Walter Benjamin, Reiner Stach,[39] Milan Kundera, and Nabokov.[40]

Max Brod wrote that "since the *Book of Job*, there has been no such fierce dispute with God as in Kafka's *The Trial* and *The Castle*."[41] Indeed, in these works, as in the *Book of Job*, God behaves toward man in ways that man considers absurd and unjust, demonstrating that the standards by which human beings operate are different from those used by those above. Furthermore, another analogy between them lies in doubt and confusion, guilt and innocence, justice and abuse, cruelty and compassion, which are in conflict in both Kafka and Job. "The guilty, Kafka tells us, suffer their guilt innocently, just as Job suffered his innocence with harsh trials."[42]

3.2.2.2 Psychoanalytic Interpretation

Kafka's *Letter to the Father* is overshadowed by the Oedipus complex, popularized by psychoanalysis, of which the author himself would be a clear example. Everyone knows about the traumatic and conflictive relationship between Kafka and his father, Hermann, an authoritarian and harsh man who despised his son's literary vocation. In fact, it can be said that for Kafka, writing functioned as therapy, helping him to survive, as it did for other writers. There was a powerful rivalry between father and son, as well as conflicts with authority, which are the embodiment of conflicts with the father.

That is why some see in many of his novels, including *The Trial*, a translation of Kafka's family and personal problems and conflicts. According to these interpreters, the novel explores the internal mechanisms of the brain of a psychologically unstable man who suffers from persecution mania, without

---

39 Reiner Stach, "Kafka y sus ediciones," in *Revista de Libros*, no. 51, 2001, pp. 3–6. *Id.*, *Kafka: die Jahre der Entscheidungen*, Frankfurt/M., Fischer, 2010. *Id.*, *Kafka. Los primeros años. Los años de las decisiones. Los años del conocimiento*, trans. by Carlos Fortea Gil, Barcelona, Acantilado, 2016. *Id.*, *¿Éste es Kafka?*, trans. from German by Luis Fernando Moreno Claros, Barcelona, El Acantilado, 2021.

40 Vladimir Nabokov (1899–1977), *Curso de Literatura europea*, Barcelona, Ediciones B., 1996. Barcelona, Ediciones Grupo Zeta, 1997. *Id.*, "Franz Kafka y La metamorfosis," in *La metamorfosis*, Bogotá, Grupo Editorial Norma, 1998. *Id.*, "Franz Kafka (1883–1924)," prologue to *La metamorfosis*, trans. J. J. del Solar, Madrid, Gredos, 2011.

41 Jesús Alonso Burgos, in *La llamada al testigo (sobre el* Libro de Job *y* El proceso *de Franz Kafka)*, Seville, Thémata, 2014. Isabel Cabrera, "Kafka a través de Job, Job a través de Kafka," in *Tópicos del Seminario*, vol. 22, 2009, pp. 157–174. Ricardo Sanmartín, *De Job a Kafka, El sentido en nuestro tiempo*, Valencia, Tirant lo Blanch, 2020.

42 Anna Katharina Schaffner, "Masochism: Franz Kafka and the Eroticization of Suffering," in *Modernism and Perversion Sexual Deviance in Sexology and Literature, 1850–1930*, 23, 3, September 2014. Julio Picatoste Bobillo, *Kafka y el Derecho, op. cit.*, p. 100.

any progress in this regard throughout the plot that would allow for a glimmer of optimism: "the protagonist does not always win; in fact, he always loses."[43]

Along the same lines is the interpretation by Elias Canetti,[44] which relates two events in Kafka's life – one, his official engagement to Felice Bauer at the Bauer family home, and the other, the breaking of that engagement, which took place in a Berlin hotel – respectively, one, with the arrest of Josef K., narrated in the first chapter of the novel, and the other with the court and execution in the last chapter. Kafka was reluctant to marry, among other reasons, because he believed it could jeopardize his commitment to his literary vocation.[45]

3.2.2.3 Sociological or Sociopolitical Interpretation

According to this third interpretation of Kafka's work, modern man is surrounded by the faceless power of society, symbolized by state bureaucracy – against which Kafka takes a stand, for example, in *The Trial* – which objectifies, standardizes, and minimizes man. It is in this context that the concept and expression "Kafkaesque" was born.

The Kafkaesque man lives mired in existential problems: insecure and anguished, desolate, desperate, and uprooted. He is a man alone before and against power.[46] This can be seen in the author's work, especially in *The Trial, The Castle, Amerika, The Metamorphosis*, and *The Great Wall of China*.

3.2.2.4 Legal Interpretation

Along with the above, a legal interpretation of the Czech author's work can also be made, which is what we propose in this book, in later sections.[47]

---

43 Julio Picatoste Bobillo, *Kafka y el Derecho, op. cit.*, p. 99.

44 Elias Canetti (1905–1994), *El otro proceso. Las cartas de Kafka a Felice*, Mexico, La conciencia de las palabras, 1981. *Id.*, *El otro proceso de Kafka*, trans. M. Faber-Kaiser and M. Muchnik, Madrid, Alianza, 1983.

45 Julio Picatoste Bobillo, *Kafka y el Derecho, op. cit.*, pp. 100–101.

46 Denis Salas, *Kafka. El combate con la ley*, trans. V. Lofiego, Buenos Aires, Poder Judicial de la Ciudad de Buenos Aires. Consejo de la Magistratura, 2015.

47 This legal interpretation can be found, for example, in the works of Amador de Lorenzo Silva, *El Derecho en la obra de Kafka. Una aproximación fragmentaria*, Breviarios de Rey Lear, 2008. Madrid, Ediciones Complutenses, 2025; Juan Alfredo Obarrio Moreno – Luis de las Heras Vives, *El mundo jurídico en Franz Kafka. El proceso*, Colección "Monografías de Derecho Romano y Cultura Clásica," edited by professor Antonio Fernández de Buján, prologue by Fermín Morales Prats, Madrid, Dykinson, 2019. Also, more recently, José Andrés Álvarez Patallo, "La dimensión jurídica de la novela *El proceso* de Franz Kafka," in *Estudios de Deusto. Revista de la Universidad de Deusto*, 53, 2, 2005. David Castillo Aguirre – André Granda, "El Derecho en Kafka una muestra de redención," in *Ius Constitutionale, Revista de Derecho Constitucional*, 2, 2021. Pedro Gandolfo, "Sobre el Derecho

3.2.2.5 Interpretation in the Light of Judaism

There is another, perhaps less significant, interpretation of *The Trial*, represented by thinkers such as Hannah Arendt, Theodor W. Adorno, and Walter Benjamin, who relate the work to the problems of Judaism.[48] "Some authors have pointed out Kafka's role as a *wandering Jew*, and the writer himself often reflected on the idea of a *promised land*."[49]

Indeed, *The Trial* has a premonitory character, like a lucid mind that prophesied the advent of totalitarian regimes, serving as an anticipation and prophetic testimony – like a clock that is ahead of its time – of the approaching Nazism. Episodes such as the arrest of Josef K. in his bedroom, at home – without any information about the charges against him –, the inaccessibility of the court, or the brutal execution of the character, like a dog, as well as the lunatic logic of bureaucracy, remind us of the Jewish Holocaust.[50] Remember the violent intrusion of the Nazis into the privacy of homes for the sole reason of being of another ethnicity, without justification for any crime. The strange court in Kafka's story had a certain real parallel with the so-called Special Courts of National Socialist Germany. The adventures of Josef K. would be only a pale reflection of those of thousands of human beings in the reality of World War II.

Kafka seemed to have a precocious intuition, a kind of animal sensitivity, like that of snakes, which are said to foresee earthquakes before they occur. This idea is highlighted by Primo Levi, María Zambrano,[51] Brecht, George

---

en Kafka," in *Anuario de Filosofía Jurídica y Social*, 1985. Julio Mauricio Londoño Hidalgo, *Introducción al Derecho en la obra de Franz Kafka,* Pontificia Universidad Javeriana. Work developed in the Seminar "Literatura y ley" (2001–2002) organized by Carmena Kline and Gustavo Zafra. Joseph Peter Stern, "The Law of *The Trial*," in *On Kafka: Semi-Centenary Perspectives,* London, 1976. Susanne Maria Weber, "El Derecho en la obra de Kafka," in *Psikeba: Revista de Psicoanálisis y Estudios Culturales*, 5, 2007.

48 Diego Moldes, *Cuando Einstein encontró a Kafka. Contribuciones de los judíos al mundo moderno,* Barcelona, Galaxia Gutenberg, 2019.

49 Lorenzo Silva, *El Derecho en la obra de Kafka. Una aproximación fragmentaria, op. cit.*, p. 29.

50 Álvaro de la Rica, *Kafka y el holocausto*, prologue by Claudio Magris, Madrid, Trotta, 2009. *Id.*, "Escribir sobre Kafka parece un ejercicio de curiosidad prohibida," in the *Blog de Editorial Trotta*, http://www.trotta.es/blog/archivo/2015/ March 3, 2015.

51 María Zambrano (1904–1991), "Franz Kafka. Mártir de la miseria humana," in *Espuela de Plata* (Havana), August 1941, pp. 3–8. Also in Various Authors, *Kafka en las dos orillas,* selection, edition and introduction by Elisa Martínez Salazar and Julieta Yelin, Zaragoza, Prensas de la Universidad de Zaragoza, 2013, pp. 101–111. *Id.*, "Franz Kafka, un mártir de la lucidez," in *Asomante* (Puerto Rico), 1, January-March 1947, pp. 5–17. Also in *Aurora. Papeles del Seminario María Zambrano,* no. 3, 2001, pp. 124–132. *Id.*, "La novela-tragedia: El castillo de Kafka," in Various Authors, *Kafka en las dos orillas. Antología de la recepción crítica española e hispanoamericana*, Zaragoza, Prensas de la Universidad de

Steiner,[52] Peter Watson, Reyes Mate, Max Brod,[53] and Sultana Wahnón.[54] In fact, after the author's death, Kafka's three sisters all died in the Lager, victims of the gas chambers of the concentration camps, as did other members of his family. Perhaps that is why his work was banned in Germany, and some of his papers and books were destroyed by the Nazis.

3.2.2.6 Immanent Interpretation

Perhaps Kafka's *The Trial*, and the procedural vicissitudes of Josef K., could be considered with a certain allegorical parallelism to human life,[55] because, as Miguel de Unamuno said in *Del sentimiento trágico de la vida en los hombres y en los pueblos* (The Tragic Sense of Life in Men and Peoples), or Francisco Umbral in *Mortal y rosa* (Mortal and Rose), since we are born we live with the sword of Damocles hanging over our heads, knowing that death is inexorable, without having committed any fault or deserved guilt for it to be so. Life, like the process of the protagonist in Kafka's novel, moves inexorably forward, without time stopping. It is time "that neither returns nor stumbles." And on this journey, we are accompanied, just like Josef K., by authority, bureaucracy, the domination of state power over man, the ignorance and arbitrariness of the laws, in this case those governing the trial, and, ultimately, a feeling of guilt, inherent and intrinsic to man and his very existence.[56]

3.2.3 Legal Aspects of the Work[57]

The Trial is both a story of a legal proceeding and the narration of a personal crisis. It is a novel about obsession. The work tells the story of a simple and

---

Zaragoza, 2013. See also, Virginia Trueba Mira, "Los infiernos de lo abstracto (Kafka en Zambrano)," in *ENDOXA*, no. 41, 2018, pp. 195–212.

52 George Steiner, "Introduction," in Franz Kafka, *The Trial*, New York, Knopf/Everyman's Library, 1992. *Id.*, "Pasión intacta. Ensayos 1978–1995," in *Notas sobre* El proceso *de Kafka*, trans. M. Gutiérrez and E. Castejón, Madrid, Siruela, 1997. 2001.

53 See, Max Brod (1884–1968), *Verzweiflung und Erlösung im Werk Franz Kafkas*, Frankfurt/M., Fischer, 1959. *Id.*, "Postfacios," in *El proceso*, trans. F. Formosa, Alianza Editorial, Biblioteca Kafka, 2000. *Id.*, *Kafka*, 1982; trans. Carlos F. Grieben, 3rd ed., Buenos Aires, Emecé Editores, 2000.

54 Sultana Wahnón, "Una sentencia justa para Josef K.: sobre *El proceso* de Kafka," in *Isegoría, Revista de Filosofía Moral y Política*, 25, 2001. *Id.*, "Josef K. era inocente: sobre *El proceso* de Kafka," in *Raíces: Revista Judía de Cultura*, 49, 2001–2002. *Id., Kafka y la tragedia judía*, Barcelona, Riopiedras Ediciones, 2003.

55 José Isaacson, *Kafka, la imposibilidad como proyecto*, Madrid, Editorial Plus Ultra, 1974. *Id., La realidad metafísica de Kafka*, Buenos Aires, Corregidor, 2005.

56 Julio Picatoste Bobillo, *Kafka y el Derecho, op. cit.*, pp. 102–105.

57 María José Falcón y Tella, *Law and Literature, op. cit.*, pp. 192–198.

innocent employee, Joseph K., who one morning finds two strangers in his room that tell him he has been accused of an offense by the courts, but they refuse to specify what the offense in question is. They only tell him that he must present himself to make a statement. It is the story of a man who is accused and convicted of a crime that he has not committed, and which is never explained to him. Though he attends his trial and defends himself, it never becomes clear what he has been accused of. Joseph K. is not imprisoned, yet driven by a mysterious force, he attends all the questioning, and his life becomes a painful hell. His absolute conviction that he is innocent transforms over time into a feeling that he must be guilty of something, though he does not know what it is. To complete the nightmare, two anonymous individuals, like those he found in his bedroom, take him to a suburb and stab him there "like a dog."

Almost all the compulsion in *The Trial* is within K.'s mind. Much of what happens to Kafka's characters is completely consensual, under the influence of disordered mental states. Moreover, though one may believe in the existence of completely free choices, the reality is that all choices metaphysically involve a degree of coercion and involuntariness. All decisions are difficult; they involve not submitting to authority. Reflecting on the neuroses of Kafka and his work, such neuroses are embodied in his status as a German-speaking Czech in the disintegrating Austro-Hungarian Empire (Kafka died in 1924), marked by a high degree of submission. Submission to authority, fear of change, and masochistic submission are palpable in *The Trial*. In our society, as in all, not all adults are fully competent, capable, and independent. In addition to ill and severely disabled people, many others are unhappy or neurotic, many are foolish, and many are given to self-deception. Many people do not want the burden of taking their own decisions. They prefer the government to take decisions on their behalf. The characters in Kafka's fiction are weak. For Freud, the law is beneficial for these people as it protects them from the strong. For Kafka, they are more like victims of it. This is seen in *The Trial*.[58]

Kafka describes a limit situation: the generic accusation of having committed an offense, which sets the judicial machinery in motion – machinery that, once underway, is unstoppable, with internal gears blind to anything not part of the procedure. This judicial machinery is not perceived as a guarantee of protection, but rather as a threat, entirely in contrast to what we today understand by procedural guarantees and the rule of law. The paradox that torments Kafka is how to achieve justice, when the instrument to attain it – the law – scrupulously uses all its resources to sanction injustice. Law becomes an

---

58 Richard A. Posner, *Law and Literature, op. cit.*, pp. 191–205.

immense bureaucratic apparatus – the trial – enclosing man in a labyrinth of procedural steps.

Kafka's criticism reveals shortcomings, among which we highlight:[59]

- The law, as an order alien to individuals, is insensitive to them.
- The law, as an unknown tool handled only by inaccessible insiders through incomprehensibly complex procedures, stands before the perplexed gaze of the individual who wants to know his position and never finds out.
- The distortion introduced into law by the administrative structures created by it and intended for its application, which end up taking over the norm and supplanting it with their internal rules of bureaucratic functioning.
- The gaps in the law.
- The law as the imposition of power, regardless of criteria of justice… The law is, ultimately, force.

In an article published a few years ago, Pablo Sorozábal Serrano – quoted by Lorenzo Silva – accurately referred to Kafka's work as "the wisdom of no," that of pure negation – as opposed to utopianism, which saves us from leaping into the void and encourages us to discover the absurd.[60]

Elias Canetti, winner of the Nobel Prize in Literature, dedicated one of his works, *Kafka's Other Trial*, to analyzing the reasons he felt had led the Czech author to write his novel. As mentioned before, he emphasized the connection and parallel between *The Trial* and Kafka's engagement to Felice Bauer, which was broken off.[61]

Unlike other novels such as *Les Misérables* or *The Gulag Archipelago*, Kafka does not attempt to reflect the drama that results from suffering an injustice due to negligence, error, hatred, or other causes that contribute to distorting the path of the law. Rather, what he seeks to show is more profound: he reflects a structure beyond justice, in which the categories of just and unjust lack sense, with highly rigid procedures but a complete arbitrariness for its subjects.[62] The perception that justice is only bureaucracy causes Kafka, who was also a civil servant, the pain of knowing that his case will be no more than a bundle of papers labeled with a number, over which he will have no control. This pain is reflected in the description of the closed environments that stifle

---

59 Lorenzo Silva, *El Derecho en la obra de Kafka. Una aproximación fragmentaria, op. cit.*, pp. 103–106.

60 *Ibid.*, pp. 107–109.

61 Frank Stringfellow, "Kafka's Trial: Between the Republic and Psychoanalysis," in *Cardozo Studies in Law and Literature*, vol. 7, issue 2, fall/winter 1995, pp. 173–206.

62 Parker B. Potter, Jr., "Ordeal by Trial: References to the Nightmare World of Franz Kafka," in *Pierce Law Review*, 3, 2004, pp. 195–330.

the protagonist. Kafka, it should not be forgotten, was a compulsive hypochondriac, constantly worried about the purity of the air.

The trial brought against K. inverts the burden of proof and the presumption of innocence. In the rule of law, there is a presumption of innocence for every person until the contrary is proven (the "*iuris tantum*" presumption), and all citizens have the right to a fair trial with all the procedural guarantees of impartiality; in addition, nobody can be punished except for an action previously categorized as an offense ("*nullum crimen, nulla poena sine praevia lege poenale*"). In the absence of all of this, K. understands that his only hope is to make use of the "traffic of influences," represented by the lawyer Huld and by the painter Titorelli.

Kafka devastatingly criticizes the judicial structure and official apparatus, employing irony and black humor to do so. We find an example of this in the foolish requirement that the examinations be carried out on Sunday, so that the defendant – who does not work on this day – can attend. In effect, he makes a strong criticism of the oppressive bureaucracy that reigns over the decrepit Austro-Hungarian Empire, with its interminable ordinances and levels, procedures that are inaccessible both to those outside the structure and to members of the organization itself.[63]

However, Kafka does not rebel in the face of this bleak situation (as does Camus). Rather, he remains in a state of helplessness before power. Kafka did not find answers to the meaning of life in rebellion (Camus) or compromise (Sartre), but instead, like Wittgenstein, feeling incapable of transmitting the truth in words – it is better not to speak of what cannot be known – he resorted to paradox and aphorism as a means of expression. Having scrutinized the institutions and culture that surrounded him, greatly disappointed, Kafka turned his gaze toward religion as the only possible route to salvation in a hostile, insane, absurd, and bureaucratized world.

Our whole existence is regulated by procedural steps, full of inhumane classifications: suitable-unsuitable, guilty-innocent, citizen-foreigner, and so forth. Bureaucracy ends up becoming the greatest of obstacles to achieving justice, truth, and law. The trial thereby constitutes, paradoxically, an obstacle, meaning that law never finds justice.[64]

Work is an insistent and almost obsessive theme for Franz Kafka. It is ever-present in his work, particularly in his great stories – *Metamorphosis*, *Amerika*, *The Trial*, *The Castle*. The characters in these works find themselves engaged in

63 Fabrizio Sciacca, "La legge nascosta. Il paradosso di Kafka," in *Rivista Internazionale di Filosofia del Diritto*, 2, 1993, pp. 222–236.

64 Pedro Talavera, *Derecho y Literatura*, *op. cit.*, pp. 163–191.

an anguished search for a comfortable social position, of which holding an office is evidence. So, in *The Trial*, K. congratulates himself by stating: "I now have a home, a situation and a real job."

Also in *The Trial*, the audience hall and its surroundings are made up of a labyrinth of corridors, rooms, patios, employees of the curia, maids preparing meals, and children playing on the stairs. Kafka uses this labyrinth, underlining the chaos of judicial endeavor, to talk about the hermetic and sacred world of the administration of justice.[65]

The Trial has been linked to *Michael Kohlhaas*. Kafka admired Von Kleist's writing and may have taken details from his works. The interview between Joseph K. and the chaplain is reminiscent of that between Kohlhaas and Martin Luther, and the somber, closed world in which Kohlhaas fights to obtain justice is like the closed world that Joseph K. inhabits. Wherever Kohlhaas goes, there are reminders of the cause of his problems. In the same manner, wherever K. turns, everything is connected to his trial. But the works differ in that, while Kohlhaas attempts a traditional act of vengeance, with the consequent problem when the vengeance goes too far, Joseph K. is a fly caught in a spider's web, who reacts not with vengeful fury but with futile and comical gestures.[66]

Joseph K.'s trial is effectively a "unique" one: both surprising and irreducibly personal at the same time. The German term *Prozess* is itself a word with a double meaning: it refers to a legal action and to a morbid process susceptible to change. In this regard, K. is at the same time the object of a (legal) proceeding and of a (pathological) process, without one fully knowing whether he is ill because of his guilt or guilty because of his illness.

One Sunday, Joseph K. appears before the court and, though he has not been told of a specific time to arrive, he is reprimanded for arriving late. It is also an open question as to when the trial has begun, and when the verdict finally arrives it is unannounced, unexpected, issued by anyone at any time.

Time in Kafka's *The Trial* is different from time in ordinary life. Justice is carried out through an infinitely casual process, without a real beginning or a distinguishable end.

Unpredictably, there is an inverse timeline in *The Trial*. As opposed to the classical sequence, the sentence precedes the accusation, as the execution precedes the trial, as if Joseph K. had been condemned from the start, as if the process – that of the metamorphosis of the character – was merely aimed at making him aware of the truth of his sentence.

---

65 Alfredo Montoya Melgar, *El trabajo en la literatura…, op. cit.*, pp. 115–120.

66 Richard A. Posner, *Law and Literature, op. cit.*, p. 139.

Similarly amorphous is the legal space of *The Trial*. Ordinary justice is confined to a determined space, clearly defined and outside of everyday life. The contrary is the case in *The Trial*, where justice is omnipresent, defying centrality and visibility, always on the periphery, in properties in distant neighborhoods.

The Trial follows its own course. Though without meaningful actions and without progress, it is necessary to act quickly. Urgency and the lack of time are constant throughout the novel. One must react rapidly and not waste time. "Finish the trial quickly in the interests of all" is the route proposed by the agents with whom K. initially has contact. It is a blurred timeline, full of setbacks; a virtual, discontinuous, infinite, and circular law, without limits. The desire of the main character to enjoy a breath of fresh air is clear – but the doors and windows, though they appear real, are often sealed and immovable.[67]

Nor would it be so difficult in the real contemporary legal environment to frequently encounter realities that are as Kafkaesque as those described by Kafka himself in his work.[68] Yet, beyond these situations, and as almost all interpretations of Kafka maintain, two preoccupations underpin his work: the threatening presence of his father and the equally threatening absence of God. The trial is hence situated between law and metaphysics. Kafka uses law as a metaphor to talk about his favorite obsessions: hidden law, secret guilt, the retribution that punishes without one knowing why and with no possible appeal for forgiveness, the salvation that barely shows itself and again becoming hidden and unattainable. As such the title of the work could also be along the lines of *Kafka's trial and the mystery of guilt*, or even *Kafka's trial or the obscenity of the sacred*. The theme of the book is essentially the breakdown of the judicial authority that is supposed to judge, as if God were prepared to permit these foolish actions.

The metaphysical element of the story lies not in surrealism, but rather in a negligible and petty reality. There are no solemnity and majesty whatsoever in the proceeding of which K. is the victim. Moreover, it appears that his persecutors cannot do anything to him. The agents that arrive at his house declare him arrested and threaten him with the confiscation of his property, but they leave shortly after, leaving everything apparently as it had been before they

---

67 François Ost, "L'invention du tiers, Esqhyle et Kafka," in *Esprit*, August-September, 2007, pp. 147–165. *Id.*, "Kafka, ou l'en deçà de la loi," in François Ost – Laurent van Eynde – Philippe Gérard – Michel van de Kerchove, *Lettres et lois. Le droit au miroir de la Littérature, op. cit.*, pp. 179–181. Antoine Garapon, "Kafka ou le non-lieu de la loi," in *Revue Interdisciplinaire d'Études Juridiques*, 28, 1992, pp. 1–17.

68 Albert Fina Sanglas, *Justicia y Literatura, op. cit.*, pp. 31–32.

arrived. The accused party is given the freedom to choose the date of his hearing and to decide whether he will appear. During his appearance before the court, he perceives an image of misery and impotence. The court is situated on the periphery, in a humble proletarian room, in a narrow and stifling area, full of badly dressed people. Every time that K. must see them again with the court, its office, and its employees, he finds the same atmosphere: a suffocating heat, little space, stale air – a kind of hell, inhabited by diabolical creatures.

K.'s situation contrasts with the foregoing: he has a good social position, a comfortable and dignified life, a beautiful office in a large bank, and he is an honest and blameless man, while his judges work in a state of moral and physical degradation, between poverty and corruption, in their absurd offices. Despite this, K. soon realizes that he is part of a gigantic moving machine, which works in the shadows in a literal sense, and has its own sense of the rules and an infallible efficiency. This is why there is truly nothing that can be done. The court and its actions are outside and above time and space: they do not belong to the common world, and neither, perhaps, does K., since all the people he coincides with appear to know more than him about the court and find all its procedures entirely natural. The court is immense, infinite, because it does not have official premises and is not an institution.[69]

The protagonist's name, Josef, was probably taken from Emperor Franz Joseph I, and K. appears to be the initial behind which Kafka, in many of his writings and diaries, hid his own personality. *The Trial* is a work that is contemporaneous with *Ulysses* by Joyce, *The Magic Mountain* by Mann, and Céline's *Journey to the End of the Night*. The work has been reproduced in cinema, theater, and opera. Perhaps the best-known cinematographic version was directed by Orson Welles in 1962, with Anthony Perkins as the lead, in which the ending was changed.

3.2.4 Existence of Suffering, Displeasure, Pain, or Evil

3.2.4.1 General Concepts

If we should come to discover that prison was experienced by its occupants as a pleasant way of life, the prison would cease to figure as a punishment. This characteristic feature of punishment differentiates it from other coercive measures which the state may adopt, and which might, though not easily, be confused with it. The state intentionally causes some suffering, unpleasant-

69 Luigi Alfieri, "Il 'Processo' di Kafka tra diritto e metafísica," in Carla Faralli – Maria Paola Mittica (eds.), *Diritto e Letteratura. Prospettive di Ricerca*, Roma, Aracne, 2010, pp. 195–220, esp. pp. 196, 199–200, 203–205 and 210.

ness, pain, or evil to the offender with a specific end in view, or as a means to that end. This distinguishes it from other coercive state measures such as quarantine, where the suffering caused is not intentional, but rather a by-product, a necessary consequence of an unlooked-for deprivation.

The idea of manipulated pain is not exclusively covered by physical pain or suffering but spreads to all imaginable situations involving the *frustration of personal desires* of whatever kind. We might speak of *evil* rather than of pain, insofar as the privation of good is concerned. This is clearly seen in the evolution of punishment from Antiquity to present-day societies. The gamut runs from the death penalty, as the ruling punishment, passes through prison and, from there, to pecuniary punishments, such as a deprivation of the basic goods of life, liberty, and property. In each case, the suffering is increasingly less physical and more of a psychological or even an economic kind.

Not all deprivation of a good, however, falls within the category of punishment. A *desired good* may be involved. Hence, one might propose the substitution of the words "not desired" or "disliked" for the word *evil*. This sets certain problems for individuals who fall outside the common pattern. Think of the fanatic who does not mind suffering the evil which the punishment consists in since what he seeks is simply publicity for his cause; of the tramp who commits small, legal infractions in order to assure himself the shelter and sustenance to be found in prison; or, even, the extreme case of the person of masochistic tendencies who finds pleasure in corporal punishment. In all these cases, what is in principle an evil is experienced as something desired and wished for, already in itself at the service of the end sought.[70]

In such cases can we still speak of punishment? To answer this question, it will prove useful to distinguish between *objectively* considered punishment and the *subjective*, individual representation of how the punishment might affect its addresses. Actions which objectively fulfill all the requirements of punishment may not be experienced as such by the specific person to whom they are applied, in a definite case.

Another interesting question is that of how we legitimate inflicting evil on others, even should it be done in the name of the state. To admit that there exists an *authority* within the legal system *for the infliction of evil* would seem incompatible with the very idea of law. A crime has been committed. By this action an evil has been produced in three senses: as concerns the victim – physical pain; as concerns society – a breach of order; and, even, as concerns the soul of the offender – a moral evil. Still, will the situation be improved by

70 Sidney Gendin, "The Meaning of Punishment," in *Philosophy and Phenomenological Research*, XXVIII, 1967–1968, pp. 236–237.

the addition of a fourth evil, that is, causing harm or pain to the offender? This fourth evil, in principle, leads to no good effect either for society or for the offended, since evil is only overridden by a good counteracting the evil, not by the infliction of another evil.

We might claim that evil is never justified, it is never good. What evil might be is legally excused. The distinction between the *justification* – on the moral plain – and the *excuse* – on the legal – rests in the fact that the justified is morally good, while excused conduct is merely not reprehensible at a legal level, even though ethically it might be objectionable. In other words, the evil that punishment brings in its wake is 50% evil. It does not represent unqualified *evil*, but neither does it constitute an absolute good. It is an evil in the service of a good, always so long as it meets certain requirements and demands. It must be a necessary measure; it must be proportional; imposed by a legitimate authority; there must be no desire for vengeance; and it must achieve some end. It must not be an end in itself. While it might not achieve the goal according to theological postulates, that is, the moral improvement or expiation of the offender, it should at least try to help in his re-education and social reinsertion and ensure that his outward behavior does no harm to the social order. None of this happens in *The Trial*.

3.2.4.2 Application to the Studied Work

According to the Spanish *RAE Dictionary*, the third definition of Kafkaesque is "an absurd and distressing situation," that is, intricate, difficult to solve, labyrinthine, and convoluted, in which the individual is absorbed by a mechanism that escapes his control and overwhelms him, with an added component of unease and danger, situations in which man feels helpless and alone, defenseless before an unknown power.[71] The individual then finds himself trapped and surrounded by a maelstrom of vicissitudes and circumstances that prevent him from achieving his goal, and even though he strives to move forward, the goal recedes further and further away until it becomes unattainable. As we shall see, this is what happens in *The Trial*, in which the protagonist never learns what crime he is accused of nor does he ever see the court.

It is similar to a dreamlike distortion, like those we sometimes experience in our dreams, or rather nightmares, when we are asleep and find ourselves immersed in unusual, strange, even extravagant situations.[72] This dreamlike

---

71 Alejandro Nava Tovar, "Franz Kafka y el estado de indefensión," in *Fuentes Humanísticas*, vol. 18, no. 33, July-December 2006. Issue dedicated to "Estudios sobre Benito Juárez y el Liberalismo en el bicentenario," pp. 153–164.

72 Julio Picatoste Bobillo, *Kafka y el Derecho*, *op. cit.*, pp. 65–67.

texture is very clearly evident in *The Trial*, which abounds with distorted, shocking, absurd,[73] grotesque, and distressing characters and settings. The reader perceives this thick, heavy, disjointed nightmare, but the characters in the novel do not. It is like in dreams, where while we are in them, we experience abnormal situations naturally, and it is only when we wake up and remember them or tell someone else that they seem grotesque to us.[74]

In *The Metamorphosis*, as in *The Trial*, the reader and the protagonist are introduced into the story unexpectedly, receiving a big surprise. In the first of these novels, Samsa suddenly finds himself mutated into a huge and repulsive insect.[75] In the second, Josef K. is arrested. And everything happens in the morning, when the protagonists are in bed in their rooms.[76] Both Samsa and K. wake up from sleep, and a nightmare begins for them. Samsa wakes up and finds himself turned into an insect. Josef K. is awakened by the agents and treated like an insect. In both works, the protagonist is belittled. This can be seen in the contemptuous way in which the agents treat K. The reader witnesses the character's feelings of helplessness, vulnerability, and defenselessness, as he becomes a victim.[77] The fact is that "waking up is the moment of maximum vulnerability, because it prolongs the state of defenselessness inherent in sleep."

Following Denis Salas we can say: Josef K. has no surname, no religion, no nationality. He is a man among men. In him, the Jewish condition is mixed with that of all innocent people to represent a universal experience.[78] "Neither named nor located, but omnipresent, this is how the Court appears in *The Trial*."[79]

73 Albert Camus (1913–1960), "La esperanza y lo absurdo en la obra de Franz Kafka," in *El mito de Sísifo*, trans. E. Benítez, Madrid, Alianza, 1985. 2012. Jules Chaix-Ruy, *Kafka o el miedo al absurdo*, Madrid, Ibérico Europea de Ediciones, S.A., 1969.

74 Julio Picatoste Bobillo, *Kafka y el Derecho, op. cit.*, pp. 113–116.

75 Óscar Jairo González Hernández, "A propósito de los cien años de La Metamorfosis, de Franz Kafka," in *Ciencias Sociales y Educación*, vol. 4, no. 7, 2015, pp. 389–401.

76 Related to this idea, in a letter to Felice on June 26, 1913, Kafka says: "I have always been afraid of people, not afraid of human beings themselves, no, but afraid of their intrusion into my weak nature. The fact that someone enters my room, even if it is a person with whom I have the greatest friendship, has always terrified me; for me, it was more than just a symbol of my fear."

77 Michael Löwy, "De Mendel Beiliss, el judío paria, a Joseph K., la víctima universal. Una interpretación de 'El proceso' de Kafka," in *Acta poética*, 24–2, fall 2003.

78 Denis Salas, *Kafka. El combate con la ley, El bien común* collection, edited by Antoine Garapon for Editorial Michalon, France, translation from the French original by Vivian Lofiego, supervised by Ariel Dilon, Buenos Aires, Editorial Jusbaires, 2015, p. 64.

79 *Ibid.*, p. 65.

"From the outset, he experiences an accusation that degrades him through anguish (detained without an arrest warrant, he is unaware of the charges against him), debt (his personal belongings and money are taken from him), and shame (he is detained in public). They make him understand that his possessions are precarious, that his identity and image are damaged. These are, says François Tricaud, 'the three defeats of any human project'... Anxiety plunges him into an infinite threat; debt places him in destitution; shame exposes him to public censure. On the day of his execution, Josef K. will dress in black as if to carry out for himself the project of an immanent justice, already present from the moment of his arrest." "It is an immanent justice; the procedure is useless. It is not justice that seeks out the accused, but the accused who present himself to it... From now on, his trial will take place wherever he goes. There will be no refuge for him."[80]

"His fate resembles that of Prometheus... Punished by Zeus for his disobedience, Prometheus is chained to the top of the Caucasus where eagles devour his liver. 'Prometheus, wanting to escape the pain caused by the pecking, pressed himself closer and closer to the rock until he merged with it'... Prometheus is tormented by a pain that literally petrifies him and dissolves him into stone. Josef K. is also gradually mineralized by guilt. The grief that overwhelms them engenders the organ of its realization: the liver that is incessantly reborn in one, the guilt that corrodes his resistance in the other."[81]

3.2.5 Existence of a Previous Legal Offense

3.2.5.1 General Concepts

A second requirement for the definition of punishment is that there should exist a prior harmful action or omission. Such action or omission might be owing to two causes: either because a breach of a rule of conduct has taken place, no matter what the moral motives for the conduct in question – an *objective* focus on the illicit; or, because a moral flaw on the part of the agent is present, because he has failed to live up to his own convictions and principles, irrespective of whether or not a breach of conduct has taken place – a *subjective* focus on the illicit.

According to J. D. Mabbott, the first focus should be foremost. One would have to give value to an objective and legal concept of punishment, independently of moral motives. *The criminal would be a man who breaks the law and not the bad man; the innocent is he who has not broken the law and is not*

80 *Ibid.*, pp. 65–69.
81 *Ibid.*, p. 72.

necessarily a good man. A person may be innocent of an offense despite being a bad person or even have broken other laws. Therefore, for Mabbott, punishment would be restricted to offenses going *exclusively against legal norms.* This would allow the denial of any punishments based on retroactive laws, in contradistinction to moral offenses, which must be punished both before and after they are entered on the books as crimes, always given that such offenses exist. Along similar lines, of not punishing individuals for their wickedness, but rather for their specific transgressions of the law, are to be found the ideas of H.L.A. Hart, A. Ross, J. Rawls, and S.I. Benn.[82]

There is the danger of *circularity* in any definition of punishment whose meaning is made to depend upon the definition of crime or offense. The problem arises when we wish to define the concept of *offense,* since it would be difficult to give a definition of the latter which would not require as some necessary element a reference to the definition of punishment. It is difficult to account for the concept of punishment without connecting it with the definition of crime and, likewise, to define crime without alluding to punishment. To overcome the danger of circularity, some authors have suggested characterizing *offenses against legal norms* as *transgressions of legal duties,* rather than as presuppositions of punishment. The trouble is not every breach of a legal duty constitutes a crime. Crime is a subclass of types of behavior which constitute the antecedent of punishments. A second solution to the problem might be the abandonment of legal criteria to characterize crime and their substitution with moral criteria.[83]

The concept of *penalty* would have to be separated from that of *punishment.* The former embraces all kinds of disparate coercive measures, such as fines, disqualifications, and sports penalties. The latter would have moral connotations. Penalization of a person who infringes upon some legal norm would then constitute a crime only when the said person is considered morally guilty. Being punished would bear with it a *stigma,* stemming from the moral condemnation of the offender, something lacking when one is merely penalized.

For others, the difference between the foregoing concepts would lie in the fact that penalization would be the form or *formal expression* of the punishment. Finally, there are also those who distinguish between penalties, usually in reference to less serious offenses, and punishments, which represent a greater *degree of seriousness.*

---

82 Cf. Jerónimo Betegón, *La justificación del castigo, op. cit.*, pp. 159–163.

83 Richard Wasserstrom, "Some Problems in the Definition and Justification of Punishment," in A. Goldman – J. Kim (eds.), *Values and Morals*, Dordrecht, Reidel, 1978.

3.2.5.2 Application to the Studied Work

There are unanswered questions surrounding Josef K.'s arrest. Not only is he not informed of the reason for his arrest, but he also does not know the law on which it is based. Julio Picatoste Bobillo says: "Josef K. proclaims his innocence,[84] he finds no fault for which he can be accused, he asks why he is being arrested, who is the authority conducting the proceedings, who is bringing the charges. The officers do not answer his questions; they only respond in the gruff tone of bureaucratic enforcers: 'they are not authorized to tell him, he will be informed in due course, they know almost nothing about the matter, they do not even know if he is actually charged, only that he is under arrest.'"[85] The state apparatus thus shows itself to be harsh, even at the moment of arrest.

The arbitrariness of K.'s arrest is merely a prelude to the abuses of the trial that will follow, which is nothing more than a grotesque accumulation of violations of the most basic guarantees of the due process of law and the rule of law in which the protagonist lived – at least until then.[86] Thus, for example, the preliminary investigation focuses exclusively on the guilt of the accused, ignoring the objective facts of the case. There is no oral trial before the court. There is a conviction without a prior trial. The investigation leads directly to a conviction, with no intermediate steps.[87]

As we have said, many authors attribute to *The Trial* a premonitory character of totalitarianism. A reflection of this lack of procedural guarantees, which Josef K. suffered, is manifested in the German doctrine (Jakobs) of "enemy criminal law," which is reflected in the reaction of the U.S. government after the September 11 attacks on the Twin Towers. According to this doctrine, anyone who has permanently fled from the law is considered an enemy, distinguishing between a system of guarantees for "normal" people and another, without the classic rights and guarantees, for enemies, who are considered non-persons and are measured by a different yardstick.[88]

This permanent silence and lack of information on the part of the court regarding the crime actually committed responds not only to a desire for concealment and misinformation, but also to the non-existence or real absence of an attributable crime. This would be an example of what will eventually

---

84 Alexandre Vialatte, *Kafka ou l'innocence diabolique*, Paris, Les Belles Lettres, 1998.

85 Julio Picatoste Bobillo, *Kafka y el Derecho, op. cit.*, pp. 116 ff, quote on p. 120.

86 Mariana Gil Bartomeu, "Las violaciones de los derechos fundamentales del Señor K. en *El proceso* de Franz Kafka," in A. Hernández Cervantes (ed.), *Derecho y Literatura. Una alianza que subvierte el orden*, Mexico, Bonilla Artiga Editores, 2017.

87 Miguel Catalán, *Kafka o la acusación como condena*, Madrid, Sequitur, 2016.

88 Julio Picatoste Bobillo, *Kafka y el Derecho, op. cit.*, pp. 112–113.

become known as "criminal law of the author," as opposed to "criminal law of the act." The fact is that K. is not being persecuted for having committed criminal acts, for his unlawful conduct, for what he did, but for what he is, because he is considered, as can be deduced from several passages in the novel, a dangerous dissident and, therefore, an undesirable subject, a persecution with political connotations. This punishment not for what one has done, but for what one is, is characteristic of authoritarian regimes, as opposed to criminal law based on the act, which is an achievement of liberal and democratic regimes, of the rule of law. The judge should not judge the morality of the defendant (though it is not a crime), but rather the commission of external acts contrary to the law, that is, crimes or misdemeanors.[89]

In internal life, the principle of freedom of conscience prevails. The law concerns only social life, to ensure peaceful coexistence in society. As mentioned before, a person may be morally very bad, but if they have refrained from breaking the law, the law should not punish them (moral sanctions in a hypothetical future or afterlife are another matter). Conversely, a good person who has, through carelessness or unintentionally, broken the law is liable to criminal prosecution.

3.2.6 Punishment Must Be Inflicted upon the Author of the Offense: Punishment of the Innocent as a Form of Victimization

3.2.6.1 General Concepts

The controversy surrounding the possibility of *punishing the innocent* has occupied a great deal of literature dealing with the moral justification of punishment. Here, an important distinction should be highlighted. The problem basically arises when, *being conscious* of their innocence, innocent people are punished. If those who punish the innocent do so because they consider them guilty, we should be faced with a supposed *error*. However, when we knowingly inflict a punishment upon someone who does not deserve it, then we can speak of *victimization* in the strict sense of the term. The idea that we may only refer to punishment when this is directed at the person guilty of an offense has been studied in-depth by A.M. Quinton, and accepted by S.I. Benn, amongst others.[90]

Guilt through the commission of an offense figures as a *logical* prerequisite for punishment to *exist*, for us *to be able to punish*, according to the retributive

---

89 *Ibid.*, pp. 133–134.

90 From the point of view of the victim, cf. also James Morden Hough, "The Impact of Victimization: Findings from the British Crime Survey," Paper prepared for the *Third*

vision; and, as a *moral* prerequisite for punishment to be *justified*, that we *should punish*, according to utilitarianism. In our opinion, here we are treating a theoretician's position over the greater or lesser importance to award the prerequisite of guilt. Either guilt is essential, a *conditio per quam*, of punishment, a sufficient reason for the said punishment, or else, though not a sufficient reason, it is a necessary one, a *conditio sine qua non*. For some, punishing the innocent is not punishment nor can it receive the name of punishment, it is, at maximum, victimization. We are confronted with an essential problem of logical, conceptual definition. Unjust punishment would not be punishment, but victimization. For others, even if only conceptually, there is room for the distinction between just and unjust punishments, according to as punishment is applied to the guilty or the innocent, although, at the moral level, only punishment of the guilty would be justified. It is not that we *cannot* punish the innocent, that to do so would represent a *contradictio in terminis*, but rather that we *must not* do so. This is because not everything that we can do, on the factual plane, we should do, on the ethical plane. The best solution would be to accept a *wide* definition of punishment, which would include punishment of the innocent, even if only nosologically and conceptually, though it might well be excluded from the moral point of view, not being ethically justified. The desert of punishment does not so much affect its quality as it affects its just application to a particular individual.

This would appear a more correct approach than that which consists of proposing an eclectic approach, *quantitative* rather than qualitative, in line with which punishment of the innocent would be explained as happening in *isolated and exceptional* cases. The eclectic approach does not seem adequate to us, not even considering the idea of the *exceptional* as a *qualitative* discriminatory criterion – as the exceptionally justified – not to mention using it as a mere statistic and quantitative datum – as the unusual, infrequent or rare. The punishment of the innocent would never be justified, even though it may exceptionally take place.

Another possible way of solving the problem of the, in principle, implicit contradiction which exists in the expression "punishing the innocent" might stem from the distinction between concepts in a *weak* sense and concepts in a

---

International Institute of Victimology, Lisbon, 1984. James Morden Hough – Path Mayhew, *Taking Account of Crime: Key Findings from the Second British Crime Survey*, London, Her Majesty's Stationery Office, 1985. James Morden Hough – D. Moxon, "Dealing with Offenders: Popular Opinions and the Views of Victims," in *Howard Journal*, 24, 3, 1985, pp. 160–175. James Morden Hough – Julian Roberts, *Attitudes to Punishment: Findings from the British 1996 Crime Survey*, London, Home Office, 1998. Andrew Karmen, *Crime Victims. An Introduction to Victimology*, Belmont, California, Wadsworth, 1984.

strong sense, according to the degree of propriety with which we handle them. A concept in the weak sense is when it is used in a somewhat improper or inexact fashion, as opposed to the technical, proper or strong sense of the concept. For instance, after a long day of training, an athlete may exclaim: "I'm half dead." In any strong sense, this would be rejectable, since life is a legal good not open to grading. One cannot speak of a percentage of life. A person is either alive or dead. It is another thing when a very old person may have a lesser quality of life. Nevertheless, in a weak sense there is room for the "half dead" expression to denote tiredness. In a similar way, to speak of the punishment of innocents is like speaking of "*punishing someone for something he has not done.*" In any strict sense, this would be a contradiction. In a weak sense, its existence could be conceived of as arising in miscarriages of justice or when, deliberately, there is a flagrant injustice committed. Though erroneous or unjust, punishment of the innocent can, in fact, take place. When it does, we use the expression "punishment" in the weak, not in the strong, sense. This would be the case in Kafka's *The Trial.*

3.2.6.2 Application to the Studied Work

In *The Trial* the presumption of innocence – according to which everyone is innocent until proven guilty – is ignored. It is the defendant who must strive to convince the court of his innocence. The fact that the burden of proof rests on the defendant takes us back to a criminal law typical of archaic times. Let us remember the ordeals or trials by God, in which it was the defendant who had to "purgate the accusation."

There is no doubt that Josef K. is innocent. The first words of the novel state: "Someone must have slandered Josef K., because without having done anything wrong, he was arrested one morning." In other words, the trial against him is based on slander, on a false accusation. From the outset, the trial is corrupted by lies. It is motivated by political reasons, by ideological persecution. This assertion can be argued on the basis that:

1. The story is set in a scenario of exceptional. Who else would dare to assault him in his own home?
2. According to the owner of the boarding house where Josef K. is staying, his arrest is not carried out in the ordinary manner, as would be the case, for example, with a thief. In K.'s arrest, there is no physical contact or threat. He is not restrained, handcuffed, or immobilized. In the height of incongruity, he is allowed to return to work and move about without restriction, as if he had not been arrested.
3. The uniforms worn by the agents who arrest him are more reminiscent of paramilitary groups than the police.

4. His situation reaches the ears of his colleagues at the bank. He also receives a visit from his uncle Karl, who is concerned about the news of the proceedings against his nephew, and K. informs him that "this is not a trial before an ordinary court," leaving the suspicion in the air that the protagonist is the target of some kind of political persecution. When, at his uncle's initiative, he goes to speak to the lawyer Huld for advice, K. exclaims: "I didn't know that in a case like this you could call on a lawyer." His uncle also warns him that if he loses the case, he will be "eliminated." There is no mention of the imposition of a penalty, but rather the term "eliminate," annihilate, is used, with connotations of political stigmatization of an alleged dissident.
5. At some point in the novel, the idea of a certain political activism on the part of the protagonist seems to be suggested, a certain dissidence against a society he considers sick, flawed, corrupt. K. presents himself as a nonconformist, revealing certain sociopolitical connotations, setting himself up in his defense before the court as a bastion and symbol of the group of other "defendants," speaking on their behalf, confronting the law that judges them.
6. Other passages in the novel seem to suggest the existence of a single power that combines the political and the judicial, as in totalitarian states, contrary to Montesquieu's separation of powers. In such regimes, uniformity and herd mentality are encouraged, as opposed to individualism and critical thinking, with mistrust of those who disagree, who are rebellious, who do not blend in with the masses. Being different, not conforming to the norm and convention, daring to be different and disagreeing, questioning dominant dogmas, is seen by authoritarian power as a challenge, which is met with hostility. In short, the "fear of difference" is cultivated, as in fascism.[91]

3.2.7 Punishment Must Be Intentionally Inflicted (in Contrast to Repentance) by Human Beings (in Contrast to Divine Punishment) Who Are Distinct from the Offender (in Contrast to Self-Punishment) and by the Institutionalized Authority to Punish (in Contrast to Private Vengeance)

3.2.7.1 General Concepts

Punishment is imposed upon the offender because of human action. We do not speak of punishment where there is no mediation by a punitive authority

91 Julio Picatoste Bobillo, *Kafka y el Derecho, op. cit.*, pp. 136–138.

exercising its will, but of *repentance*, whenever there is voluntary restitution of the benefit unrightfully obtained, or when there is compensation or satisfaction for the evil derived from the offense. Punishments are not only imposed against our will but must also be imposed by a will alien to ours, by other human beings. It is not enough that they appear unexpectedly – just happening like the pain caused to us when the dentist does not anesthetize us properly – or that they be inevitable though intentionally inflicted, as would be the case with the surgeon who, for some reason, cannot give us analgesics against the pain. On the contrary, punishments must be impositions deliberately carried out on the part of the agent or authority applying them.[92]

Natural disasters or accidental damage cannot be considered punishments, but from a *religious* point of view. We might think of the God of the Old Testament, who sent plagues and punishments upon mortals. Theory tends to coincide with the demand that punishment must be inflicted by human beings, in contradistinction to religious punishment, of *divine* origin. The contrary premise would require assuming the existence of an afterlife, which is a profession of faith, something not everyone is willing to admit. In that hypothetical future life, rewards and punishments would be distributed. Another feature of Divine Punishment would be the lack of institutionalization, both in the sense that specific rules are not necessary when determining which *actions* should count as offensive, and regarding the way the *authority* to inflict punishment arises.

On the other hand, what Divine Punishment seeks would not be *efficacy* or obedience to a system of rules and norms – as is the way with earthly punishment – since such would follow as a postponed reaction in the hypothetical context of an afterlife. What Divine Punishment would have in advantage is that it is infallible, with no place for error, it corresponds to the real and effective guilt of he who has committed the offense, given that the one inflicting the punishment has direct and absolute knowledge of the degree of guilt of he who is to suffer. God never punishes an innocent man. The possibility of collective Divine Punishment would be another question.

Again, those who apply punishment must be individuals distinct from the offender, hence *self-punishment*, which one imposes upon oneself, as in the case of Josef K., is excluded from the standard definition of punishment. There must be nothing of unintentional punishments, nothing of punishments

92 John Kleinig, *Punishment and Desert*, The Haghe, Martinus Nijhoff, 1973, p. 23.

imposed by fate, no Divine Punishments. Nor can there be punishments that we might inflict upon ourselves.[93]

Finally, a characteristic feature of punishment to be noted is that it must be imposed by people who have been *institutionally* awarded the faculty to punish – for example, a judge – as against the idea that just anyone may take justice into his own hands. The latter case is more properly considered personal vengeance which is typical of the pre-social state, before the constitution of the state.[94] What does not appear necessary is the restriction of the idea of punishment to some state organization or to the judges; the existence of any *authority* able of elaborating rules, together with *agents* to apply them, is enough.

3.2.7.2 Application to the Studied Work

The second chapter deals with the interrogation to which K. is subjected. Political motivation emerges in this chapter. It is grotesque and absurd that K. is summoned on a Sunday, so as not to interfere with his work, it is said, as well as the haphazard search, first for the building and then for the interrogation room. The court premises are in the suburbs. Once inside the building, many children swarm around the stairs. Everything is vulgarity, destitution, and poverty.

During the interrogation, Josef K. stands up to the judge, addressing him with words of extreme gravity and harshness. But curiously this will be the only time he acts with resolve and energy. In the following chapters, that vigor disappears, and he collapses, dejected, with a resignation that will ultimately lead him to follow his executioners to the open field where he will be executed.

The audience reacts with applause and laughter, "enjoying the defendant's allegations very much," as if it were a theatrical performance. Everything is staged and pure theater. There are similarities between the interrogation room and a political assembly, for, as the protagonist perceives, all those present wear the same insignia, suggesting a lack of political pluralism. They are civil servants.

During the interrogation, K. can see the judge face to face. But this judge, called to take his first statement, will later be replaced by an unknown court,

---

93 Thomas McPherson, "Punishment: Definition and Justification," in *Analysis*, 28, 1967–1968, pp. 21–27, esp. p. 22.

94 Edward L. Ayers, *Vengeance and Justice: Crime and Punishment in the Nineteenth Century American South*, New York, 1984.

which he will never see. Perhaps this contributes to the protagonist's discouragement. It is an inaccessible, unknowable, distant, and all-powerful court.[95]

The trial[96] thus becomes an absorbing and invasive reality that threatens and grips his life, becoming the center of it. He thinks only of the trial and lives only for it. It is an omnipresent nightmare in his life and he feels trapped, with no way out. "K. not only has to defend himself *in* the trial, but he also has to defend himself *against* the trial that is advancing against him." His procedural adventure has nothing to do with a normal legal proceeding.[97] It is simply a "parody of justice," a grotesque spectacle.

To begin with, he is not informed of the crime he is accused of, which leaves him completely defenseless, with his chances of defense curtailed by the court itself. As the novel itself states, sometimes "it happened that the court did not read those first requests," that the first request was misplaced or lost forever. Furthermore, the trial lacked publicity and, as a result, the defendant and his defense were also unable to access the court's documents, especially the indictment.

We would be dealing with a purely inquisitorial procedure, typical of absolute states, where the accused is the object and not the subject of the law. "Inquisitio" and "acusatio" would be confused. The court is attracted by guilt, goes out in search of the guilty, without holding an oral trial, moving from

95 Julio Picatoste Bobillo, *Kafka y el Derecho, op. cit.*, pp. 122–125.

96 Eric Lawson Marson, *Kafka's Trial. The Case Against Josef K.*, St. Lucia, Australia, University of Queensland Press, 1975.

97 Let us recall here, in the words of Luigi Ferrajoli, the procedural guarantees inherent to a state governed by the rule of law (due process of law):
- "Nulla poena sine crimine."
- "Nullum crimen sine lege."
- "Nulla lex (poenale) sine necessitate."
- "Nulla necessitas sine iniuria."
- "Nulla iniuria sine actione."
- "Nulla actio sine culpa."
- "Nulla culpa sine iudicio."
- "Nullum iudicium sine accusatione."
- "Nulla accusatio sine probatione."
- "Nulla probatio sine defensione."

On this topic in Kafka, see Matías Germán Rodríguez Romero, "Principios procesales del Derecho en *El Proceso* de Franz Kafka. ¿Qué tan lejos estamos del proceso del autor austriaco?," in *Revista Derechos en Acción*, year 5, no. 17, spring 2020, pp. 487–494.

investigation or preliminary proceedings to conviction. There are clear signs of bias and a tendency to convict. Objectivity and impartiality are lacking.[98]

In the words of Ferrajoli, the purpose of criminal law is twofold: "the punishment of the guilty, yes, but, at the same time, the protection of the innocent." Not only does the presumption of innocence not apply, but the presumption of guilt prevails. In this regard, we must recall K.'s conversation with the chaplain in the cathedral, in which both are aware that the trial is going badly. The essence of any trial is missing, namely, two opposing parties (the plaintiff and the defendant) and an impartial judge to decide.[99]

There is a sequence in *The Trial* in which the painter Titorelli, who paints portraits for the court, uses his experience to explain to Josef K. the forms of acquittal used by the court.

First, there is "real acquittal," in which the files are destroyed, and of which Titorelli knows of no case in which it has been applied.

Then there is "apparent acquittal," which is temporary, a kind of bureaucratic lethargy or state of latency, but in which no file is archived, and everything remains in force. The papers continue to move back and forth, from the lower courts to the higher courts and vice versa, but they are neither lost nor destroyed. Seen from the outside, it might sometimes seem that everything has been forgotten, but this is not the case; the court forgets nothing.

Finally, there is "indefinite postponement," which consists of permanently keeping the case in its lower procedural stages, without the proceedings moving beyond its initial phase. Here, although the trial is not interrupted, the defendant is as sure as if he were free not to be convicted. Except for the first solution, the other two are ways of keeping citizens subjugated and fearful, under constant *surveillance*, with a sword of Damocles permanently hanging over their lives, depriving them of peace and tranquility, like a fly caught in the spider's web woven by the court.[100]

Kafka has a negative and depressing view of the world of justice.[101] Although this is not the central theme of *The Trial*, the novel contains strong criticism and satire against lawyers, judges, and agents of the judicial world.

---

98 Fernando Bermejo Rubio, "'Die Lüge wird zur Weltordnung gemancht': procesos victimarios y distorsión de la objetividad en la obra de Franz Kafka," in *Revista de Filología Alemana*, 18, 2010, pp. 135–161.

99 Julio Picatoste Bobillo, *Kafka y el Derecho, op. cit.*, pp. 125–132.

100 *Ibid.*, pp. 132–133.

101 Julián Axat, *Franz Kafka para explicar la teoría del acceso a la justicia*, Excerpt from the transcript of the presentation given at the Specialized Seminar on Public Law, Facultad de Derecho, Universidad Nacional de Rosario, May 19, 2022.

Kafka highlights the fatuity, haughtiness and vanity of judges. For the Czech author, the law is inaccessible, as are the courts and the best lawyers. The petitions drafted by them or by the parties involved are met with indifference by the judges, who, he says, barely examine or study them.

Kafka has a somewhat better opinion of the officials in the intermediate bodies, who only obey the orders of their hierarchical superiors. Perhaps his more benevolent judgment of them is because the author himself held a position as a civil servant at the Labor Insurance Institute. This condescending treatment can be seen in the passage in which Josef K. exonerates the agents who arrested him when they are whipped precisely because of his complaint.

But it is undeniable that the protagonist of *The Trial* has a poor conception of the world of justice, which, in his opinion, is corrupt and rife with bribery and influence peddling. Furthermore, the novel reveals a lack of material resources, a poor justice system, and undignified settings. The courts are in the suburbs of the city, in mediocre buildings.[102]

3.2.8 Desert as an All-Encompassing Concept of Merit – Positive – and Its Negative Version – Demerit – as a Justification for Punishment: Can We Speak of Punishment as Reward?

3.2.8.1 General Concepts

When considering punishment as just and legitimate, a central idea is that of deserving.[103] The absence of certain typical or defining qualities of punishment may cause it to be characterized as unjust or undeserved punishment. Nevertheless, the subject of desert has usually been studied in relation to questions of social justice or distributive justice,[104] rather than in relation to studies and researches into the justification of punishment.[105] This does not

102 Julio Picatoste Bobillo, *Kafka y el Derecho, op. cit.*, pp. 139–143.

103 On the subject, cf. Ted Honderich, *Punishment. The Supposed Justification, op. cit.*, 1969, pp. 26–47.

104 Cf. on the subject, among others, Robert Nozick (1938–2002), *Anarchy, State and Utopia*, Oxford, Basil Blackwell, 1974; and Michael Sandel, *Liberalism and the Limits of Justice*, Cambridge, Cambridge University Press, 1982.

105 Cf. on desert, Joel Feinberg (1926–2004), *Doing and Deserving*, New Jersey, Princeton University Press, 1970; Wojciech Sadurski, *Giving Desert Its Due*, Dordrecht, D. Reidel Pub. Co., 1985; George Sher, *Desert*, New Jersey, Princeton University Press, 1987. John Braithwaite – Philip Pettit, *Not Just Deserts. A Republican Theory of Criminal Justice*, Oxford, Clarendon Press, 1990. Richard W. Burgh, "Do the Guilty Deserve Punishment?," in *The Journal of Philosophy*, vol. 79, no. 4, 1982, pp. 193–210. Douglas N. Husak, "Why Punish the Deserving?," in *Nous*, 26, 1992, pp. 447–464. Frederick Hussey, "Just Deserts and Determinate Sentencing: Impact on the Rehabilitation Ideal," in *The Prison Journal*,

prevent for the application of some characteristic features attributed to the idea of desert – or not deserving, in its negative guise – to see what their relevance might be in relation to punishment.

The terms "deserve," or "desert" almost always reflect deeply rooted feelings or our intuitions concerning what is just, vestiges of a primitive tendency which drives us to desire good to our benefactors and ill to our detractors. Whoever has made an effort to achieve some tasks has merit and we consider their effort should be crowned with success and, contrariwise, whoever has acted badly morally does not deserve any triumph in his undertakings.

Judgments of desert are characterized by their reference to the past;[106] their apparent tie to the idea of obligation; and their being judgments about people.

To deserve something is not equivalent to *having a right to* that something.[107] When dealing with rights, the personal circumstances of the subject are completely irrelevant. One might be an owner despite being lazy and not deserving to have that property right at all. One must distinguish between *deserving X* – a moral concept –, *having a title to X* – a legal concept –, and *affirming the necessity of X* – a factual concept. Each one of these three criteria is conceptually independent.

A deterministic vision of the world and of the individual in society, where the individual is compelled, by factors external to his will, to commit crimes, is apparently incompatible with the idea of deserving and undeserving. If the offender is not free to commit the offense, if he is determined thereto, he does not deserve a prize – since he does commit it – but neither does he deserve a punishment – since his action escapes the control of the human will, in part denying the role played by intelligence, talent, will-power, self-control, and so on. There, one would have to give up the retributive idea of punishment as deserved and just consequence of a moral offense committed by a free subject. There, the existence of the illicit or of an offense would be enough to immediately set the blind punishing mechanism of the state in motion. It would be enough to commit the forbidden to acquire a right to be

---

LIX, 2, fall-winter 1980, pp. 36–47. Richard G. Singer, *Just Deserts: Sentencing Based on Equality and Desert*, Cambridge, Massachusetts, Ballinger, 1979. Martin Wasik – Andrew von Hirsch, "Non-Custodial Penalties and the Principles of Desert," in *Criminal Law Review*, 1988, pp. 555–572. Laurence Stern, "Deserved Punishment, Deserved Harm, Deserved Blame," in *Philosophy*, 45, 1970, pp. 317–329. Andrew von Hirsch – Andrew Ashworth, "Not Just Deserts: A Response to Braithwaite and Pettit," in *Oxford Journal of Legal Studies*, 13, 1992, pp. 83–96. Jerónimo Betegón, *La justificación del castigo, op. cit.*, pp. 205–321.

106 Cf. Wojciech Sadurski, *Giving Desert Its Due, op. cit.*, p. 118.

107 Cf., on the subject, John Deigh, "On the Right to Be Punished: Some Doubts," in *Ethics*, 94, 1984, pp. 191–211.

treated after a pre-determined fashion – a normative consequence.[108] The imposition of a punishment would be a function of what an individual does and not of what he is.[109]

Already in his *L'éducation morale*, Émile Durkheim distinguished between two large groups of punishments: *negative* sanctions and *positive* sanctions. Negative sanctions are *punishments* and positive sanctions are *rewards*. What they have in common is that they reinforce the fulfilling of norms. They do this antagonistically: in the case of negative sanctions, by punishing the malefactor; in the case of the positive, they reward those who fulfil their duties. Within negative sanctions are included both *repressive* or criminal punishments and *restitutive*, civil or administrative sanctions. Positive sanctions are, for instance, those existing in schools when better marks or distinctions are awarded to the most outstanding pupils. The same also occurs in morally healthy societies. Nevertheless, the number of punishments is always much greater in comparison with the much lesser importance of the prizes. Hence, when speaking of legal sanctions, we think of punishments first and foremost. In fact, there is no Prize Code which would parallel the Criminal Code. Positive sanctions rather deserve the name of *incentives or advantages* than sanctions properly speaking, even though there are those who use the not very common, and even at first sight contradictory, term "*sanction as reward*."[110]

3.2.8.2 Application to the Studied Work

In Kafka's work, unlike what happens to Raskolnikov in *Crime and Punishment*, it is not that the offense seeks punishment, but rather that the accused eagerly seeks his guilt, because he is completely unaware of it, and it is from this insecurity and lack of legal certainty that self-blame arises. The scene of the intrusion into Josef K.'s bedroom completely changes his life in a matter of seconds, transforming him from an anonymous citizen into a man under *sur-*

---

108 Jerónimo Betegón, *La justificación del castigo, op. cit.*, pp. 236 ff.

109 Wojciech Sadurski, "Distributive Justice and the Theory of Punishment," in *Oxford Journal of Legal Studies*, 5, 1, 1985, p. 47. *Id., Giving Desert Its Due, op. cit.*, 1985, p. 225.

110 Cf. on the subject Gregorio Robles, *Crimen y castigo (Ensayo sobre Durkheim), op. cit.*, pp. 61–63. Mario Alberto Copello, *La sanción y el premio en el Derecho*, Buenos Aires, Losada, 1945. Luis Jiménez de Asúa, "La recompensa como prevención general – El derecho premial," in *Revista General de Legislación y Jurisprudencia*, vol. 125, pp. 5–32 and 353–394. Angelo de Mattia, "Merito e ricompensa," in *Rivista Internazionale di Filosofia del Diritto*, XVII, VI, pp. 608–624. Jeremy Bentham (1748–1832), *Tratados de Legislación penal y civil*, I, pp. 66–95, and IV, pp. 311–314, Villalpando, Madrid, 1821. Jacinto Dragonetti, *Tratado de las virtudes y de los premios*, in Beccaria, *Dei Delitti e delle pene*, Villamil, Madrid, 1836. Frédéric Holbach, *Justice laudative*, Larcier, Pedone, Brussels-Paris, 1904.

veillance who, from that moment on, loses all his privacy and for whom all guarantees disappear. It is as if the protagonist's life has come to a standstill. The novel says that the cook does not bring him breakfast and that "it was the first time this had happened." One wonders how someone can be arrested and not even be told the reason for their arrest or what their rights are. The atmosphere is like a fog, in which, knowing nothing, one speculates even more (Who are these agents, what agency do they belong to, what are their functions?). When, a few minutes later, the agents wash their hands of the matter, Josef K., as if in premonition, considers the advisability of suicide.

Later, the protagonist of *The Trial* states: "I am not familiar with that law," the law under which he is being charged. And although everyone is familiar with the aphorism that "ignorance of the law is no excuse for non-compliance," in this case, what K. does not know is not so much the law itself, but its very existence, as it is a law that no one knows because it is unattainable. How, then, should one act if access to the laws is not allowed?

Here it is worth recalling the words Kafka wrote to his father in *Letter to the Father*, in which he acknowledges that his entire life he has been the victim of a trial, his father's, which led him to feel immense guilt and a loss of self-confidence, feeling accused and irreversibly condemned, his innocence impossible to prove because the Law, his father's Law, only allows for guilt.[111]

There is also an anomaly in the way Josef K. is notified of the court summons: by telephone. And in the day chosen for the start of the trial: a Sunday, when everyone knows that the courts are closed on public holidays. There is also uncertainty about the time he is to appear ("we forgot to agree on the time", despite which, once inside, the judge reproaches him: "You should have been here an hour and five minutes ago," and it is because of this "undue delay" that the investigating judge, a tiny little man, reconsiders his refusal to question him), and in the place where he must go: a distant suburb where K. had never been, instead of a court located in a familiar part of the city. Although he is told that the proceedings will be "brief," it is added that the interrogations will be detailed. Josef K. also has no access to the court document containing his indictment, which is beyond his reach. And, after his court appearance, yet no one arrests him, leaving him, as a desolate defendant, with no choice but to leave the room.

From the moment the protagonist is arrested, he is accompanied by a feeling of shame and fear that leads him to keep everything "as secret as possible." Little by little, he realizes that he "has no right to have rights," as happened to

111 Juan Alfredo Obarrio Moreno – Luis de las Heras Vives, *El mundo jurídico en Franz Kafka. El proceso*, Madrid, Dykinson, 2019, pp. 89–106.

Socrates,[112] Josef K.'s words sounding like those of the Greek philosopher in the *Apology*: "harsh, but at the same time fair." As in the case of Socrates, slander and gossip hang over him like a stain. The protagonist of *The Trial* is faced with a clear violation of his right to defense, to remain silent, to be assisted by a lawyer, and to see the case file during the trial. In this phantasmagorical world, anguish takes hold of the young Josef K., his confidence falters and vanishes. After the first interrogation, he not only feels a great distrust of justice, but also an immense feeling of helplessness in the face of it. For this reason, the only solution, rather than fighting, seemed to be resignation. To win the case, as Josef K. was informed (in his meetings with lawyer Huld and painter Titorelli), contacts, a kind of clientelist relationship, were more important than the expertise demonstrated in the trial. Success, if achieved, would be accidental rather than causal. The trial is thus presented as "an impossible achievement."[113]

The passage "Before the Law" is famous in the novel *The Trial*. Rather than describing it, what we want to do here is to show the conclusion or moral that seems to be drawn from it: If we stop at what worries, distresses, or frightens us, without being able to rebel to protect our rights, we have no alternative. We can wait sitting down, watching life pass us by without having lived it, or we can cross the threshold and face our fears, those that haunt all human beings, to "cross doors that were created for us to dare to cross them. For this reason, when we do not enter the door we have chosen, it closes forever."[114]

At the heart of the parable "Before the Law" lie the traps of "voluntary servitude," which Étienne de La Boétie discussed in his famous work of the same title. As Michael Löwy says, the peasant in the fable "has failed because he did not want to take the path of the law by crossing the threshold *without authorization*." It was he himself who put on his own chains. But Josef K, unlike the man from the countryside, chooses to fight the law. "While the peasant resigns himself, Josef K. will resist, he will unmask the mysterious Law... In short, faced with a law that has the last word, he will oppose the force of *interpretation*."[115]

---

112 See José Iturmendi Morales, "Proceso y muerte de Sócrates. Un sabio ante la justicia de su tiempo," in *Grandes abogados, grandes procesos que hicieron historia*, Pamplona, Aranzadi, 1997, pp. 155–159.

113 Juan Alfredo Obarrio Moreno – Luis de las Heras Vives, *El mundo jurídico en Franz Kafka…, op. cit.*, pp. 107–119, 136–139 and 148 ff.

114 *Ibid.*, pp. 159 ff., quote on p. 166.

115 Michael Löwy, *Franz Kafka, rêveur insumis*, Paris, Stock, 2004. Denis Salas, *Kafka. El combate con la ley, op. cit.*, pp. 81–82 and 84.

Josef K. is sentenced to death. He is not notified of the sentence. Nor does the reader know it. Both the protagonist and the reader learn of the sentence through its execution. Kafka's narrative is an unequivocal plea against capital punishment, which he considers barbaric and cruel. In executions subject to the law, capital punishment is regulated and standardized, which gives it a certain civility. In contrast, in *The Trial*, K.'s execution is anything but solemn; it is an act stripped of all legal formalism, which makes it a true "legal murder," an inhuman and ferocious act. This is seen in the last words, which serve as the closing of the novel: "Like a dog! It was as if shame should survive him."[116]

In the end, the protagonist submits, and what is most remarkable in this work about guilt and punishment is that his submission is not forced by violent means, but "by the growing feeling of guilt that germinates within him" as a result of the entire process he undergoes. In short, it is the idea that "after all, no human being is free from guilt": "He must have done something," it seems to imply.[117]

3.2.9 Bureaucracy

Bureaucracy is the central theme of *The Trial*.[118] Kafka himself, as an insurance clerk, knew well what it was. He knew it, therefore, as an active subject, but also, undoubtedly, as a passive subject, observer, and qualified critical witness to the injustices it produced. "Franz Kafka remains in the literary Olympus as one of the writers who best exposed the bureaucratic nightmare."[119]

Picatoste Bobillo says: "If any image evokes the word Kafkaesque in us, it is precisely the world of bureaucracy, its thickness, the density of its atmosphere, its labyrinthine multiplication and dispersion, its mechanization and its metastasis, all of which are scourges that weave a web in which the citizen, powerless, finds himself trapped. Citizens rebel against the absurd and obsolete demands of bureaucracy, which are sometimes contrary to reason and maintained because of an inertia that no one challenges; it is the feeling of

116 Gerardo Córdoba Ospina, "La 'metáfora' como dadora de muerte. Acerca de la última frase de El Proceso de Kafka," in *Álabe*, no. 11, 2015.

117 Guillermo Sánchez Trujillo, "Crimen y castigo de Franz Kafka," in *The Kafka Project*: http://www.kafka.org/essays/crimen.htm. Julio Picatoste Bobillo, *Kafka y el Derecho, op. cit.*, pp. 143–147.

118 María Lourdes Gasillón, "Ezequiel Martínez Estrada y Franz Kafka, narradores de la máquina burocrática," in *Cuadernos del Sur-Letras*, 44–45, 2014–2015, pp. 41–69.

119 Julio Picatoste Bobillo, *Kafka y el Derecho, op. cit.*, pp. 171–172.

anguish caused by the representation of intricate procedures that must be overcome to reach a distant administrative goal."[120]

Another author who masterfully addressed the subject of bureaucracy was Max Weber, this time from the objective perspective of the sociologist, conceiving it as a rational organizational apparatus at the service of the state, with a body of civil servants who, in the opinion of this thinker, would perform their duties in an impersonal, unpredictable, but undoubtedly effective manner.

This Weberian view is diametrically opposed to the Kafkaesque one studied here.[121] The former is an *internal* view of the problem, *from above*, from the point of view of the state. Kafka's is an *external* perspective, *from below*, putting himself in the shoes of the individual victim of the absurd, oppressive, and authoritarian way of operating of said bureaucracy.[122]

To conclude and looking back at the current judicial situation in Spain and, we assume, in many other countries, it is worth noting that the bureaucratization of justice is an increasingly prevalent complaint, a real threat, as reflected by Kafka in the adventures of Josef K. narrated in *The Trial*.

---

120 *Ibid.*, p. 170.

121 José María González García, *La máquina burocrática* (*Afinidades electivas entre Max Weber y Kafka*), Madrid, Visor, 1989. *Id.*, "Jaulas, máquinas y laberintos (Imágenes de la burocracia en Kafka, Musil y Weber)," in *Observaciones Filosóficas*, no. 4, 2007. http://www.observacionesfilosoficas.net/Kafkaylaneurosis.htm.

122 Julio Picatoste Bobillo, *Kafka y el Derecho*, *op. cit.*, p. 172.

Bibliography

Abrahamsem, David, *The Psychology of Crime*, New York, Columbia University Press, 1960.

Adamiak, Richard, *Justice and History in the Old Testament: The Evolution of Divine Retribution in the Historiographies of the Wilderness Generation*, Cleveland, J. T. Zubal, 1982.

Adorno, Theodor Ludwig Wiesengrund (1903–1969), "Apuntes sobre Kafka," in *Prismas. Crítica de la cultura y la sociedad*, translation by Manuel Sacristán, Barcelona, Ariel, 1962, pp. 260–292.

Aeschylus (525 B.C.–456 B.C.), *La Orestiada*, translation by Álvaro del Amo, Madrid, Instituto Nacional de las Artes Escénicas y de la Música, 1990.

Aguilar, Alberto, *Fedor Dostoiewski Los hermanos Karamazov*, pdf.

Aguilera Barchet, Bruno, "El Derecho en el *Quijote*. Notas para una inmersión jurídica en la España del Siglo de Oro," in *Anuario de Historia del Derecho Español*, 76, 2006, pp. 173–214.

Aguirre Martínez, Guillermo, "Gide, Kafka,Woolf. Iluminación de su vida y obra a través de los diarios," in *Tropelías. Revista de Teoría de la Literatura y Literatura Comparada*, vol. 18, no. 1, 2012, pp. 168–203.

Alborg, Juan Luis (1914–2010), *Historia de la Literatura española*, 2nd. ed. with index, vol. II, *Época barroca*, Madrid, Gredos, 1970.

Alcoriza Vento, Javier, *Dostoyevski y su influencia en la cultura europea*, Ed., Verbum, 2005.

Alemán Páez, Francisco A., "Trabajo y Derecho," in *Trabajo y Derecho en* El Proceso *de Franz Kafka* (*I y II*), 18 and 19, 2016.

Alenza García, José Francisco, "Leer a Cervantes para aprender Derecho," Introduction by José Francisco Alenza García (Dir.), *Cervantes y el Derecho. Ideas cervantinas para el aprendizaje del Derecho*, Colección Facultad Ciencias Jurídicas UPNA, no. 2, Cizur Menor (Navarre), Thomson Reuters Aranzadi, 2016, pp. 35–68.

Alfieri, Luigi, "Il 'Processo' di Kafka tra diritto e metafísica," in Carla Faralli – Maria Paola Mittica (dirs.), *Diritto e Letteratura. Prospettive di Ricerca*, Roma, Aracne, 2010, pp. 195–220.

Alonso Burgos, Jesús, in *La llamada al testigo* (*sobre el* Libro de Job *y* El proceso *de Franz Kafka*), Seville, Thémata, 2014.

Alonso Rimo, Alberto, *Víctima y sistema penal: Las infracciones no perseguibles de oficio y el perdón*, Valencia, Tirant lo Blanch, 2002.

Altamirano, Manuel, *Justicia y Derecho en* El Proceso *de Kafka. Una lectura derridiana sobre la literatura, la ley y el origen*, UNC-Conicet, 2013.

 HTTPS://DOI.ORG/10.1163/9789004766006-009

Álvarez González, Norberto, *La tendencia a sufrir el castigo: Una contribución a la teoría de la culpa*, Alcalá, Universidad de Alcalá de Henares, Servicio de Publicaciones, 1996.

Álvarez Lopeztello, José Luis, "Cioran y Dostoyevski. El despertar de la conciencia y la lasitud de estar despierto," in *Revista de la Sociedad Iberoamericana de Antropología Filosófica*, vol. 3, no. 2, 2021, pp. 123–140.

Álvarez Patallo, José Andrés, "La dimensión jurídica de la novela *El proceso* de Franz Kafka," in *Estudios de Deusto. Revista de la Universidad de Deusto*, 53, 2, 2005.

Álvarez Sánchez, Gustavo, "Kafka, en el límite," in *En-claves del Pensamiento*, vol. 7, no. 13, 2013, pp. 11–22.

Álvarez Vigaray, Rafael, *El Derecho civil en las obras de Cervantes*, Foreword by Rafael Gibert Sánchez de la Vega, Granada, Comares, 1987.

Amat, Nuria, *Todos somos Kafka*, Madrid, Anaya & Mario Muchnik, 1993.

Ana Isabel, *El gran inquisidor Fiodor Dostoievski*, Colombia, Ediciones La Cueva.

Anders, Günther, *Kafka. Pour et contra*, Strasbourg, Circé, 1990.

Anderson, Mark (ed.), *Reading Kafka. Prague, Politics and the fin the siècle*, New York, Schocken Books, 1989. With "Introduction" by the author, and contributions by Christoph Stölzl, "Kafka: Jew, Anti-Semite, Zionist"; by Gerhard Kurz, "Nietzsche, Freud and Kafka" (pp. 143 ff.); or Klaus Wagenbach, "Prague at the Turn of the Century."

Andler, Charles, "Nietzsche et Dostoievski," in *Mélanges offerts à Fernand Baldensperger*, vol. I Paris, Honoré Champion, 1930.

Andrade Boué, Pilar, "La figura del idiota de Dostoievski y sus reescrituras literarias y cinematográficas," in *Anuario de la Sociedad Española de Literatura General y Comparada*, 4, 2014, pp. 129–151.

Anonymous, "Zenda recomienda: Diarios, de Franz Kafka," in *ZendaLibros.com*, January 13, 2024.

Añoveros Trías de Bes, Xabier, "El Derecho y la justicia en la obra de Cervantes," in *Digestum Legal*, and in http://digestum.es/el-derecho-y-la-justicia-en-la-obra-de-cervantes/.

Aparicio Belmonte, Juan, "Kafka, entomólogo," in *20 Minutos*, June 9, 2024.

Aparicio Maydeu, Javier, *Lecturas de ficción contemporánea. De Kafka a Ishiguro*, Madrid, Cátedra, 2020.

Arendt, Hannah (1906–1975), *Franz Kafka revalorado*, translation by J. Parra, in Franz Kafka, *Obras completas, t. I: Novelas*, Galaxia Gutenberg-Círculo de Lectores, 1999, pp. 173–193.

Aristodemou, Maria, "Seduction of Mimesis: Theater as Woman and the Play of Difference and Excess in Aeschylus's *Oresteia*," in *Cardozo Studies in Law and Literature*, vol. 11, issue 1, summer 1999, pp. 1–34.

Arrieta Burgos, Enán, "Literatura y Derecho: Kafka y las ficciones de la justicia," in *Pólemos*, April 27, 2020.

Arroyo Zapatero, Luis, "Delitos y penas en el *Quijote*," blog.uclm.es, 1993.

Arséntieva, Natalia, "Tomar conciencia y expresarlo: 'El realismo en un sentido amplio' como método artístico de Dostoievski," in *Mundo Eslavo*, no. 5, 2006, pp. 251–252.

Arséntieva, Natalia, "Dostoievski: Clave del 'Código Cervantes'," in Miguel Ángel Garrido Gallardo – Luis Alburquerque García (eds.), *El* Quijote *y el pensamiento teórico literario: Actas del Congreso Internacional celebrado en Madrid los días del 20 al 24 de junio de 2005*, 2008, pp. 353–372.

Arséntieva, Natalia, "Dostoievski," in *Materiales e Investigación*, no. 20, Saint Petersburg, Nestor Historia, 2013.

Arsuaga Acaso, Teresa, *Derecho y Literatura: James Boyd White y Richard H. Weisberg. Dos modelos de crítica literaria aplicada al Derecho*, PhD dissertation, supervised by Paloma Durán y Lalaguna, Madrid, Departamento de Filosofía del Derecho, Moral y Política I, Facultad de Derecho, Universidad Complutense de Madrid, 2015.

Arsuaga Acaso, Teresa, "La literatura en la formación de jueces y abogados," in *Anuari de Filologia. Estudis de Lingüística*, 7, 2017, pp. 125–148.

Arteaga Padilla, Edwin, "Editorial. Hacia una quijotización del Derecho Penal," in *Justicia*, 30, December 2016, pp. 9–12.

Asensi, Alfredo, "2024, el año más kafkiano: el autor de 'La metamorfosis' vuelve a la primera línea editorial," in *El Español. El Cultural*, December 31, 2023.

Axat, Julián, *Franz Kafka para explicar la teoría del acceso a la justicia*, Fragmento de la desgrabación de la ponencia expuesta ante el Seminario especializado en Abogacía Pública, Facultad de Derecho, Universidad Nacional de Rosario, May 19, 2022.

Ayala, Rubén, *Crimen y castigo Fyodor Mikhailovich Dostoyevsky v1...* pdf.

Ayers, Edward L., *Vengeance and Justice: Crime and Punishment in the Nineteenth Century American South*, New York, 1984.

Azorín (José Martínez Ruiz) (1873–1967), "Cervantes y América," in *Con permiso de los cervantistas*, Madrid, Biblioteca Nueva, 1948.

Babelia, "Los libros del centenario de Franz Kafka," in *El País. Babelia*, May 4, 2024.

Bajtín, Mijaíl Mijaílovich, *Problemas de la poética de Dostoievski*, translation by Tatiana Bubnova, Mexico, Fondo de Cultura Económica, 1986. Buenos Aires, F.C.E., 1993.

Bajtín, Mijaíl Mijaílovich, *Dostoevskij: poetica e stilistica*, translation by G. Garritano, Turin, Einaudi, 1968.

Balderston, Daniel, "Borges y sus precursores," in *Itinerarios*, vol. 14, 2011, pp. 113–120.

Baldovinos, Ricardo Roque, *Lo kafkiano en clave histórica: para una lectura crítica de "La metamorfosis,"* in Biblioteca "P. Florentino Idoate, S. J.," Universidad Centroamericana José Simeón Cañas, 1997.

Balint, Benjamin, *El último proceso de Kafka. El juicio de un legado literario*, Barcelona, Ariel, 2019.

Banakar, Reza, "In Search of Heimat: A Note on Franz Kafka's Concept of Law," in *Law & Literature*, vol. 22, issue 3, fall 2010, pp. 463–491.

Barcia Lago, Modesto, *Polis y "leyes no escritas": claves iusfilosóficas de la tragedia* Antígona *de Sófocles*, PhD dissertation, supervised by professors José Iturmendi Morales and Agapito Maestre Sánchez, Complutense University of Madrid, defended on September 9, 2022, released in November of that same year by Bosch Publishing.

Barón Crespo, Enrique, *Europa y el cristianismo. En torno a* Ante la Ley *de F. Kafka*, Barcelona, Anthropos, 2013.

Barrault, Jean-Louis, "Cas de conscience devant Kafka," in *CCRB 5, Franz Kafka. Du Procès au Château*, 20, October 1957.

Barreiro González, Germán José María, "El Derecho en la Literatura. ¿Cervantes iurisperito?," in *Gacetilla Colegial, Colegio de Graduados Sociales de León*, 79, 2004.

Barreiro González, Germán José María, "Don Quijote. Caballero andante jurisperito," in *Revista del Consejo General de Graduados Sociales de España*, 4, 2005.

Barreiro González, Germán José María, "Cervantes y Don Quijote Jurisperitos," in *Anales de Derecho: Colección Huarte de San Juan*, 6, 2005, pp. 13–38.

Barreiro González, Germán José María, "Cervantes y Don Quijote Jurisperitos (Una visión literaria del Derecho en Don Quijote de la Mancha)," in *Anales de Derecho, Universidad Pública de Navarra*, 6, 2005.

Barreiro González, Germán José María, "El Derecho como recurso literario en el *Quijote*: Cervantes y el ingenioso caballero jurisperito," in Homenaje a Don Miguel de Cervantes Saavedra con motivo del IV Centenario del nacimiento de Don Quijote, *Anuario da Facultade de Dereito*, 2005.

Barreiro González, Germán José María, "Ius quijotescum (El Derecho como recurso literario en el *Quijote*: Cervantes y el Ingenioso Caballero Jurisperitos)," in *Anuario da Facultade de Dereito da Universidade da Coruña*, 9, 2005.

Barthes, Roland, "La respuesta de Kafka," in *Ensayos críticos*, Barcelona, 1983.

BBC News MUNDO, Redacción, "Orwelliano o kafkiano: qué significan realmente y cómo eran los escritores detrás de esos populares adjetivos," in *News Mundo*, June 30, 2024.

Begley, Louis, *El mundo formidable de Kafka. Ensayo biográfico*, translation by I. Villaro, Barcelona, Alba Editorial, 2009.

Benjamin, Walter (1892–1940), "Dos iluminaciones sobre Kafka," in *Imaginación y sociedad. Iluminaciones*, Madrid, Taurus, 1988, pp. 203–204.

Benjamin, Walter, *Sobre Kafka. Textos, discusiones, apuntes, Eterna Cadencia*, ed. H. Schweppenhäuser, translation, foreword and notes by Mariana Dimópulus, Buenos Aires, 2014.

Bentham, Jeremy (1748–1832), *Tratados de Legislación penal y civil*, vol. I, and vol. IV, Villalpando, Madrid, 1821.

Benzo Mestre, Fernando, *Las ideas jurídicas de Don Quijote*, Discurso pronunciado en la toma de posesión como académico numerario de la Real Academia de Doctores el día 4 de febrero de 2005. Contestación del Académico Excmo. Sr. Dr. D. Jesús López Medel.

Berdiaev, Nicolás, *El espíritu de Dostoievski*, Buenos Aires, Carlos Lohlé, 1978. Translation into Spanish by Olga Trankova, with Sebastián Montiel and Artur Mrwczynski-van Allen, Granada, Editorial Nuevo Inicio, 2008.

Berdiaev, Nicolás, *Sobre el Gran Inquisidor: Dostoievski y los siguientes*, Moscow, Joven Guardia, 1991.

Beristain, Antonio, *La pena-retribución y las actuales concepciones criminológicas*, Introductions by Elías Neuman and Eugenio Raúl Zaffaroni, Buenos Aires, Depalma, Criminología Contemporánea, 1982.

Bermejo Rubio, Fernando, "'Die Lüge wird zur Weltordnung gemacht': procesos victimarios y distorsión de la objetividad en la obra de Franz Kafka," in *Revista de Filología Alemana*, 18, 2010.

Bernardete, Mair J., "Los galeotes (I, 22, 23, 25, 29): el criminal y la sociedad," in *Revista Hispánica Moderna* (*Columbia University Hispanic Studies*), 31, 1965.

Bernardo de Quirós, Constancio (1873–1959), "Figuras delincuentes en el *Quijote*," in *Anales de la Universidad de Santo Domingo*, 12, 1947.

Betegón, Jerónimo, *La justificación del castigo*, Madrid, Centro de Estudios Constitucionales, 1992.

Betz, Joseph, "Can Civil Disobedience Be Justified?," in *Social Theory and Practice*, vol. I, no. 2, fall 1970, pp. 13–30.

Bienstock, J.-Wladimir, *Les inédits de Dostoievski*, translation into French by J.-Wladimir Bienstock, Paris, Librairie Stock, 1923.

Bienstock, J.-Wladimir, "Dostoievski et Balzac," in *Mercure de France*, December 1, 1924. Supplement of the *Diario de La Marina*, June 12, 1927.

Bible, The, The Pentateuch, First Kings.

Blackmore, Jonathan, "An Examination into the Influence of Franz Kafka on American Jurisprudence," in *The Journal of Jurisprudence*, 4, 2009, pp. 307–332.

Blanco Sarto, Pablo, "Los Karamazov discuten. *Dios y el mal* en Dostoievski," in *Espíritu*, Notas, Textos y Documentos, LIII, 2004, pp. 77–85.

Blanchot, Maurice, "Reading Kafka," in *Twentieth Century Interpretations of the Trial*, New Jersey, 1976.

Blanchot, Maurice, *De Kafka a Kafka*, translation by J. Ferreiro, Mexico, Fondo de Cultura Económica, 1999. 2018.

Blázquez Ruiz, Francisco Javier, "El sentido de la dignidad. Libertad, justicia y utopía según D. Quijote," in José Francisco Alenza García (dir.), *Cervantes y el Derecho. Ideas cervantinas para el aprendizaje del Derecho*, Colección Facultad Ciencias Jurídicas UPNA, no. 2, Cizur Menor (Navarre), Thomson Reuters Aranzadi, 2016.

Blockeel, Francesca, "*Don Quijote*: realidad, ficción y elogio de la locura," en Various Authors, *Tras las huellas de Don Quijote. Actas de la Jornada dedicada a* Don Quijote de la Mancha, Antwerp, Lessius Hogeschool, December 9, 2005, edited and translated by Lieve Behiels, Ministerio de Educación y Ciencia de España – Lessius Hogeschool (Associatie K. U. Leuven), 2007, pp. 131–139.

Bloom, Harold, "Kafka," in *Acta Poética*, spring-fall 1989, pp. 361–384.

Bloom, Harold (ed.), *Fyodor Dostoievsky's Crime and Punishment*, New York, Chelsea House Publisher's, 1988.

Bombachi, Tomás,"F. M. Dostoievski, entre el hacha y el martillo. La praxis en las ideas de Rodión Raskólnikov", in *Rus* (Sao Pâulo), vol. 13, 2022, pp. 71–87.

Boneva, Preslava, "De Gabo a 'Gladiator 2' pasando por Kafka: lo más esperado de 2024," in *The Objective*, January 5, 2024.

Borges, Jorge Luis (1899–1986), "Kafka y sus precursores," in *Id., Obras Completas*, Buenos Aires, Emecé, 1974. Also in *Otras inquisiciones*, Destino, 2007.

Borges, Jorge Luis, "Prologue" to *Biblioteca personal Franz Kafka. América. Relatos breves*, Barcelona, 1988.

Borges, Jorge Luis, *Las pesadillas y Franz Kafka, Textos recobrados (1931–1955)*, Buenos Aires, 1996.

Borrell Merlín, María Dolores, "La justicia y la paz en el *Quijote*," in *Cuadernos de Estudios Manchegos*, 29, 2005.

Boruchoff, David A., "On the Place of Madness, Deviance, and Eccentricity in Don Quijote," in *Hispanic Review*, 70, 1, 2002, pp. 1–23.

Braithwaite, John – Pettit, Philip, *Not Just Deserts. A Republican Theory of Criminal Justice*, Oxford, Clarendon Press, 1990.

Breger, Louis, *Dotoevsky: The Author as Psychoanalyst*, New York, New York University Press, 1989.

Brisset, Demetrio E., in *Las puestas del poder. El proceso de Kafka y Welles como gestos de rebeldía*, translation by Román Gubern, Barcelona-Málaga, Luces de Gábilo (Gorbs Ediciones S.L.), 2013.

Brod, Max (1884–1968), *Verzweiflung und Erlösung im Werk Franz Kafkas*, Frankfurt/M., Fischer, 1959.

Brod, Max, "Postfacios," in *El proceso*, translation by F. Formosa, Alianza Editorial, Biblioteca Kafka, 2000.

Brod, Max, *Kafka*, 1982; translation by Carlos F. Grieben, 3rd. ed., Buenos Aires, Emecé Editores, 2000.

Brod, Max, *Franz Kafka. Una biografia*, Passigli Editore, 2020.

Brombert, Victor, "Kafka: The Death-Journey in the Everlasting Present," in *The Hudson Review*, vol. 64, no. 4, 2012, pp. 623–642.

Brontë, Emily (1818–1848), *Cumbres borrascosas*, Harmondsworth, Penguin, 1965. There is an edition by Paz Kindelán, translation by Rosa Castillo, Madrid, Cátedra, 2011. There is also a translation by Carmen Martín Gaite, Barcelona, Alba Editorial, 2010. Also in Madrid, Siruela, 2007, with foreword by Alejandro Gándara, translation and notes by Cristina Sánchez-Andrade.

Brook, Thomas, *Cross-Examinations of Law and Literature: Cooper, Hawthorne, Stowe, and Melville*, Cambridge-New York, Cambridge University Press, 1987.

Budánov, Nikolai, *Dostoievski y Turguénev. Tvorcheski dialog*, Leningrad, 1988.

Burgh, Richard W., "Do the Guilty Deserve Punishment?," in *The Journal of Philosophy*, vol. 79, no. 4, 1982, pp. 193–210.

Burns, Robert P., *Kafka's Law. "The trial" and American Criminal Justice*, Chicago, University of Chicago, 2014.

Butler, Rex, "Re-reading 'Kafka y sus precursores'," in *Variaciones Borges*, University of Pittsburg, vol. 29, 2010, pp. 93–105.

Buytendijk, Frederic Jacobus Johannes, *La psicología de la novela: estudios sobre Dostoievski*, Buenos Aires, Carlos Lohlé, 1961.

Cabello Bustos, María Jesús, *De las referencias e influencias musicales, literarias, pictóricas y cinematográficas en el cine de Woody Allen. El caso Match Point* (2005), PhD dissertation supervised by Pedro Poyato Sánchez, Córdoba, Universidad de Córdoba, 2020.

Cabrera, Isabel, "Kafka a través de Job, Job a través de Kafka," in *Tópicos del Seminario*, vol. 22, 2009, pp. 157–174.

Calasso, Roberto, *K.*, translation by E. Dobry, Barcelona, Anagrama, 2005.

Calvet Botella, Julio, "Don Quijote y la justicia o la justicia en Don Quijote," Lecture, in Biblioteca Virtual Miguel de Cervantes, http://www.cervantesvirtual.com/obra-visor/don-quijote-y-la-justicia-o-la-justica-en-don-quijote-conferencia-0/html/00921af6-82b2-11df-acc7-002185ce6064_3.html.

Calvo González, José, "'Levanto las manos separando los dedos'. Leer a Kafka desde Goya," in *Revista Europea de Historia de las Ideas Políticas y de las Instituciones Públicas*, 13, 2018.

Calvo González, José, "Los guanteletes de Kafka. Manos y dedos en el discurso kafkiano de escritura y lectura de la letra de la ley," in *Anales de la Cátedra Francisco Suárez*, 54, 2020, pp. 237–263.

Callejas Berdonés, José María, *Persona y ética en el* Quijote, research paper supervised by professor Ana María Layra, Madrid, May 13, 2003, Universidad Complutense de Madrid.

Camargo, Ángeles, "Introducción," in *F. Kafka. La metamorfosis y otros relatos*, Madrid, 1985.

Camus, Albert (1913–1960), "La esperanza y lo absurdo en la obra de Franz Kafka," in *El mito de Sísifo*, translation by E. Benítez, Madrid, Alianza, 1985. 2012.

Canal, Jordi, *Con permiso de Kafka. El proceso independentista en Cataluña*, Barcelona, Ediciones Península, 2018.

Canavaggio, Jean, "Burlas y veras en la aventura de los galeotes. Nueva reflexión sobre un episodio del *Quijote*," in *Anales Cervantinos*, 18, 1979–1980.

Canetti, Elias (1905–1994), *El otro proceso. Las cartas de Kafka a Felice*, Mexico, La conciencia de las palabras, 1981.

Canetti, Elias, *El otro proceso de Kafka*, translation by M. Faber-Kaiser and M. Muchnik, Madrid, Alianza, 1983.

Canetti, Elias, *Sobre Kafka. El otro proceso*, Barcelona, Galaxia Gutenberg, 2023.

Cansinos Assens, Rafael, *Obras completas de Fiódor M. Dostoievski*, Madrid, Aguilar, 1961.

Caparrós, Nicolás, "Dostoievski, un literato de la complejidad," in *Norte de Salud Mental*, vol. 16, no. 61, 2019, pp. 68–73.

Capó, Daniel, "Kafka en España," in *The Objective*, June 11, 2024.

Caprio Leite de Castro, Fabio, "El profetismo de la colonia penitenciaria de Kafka: aparato de justicia y Biopolítica," in *Franz Kafka: culpa, ley y soberanía*, Medellín, 2017.

Carballa Rivas, Noa María – Urchaga Litago, José David, "La presencia de Fiódor Dostoyevski en los estudios científicos publicados en España," in *Tonos digital: Revista de estudios filológicos*, 34, 2018.

Cardona Castro, Francisco, *Kafka*, Barcelona, Iberlibro, 1991.

Carosio, Enrico, "Un enigma di nome K.," in *The Kafka Project*: http://www.kafka.org/essays/artikeln/enigma-art.htm.

Carr, Edward Hallet, *Dostievski, 1821–1881: lectura crítico-biográfica*, Barcelona, Laia, 1972.

Carrera, Mario Alberto, "La poética intimista pero también social de F. Kafka," in *LaHora.gt*, June 17, 2024.

Carrouges, Michel, *Kafka contra Kafka*, translation by M. T. Vernet, Barcelona, Eler, 1965.

Casanova, Pascale, *Kafka en colère*, Paris, Seuil, Fiction & Cie, 2011.

Cassese, Antonio, *Kafka é stato con me tutta la vita*, Bologna, Il Mulino, 2014.

Castilla del Pino, Carlos, *Cordura y locura en Cervantes*, Barcelona, Península, 2005.

Castillo Aguirre, David – Granda, André, "El Derecho en Kafka una muestra de redención," in *Ius Constitutionale, Revista de Derecho Constitucional*, 2, 2021.

Catalán, Miguel, *Kafka o la acusación como condena*, Madrid, Sequitur, 2016.

Cattaneo, Mario A., "Un tentativo di giustificazione della pena giuridica. Nota su un libro di Igor Plimoratz," in *Rivista Internazionale di Filosofia del Diritto*, 2, 1991, pp. 414–427.

Cedillo, Jaime, "Los cuentos de Kafka, el corazón de su obra y la mejor puerta para entrar en su fascinante universo," in *El Español, El Cultural*, April 19, 2024.

Cêrmák, Josef, *Franz Kafka, ficciones y mistificaciones*, Buenos Aires, 2008.

Cervantes Saavedra, Miguel de (1547–1616), *Don Quijote de La Mancha* (1605–1615), edited by John Jay Allen and illustrated by Jean Mosnier, Madrid, Cátedra, 2015. There is also an edition by Florencio Sevilla Arroyo and Antonio Rey Hazas, Alcalá de Henares, Centro de Estudios Cervantinos, 1993; Madrid, 2005. Other noteworthy editions are those of Diego Clemencín of 1833–1839 (whose notes were incorporated in the 1966 Madrid edition published by Ediciones Castilla and for which the *Índice* by Carlos F. Bradford, Madrid, 1885, reprinted in 2005, is quite useful); Francisco Rodríguez Marín (Madrid, 1906–1917, 1927–1928, and 1947–1949); Vicente Gaos (Madrid, 1987); Francisco Rico (Barcelona, Crítica, 2001); Instituto Cervantes (2 vols., Madrid, 2004); and the Fourth Centennial edition (Real Academia Española and Asociación de Academias de la Lengua Española, 2004). On the editions of this work, see the catalogue of the exhibition *El* Quijote, *biografía de un libro* (Madrid, Biblioteca Nacional, 2005) and the essential *Catálogos*, 179, 180, and 184 by Luis Bardón, Madrid, 2005. All English quotations in this book, are taken from the translation by John Ormsby [1885], *The Ingenious Gentleman Don Quixote of La Mancha*, New York/Boston, Thomas Y. Crowell and Co., 1906.

Cervantes Saavedra, Miguel de, *Obras completas de Cervantes*, Madrid, Edición Oficial de la Real Academia Española, 1917 and 1923.

Césped Benítez, Irma, "Creación y comunicación de mundos en el *Quijote*," in Jean-Pierre Sánchez (ed.), *Lectures d'une oeuvre, Don Quichotte de Cervantes*, Paris, Éditions du Temps, 2001, pp. 41–84.

Cicovacki, Predrag, *Dostoevsky and the Affirmation of Life*, New Jersey, Transaction Publishers, 2014.

Citati, Pietro, *Kafka*, translation by J. R. Monreal, Barcelona, Acantilado, 2012.

Coetzee, John Maxwell, "Time, Tense and Aspect in Kafka's 'Der Bau'," in *Modern Language Notes*, 96, 1981, in David Atwell (ed.), *Doubling the Point: Essays and Interviews*, Cambridge, Massachusetts, Harvard University Press, 1992.

Coetzee, John Maxwell, "Confession and Double Thoughts: Tolstoy, Rousseau and Dostoevsky," in *Comparative Literature*, 37, 3, summer 1985, pp. 193–232.

Conchillo Martínez de la Cruz, Carlos, "La búsqueda de lo real en Kafka. Literatura y Filosofía," in *STOA*, vol. 12, no. 24, 2021, pp. 5–41.

Conejo, Ana Isabel, *El lector de Dostoievski*, Eolas Ediciones, poesía, 2018.

Copello, Mario Alberto, *La sanción y el premio en el Derecho*, Buenos Aires, Losada, 1945.

Córdoba Ospina, Gerardo, "La 'metáfora' como dadora de muerte. Acerca de la última frase de El Proceso de Kafka," in *Álabe*, no. 11, 2015.

Corngold, Stanley – Greenberg, Jack – Wagner, Benno – Patton, Eric – Hein, Ruth (eds.), *Franz Kafka. The Office Writings*, Princeton, Princeton University Press, 2008.

Corroto, Paula, "Milena Jesenká, la mujer que fue mucho más que el gran amor de Kafka (y de otras mujeres)," in *El Confidencial*, February 21, 2024.

Cortés, Rodrigo, "Kafka & Kafka," in *ABC Cultural*, June 6, 2024.

Cosi, Giovanni, *Saggio sulla disobbedienza civile. Storia e critica del dissenso in democrazia*, Milan, Giuffrè, 1984.

Coy Ferrer, Juan José, "Melville, Herman," in *GER*, vol. 15, pp. 507–509.

Cragg, Wesley, "H. L. A. Hart and the Justification of Punishment," in *Canadian Journal of Law and Jurisprudence*, V, 1, 1992, pp. 43–55.

Cristaldi, Giovanni, *Dostoevskij o la scommessa della fede*, Milan, Vita e Pensiero, 1989.

Cruz, F., "Aturdimiento, ropaje y secreto en 'El proceso' de Kafka," in *Observaciones filosóficas*, 26, 2008. Also in https://www.observacionesfilosoficas.net/n6rof2008.html.

Cubí del Amo, Pablo, "Franz Kafka, el escritor visionario: 'Sí, existe la felicidad perfecta: creer en lo indestructible que hay dentro de ti y no aspirar a ello'," in *Cuerpo Mente*, November 26, 2025.

Cusson, Maurice, *Pourquoi punir?*, Paris, Dalloz, Collection Criminologie et Droits de l'Homme, 1987.

Cyzevskyj, Dmytro, "Schiller un di 'Brüder Karamazov'," in *Zeitschrift für slavische Philologie*, vol. VI, 1929, pp. 1–42.

Chacana Arancibia, Roberto, *La familia de Kafka. Lealtad y sacrificio*, Pozuelo de Alarcón (Madrid), Plaza y Valdés, 2012.

Chacana Arancibia, Roberto, *Kafka. La lucha por ascender*, Ediciones UACh, Colección Austral Universitaria de Ciencias Sociales, Artes y Humanidades, 2018.

Chaix-Ruy, Jules, *Kafka o el miedo al absurdo*, Madrid, Ibérico Europea de Ediciones, S.A., 1969.

Choclán Montalvo, José Antonio, *Individualización judicial de la pena. Función de la culpabilidad y la prevención en la determinación de la sanción penal*, Foreword by Siro García, Madrid, Colex, 1997.

Christie, Nils, *Limits to Pain*, Oxford, Martin Robertson, 1982. We use the Spanish translation by Mariluz Caso, *Los límites del dolor*, Mexico, Fondo de Cultura Económica, 1984.

D'Agostino, Francesco (1946–2022), *La sanzione nell'esperienza giuridica*, Turin, Giappichelli, 1989.

D'Agostino, Francesco, "Giustizia e misericordia. Fondamenti filosofici e teologici della sanzione penale," in *Rivista Internazionale di Filosofia del Diritto*, 66, 1989, pp. 3–23.

Dalipagic-Czimazia, Catherine, *Dostoievski et l'Europe*, Dalipagic-Czimazia, 1993.

Dargo, George, "Reclaiming Franz Kafka, Doctor of Jurisprudence," in *Spring Issue Brandeis L. J.*, 7, 2006.

De Azúa, Félix, "Dostoievski," in Jordi Llovet (ed.), *Lecciones de Literatura Universal: siglos XII a XX*, 1995, pp. 635–644.

De Benito y la Llave, Enrique, "La criminología del 'Quijote'," in *Lecciones Universitarias del* Quijote, III, Zaragoza, Universidad de Zaragoza, 1905.

De Bruyne, Jacques "Introducción a la lectura del mejor libro de todos los tiempos," in Various Authors, *Tras las huellas de Don Quijote. Actas de la Jornada dedicada a* Don Quijote de la Mancha, Antwerp, Lessius Hogeschool, December 9, 2005, edited and translated by Lieve Behiels, Ministerio de Educación y Ciencia de España – Lessius Hogeschool (Associatie K. U. Leuven), 2007, pp. 9–22.

De Buen, Néstor, "Derecho y Justicia en Cervantes: burla burlando," in *Revista de Derecho Privado*, IV, 11, May-August 2005, pp. 3–17.

Deigh, John, "On the Right to Be Punished: Some Doubts," in *Ethics*, 94, 1984, pp. 191–211.

De la Rica, Álvaro, *Kafka y el holocausto*, Foreword by Claudio Magris, Madrid, Trotta, 2009.

De la Rica, Álvaro, "Escribir sobre Kafka parece un ejercicio de curiosidad prohibida," in *Blog de Editorial Trotta*, March 3, 2015, http://www.trotta.es/blog/archivo/2015/.

De las Heras Vives, Luis – Obarrio Moreno, Juan Alfredo, *El mundo jurídico de Franz Kafka. El proceso*, Madrid, Dykinson, 2019.

Deleuze, Gilles – Guattari, Félix, *Kafka: pour une litterature mineure*, Paris, Editions de Minuit, Critique, 1975. There is a translation into Spanish by Jorge Aguilar, *Kafka. Por una literatura menor*, Mexico, Ediciones Era, 1978 and 1990.

De Lucas, Javier, "Kafka en su centenario," in *infoLibre.es*, January 3, 2024.

Della Fraille, Nicolas, "Le spectacle littéraire d'un droit aliéné et ses possibles lignes de fuite à travers deux textes de Kafka," in François Ost – Laurent van Eynde – Philippe Gérard – Michel van de Kerchove (dirs.), *Lettres et Lois. Le droit au miroir de la littérature*, Brussels, Publications des Facultés Universitaires Saint-Louis, 2001, pp. 187–217.

De Mattia, Angelo, "Merito e ricompensa," in *Rivista Internazionale di Filosofia del Diritto*, vol. XVII, issue VI, pp. 608–624.

De Sutter, Laurent, "The Quixote Principle, or Cervantes as a Critique of Law," in *Law & Literature*, vol. 26, issue 1, 2014, pp. 117–126.

Diamant, Dora, "Mi vida con Franz Kafka. Recuerdos de Dora," in *Cuando Kafka vino hacia mi…*, edited by Hans-Gerd Koch, translated by B. Vías Mahou, Barcelona, Acantilado, 2009.

Díaz Márquez, Manuel, *Fiódor Mijáilovih Dostoievski. Existencia, sociedad y verdad*, PhD dissertation supervised by Jesús De Garay Suárez Llanos, Universidad de Sevilla, 2011.

Díez Bosch, Miriam – Micó Sanz, Josep Lluís – Sabaté Gauxachs, Alba, "Incomunicados: aislamiento espiritual en Dostoievski y su eco en la narrativa de Carson McCullers," in *Pensamiento. Revista de Investigación e Información Filosófica*, vol. 78, no. 297, January-April 2022.

Di Filippo, Mario Alario, "'El Quijote' en América," Speech delivered at the Colombian Academy of Language in Bogotá on August 6, 1975, upon taking office as a full member; in http://cvc.cervantes.es/literatura/quijote-america/colombia/alario.htm. Also in "La justicia en el *Quijote*," in *Universitas*, 49, 1975, pp. 19–30.

Djermanovic, Tamara, *Dostoyevski entre Rusia y Occidente*, Barcelona, Herder, 2006.

Djermanovic, Tamara, "Profecías de Dostoyevski," in *Claves de Razón Práctica*, 228, 2013, pp. 142–151.

Djermanovic, Tamara, "Dostoyevski y Don Quijote: poética y estética de una ilusión," in *Anales Cervantinos*, 47, 2015, pp. 9–24.

Dobre, Catalina Elena, "Apuntes del subsuelo. La crítica del orden establecido en Fiódor Dostoievski," in *Revista de Filosofía*, vol. 54, no. 153, 2022, pp. 16–45.

Domínguez, Michael Christopher, "Los Demonios de Fyódor Dostoyevski," in *Letras Libres*, September 2002.

Dostoyevsky, Aimée, *Vida de Dostoyevski por su hija*, El buey mudo, 2011.

Dostoyevsky, Fyodor Mikhailovich (1821–1881), *Obras completas de Dostoievski en tres tomos*, translation, introduction, foreword and notes by Rafael Cansinos Asséns, Madrid, Aguilar, 1958.

Dostoyevsky, Fyodor Mikhailovich, *Apuntes de la casa muerta* (1861–1862), Madrid, Alianza Editorial, 2011.

Dostoyevsky, Fyodor Mikhailovich, *Una historia desagradable* (1862), Illustrations by Kenia Rodríguez, translation by Marta Sánchez Nieves, Batiscafo Nordica Libros, 2021.

Dostoyevsky, Fyodor Mikhailovich, *Apuntes del subsuelo* (1864), Madrid, Alianza Editorial, 2005.

Dostoyevsky, Fyodor Mikhailovich, *Crime and Punishment* (1866), A six-part novel with an epilogue, translated into English by Julius Katzer, Moscow, Raduga Publishers, 1985. Translation into Spanish, *Crimen y castigo*, Madrid, Ed. Fraile, 1981. Also in Madrid, Alianza Editorial, 2013, and in Madrid, Gredos, 2011, with an introduction by Vladimir Nabokov, translation by Augusto Vidal. There is also an edition and translation by Isabel Vicente, Madrid, Cátedra, 2007. Madrid, 2017.

Dostoyevsky, Fyodor Mikhailovich, *El idiota* (1869), translation into Spanish by Gloria Martinengo, Barcelona, Juventud, 1977.

Dostoyevsky, Fyodor Mikhailovich, *Los demonios* (1872), translation into Spanish by Fernando Otero Macías, Madrid, Editorial Alba, 2016.

Dostoyevsky, Fyodor Mikhailovich, *Diario de un escritor* (1873), Barcelona, 2007.

Dostoyevsky, Fyodor Mikhailovich, *The Unpublished Dostoevsky, Diaries and Notebooks, 1860–1881*, vol. 1, New York, Ardis, 1973.

Dostoyevsky, Fyodor Mikhailovich, *El adolescente* (1875), translation into Spanish by Mariano Orta Manzano, Barcelona, Juventud, 1973.

Dostoyevsky, Fyodor Mikhailovich, *The Brothers Karamazov* (1880), New York, Penguin Books, 2003. *Los hermanos Karamazov*, edited by Marina Ujánova, translation into Spanish by Augusto Vidal and José María Bravo, Madrid, Cátedra, 2011. Also in Barcelona, Planeta, 1988, introduction by Aquilino Duque, translation and notes by Augusto Vidal Roget. Also in Barcelona, Bruguera, 9th. ed., 1974. And in Buenos Aires, Longseller, 2005. Madrid, Alianza Editorial, translation by Augusto Vidal Roget, 2006.

Dragonetti, Jacinto, *Tratado de las virtudes y de los premios* (translated into Spanish and published in Beccaria, *Dei delitti e delle pene*, by Ramón Salas), Villamil, Madrid, 1836.

Dudley, Edwards Owen, "Stevenson, Jekyll, Hyde and all the Deacon Brodies," in *FOLIO*, National Library of Scotland, issue 1, fall 2000.

Dumas, Alexandre (1802–1870), *El Conde de Montecristo*, translation into Spanish by Gregorio Cantera Chamorro, Buenos Aires, Losada, 2005. Also in Madrid, El País, 2004. And in Madrid, Debate, 2001. And in Barcelona, Folio, 2000. And in Barcelona, SAV, 2000. And in Madrid, Alhambra, 1932. There is a translation into Spanish by Belén Jáuregui, Buenos Aires, Gradifco, 2007.

Durkheim, Émile (1958–1917), *De la division du travail social*, Paris, Alcan, 1893; Paris, Presses Universitaires de France, 5th. ed., 1998.

Durkheim, Émile, *Les règles de la méthode sociologique*, Paris, Alcan, 1895; Paris, Presses Universitaires de France, 10th. ed., 1999.

Durkheim, Émile, "Deux lois de l'évolution pénale," in *L'Année Sociologique*, 4, 1902, pp. 65–95; also in *Émile Durkheim on Institutional Analysis*, edition, translation and introduction by Mark Traugott, Chicago, The University of Chicago Press, 1978, pp. 153–180: "Two Laws of Penal Evolution"; reedited as chapter 4, "The Evolution of Punishment," in Steven Lukes – Andrew Scull (eds.), *Durkheim and the Law*, Oxford, 1983.

Durkheim, Émile, *Les formes élémentaires de la vie religieuse* (*Le système totémique en Australie*), Paris, Alcan, 1912; Paris, Librairie Générale Française, 1991, with Introduction by Michel Maffesoli.

Durkheim, Émile, *L'éducation morale*, Paris, Alcan, 1925; English translation, *Moral Education*, New York, 1973; Spanish translation by M. L. Navarro, Buenos Aires, 1947.

Echevarría, Ignacio, "La mano de Kafka," in *El Cultural del diario El Mundo*, January 4, 2019.

EFE, "Una nueva traducción de 'El proceso' de Kafka incorpora un fragmento inédito en español," in *El Mundo*, May 2, 2024.

Ehrenberg, Hans, *Dostojewski. Volk und Mensch*, Frommanns, 1922.

Eichenhofer, Eberhard, *Franz Kafka und die Sozialversicherung*, Stuttgart, R. Boorberg, 1997.

Eisemberg, Daniel, "La biblioteca de Cervantes," in Riquer, *Studia in honorem prof. M. de Riquer*, 4 vols., Barcelona, 1987, II, pp. 271–328.

Etcheverry, Luis María, "El Proceso de Kafka o los umbrales vitales del sabotaje," in *Nuevo Pensamiento. Revista de Filosofía del Instituto de Investigaciones Filosóficas de la Facultad de Filosofía de la Universidad del Salvador*, área San Miguel, edited by Juan Pablo E. Esperón, vol. 1, year 1, 2011.

Euripides (480 B.C.–406 B.C.), *Electra*, edited with an introduction and comments by P. J. Finglas, Cambridge, Cambridge University Press, 2007.

Evdokimov, Paul, *Introducción a Dostoyevski (en torno a su ideología)*, translation and foreword by Alberto Colao, Cartagena, Athenas Ediciones, Colección Diapasón, 1959.

Evdokimov, Paul, *Gogol et Dostoïevski ou la descente aux enfers*, Paris, Corlevour, 2011.

Falcón y Tella, María José, *La desobediencia civil*, Foreword by Fernando Garrido Falla, Madrid, Marcial Pons, 2000. Reviews: by Pablo Iglesias Turrión, "Desobediencia civil y movimiento antiglobalización. Una herramienta de intervención política," in *Revista Telemática de Filosofía del Derecho*, 5, 2001–2002, pp. 213–251. By Guido Saraceni, in *Rivista Internazionale di Filosofía del Diritto*, 3, July-September 2001, pp. 424–426. By Paula López Zamora, in *Revista de Estudios Políticos*, 111, pp. 312–315. By Beatriz Castro Toledo, in *Revista de la Facultad de Derecho de la Universidad Complutense de Madrid*, 94, 1999–2000, pp. 243–266. By Oscar Mª Prieto García, in *Anuario de Derechos Humanos, Nueva Época*, Instituto de Derechos Humanos, Facultad de Derecho, Universidad Complutense de Madrid, 2001, pp. 1026–1035. By Juan Antonio Martínez Muñoz, in *Veintiuno. Revista de Pensamiento y Cultura*, 53, spring 2002, pp. 146–148. By Pedro Rivas, in *Anales de la Cátedra Francisco Suárez*, 34, 2000: "De nuevo sobre la desobediencia civil," pp. 447–450. There is a translation into English, of the first part: *Civil Disobedience*, by Peter Muckley, Foreword by Martti Koskenniemi, Leiden-Boston, Martinus Nijhoff Publishers, 2004 (Review in Martinus Nijhoff Publishers, Leiden-Boston, Catalogue Spring 2005, International Law, pp. 3 and 73). And of the second part, also by Peter Muckley, *A History of Civil Disobedience*, Geneva, Editions Diversités, 2004.

Falcón y Tella, María José, *Lecciones de Teoría del Derecho*, Madrid, Servicio de Publicaciones, Facultad de Derecho, Universidad Complutense de Madrid, 1st ed. 2001, 2nd ed. 2003, 3rd ed. 2006, 4th ed. 2009, 5th ed. 2011, 6th ed. 2014, 6th ed. 1st reimpr. 2018. 7th ed., 1st ed. by Tirant lo Blanch, 2020, 8th ed., 2nd ed. by Tirant, 2023. 9th ed., 3rd ed. by Tirant, 2025. There is a translation into English by Howard Shneider and Jon Randall Walden, *A Three-dimensional Theory of Law*, Boston-Leiden, Martinus Nijhoff-Brill, 2010. And translation into Portuguese by Claudia De Miranda Avena and Ernani De Paula Contipelli, in the series "Direito Europeu," directed by Antonio García-Pablos de Molina, *Liçoes de Teoria Geral do Direito*, Brazil, Revista dos Tribunais, 2011.

Falcón y Tella, María José, *La désobéissance civile face à la Philosophie du Droit*, Foreword by Alfred Fernández, Geneva, Editions Diversitès, 2004.

Falcón y Tella, María José, *Estudios de Filosofía Jurídica y Política*, Foreword by Jorge Carpizo, Mexico, UNAM, 2009.

Falcón y Tella, María José, *La justicia como mérito*, Foreword by Martín Laclau, Madrid-Barcelona-Buenos Aires-Sâo Paulo, Marcial Pons, 2014. Reviewed: – By prof. María de los Ángeles Nogales Naharro, in *International Journal of Humanities and Social Science*, vol. 4, issue 9, July 2014, pp. 134–136. – By prof. María Eugenia Pérez Montero, in *Foro. Revista de Ciencias Jurídicas y Sociales*, vol. 17, issue 1, 2014, pp. 410–414. – By prof. José López Hernández, in *Daimon. Revista de Filosofía*, 66, 2015, pp. 172–173. – In *Iuris Tantum. Revista de la Facultad de Derecho. Universidad Anahuac*, Mexico, year XXIX, no. 25, Tercera Época, 2014, pp. 389–405. – In *Anuario de Filosofía del Derecho*, XXXI, 2015, pp. 290–294. There is a translation into English, *Justice and Law*, Foreword by Martín Laclau, Leiden-Boston, Martinus Nijhoff Publishers, 2014.

Falcón y Tella, María José, *Derecho y Literatura*, Foreword by François Ost, Madrid-Barcelona-Buenos Aires-Sâo Paulo, Marcial Pons, 2015. Reviewed: In *International Journal of Education and Social Science*, vol. 2, issue 12, December 2015, pp. 41–43. – In *International Journal of Arts and Humanities*, vol 1, issue 4, December 2015, pp. 38–39. – By prof. Nuria Cuadrado Gamarra, in *Las Torres de Lucca. Revista Internacional de Filosofía Política*, no. 7, 2015, pp. 325–328. – By prof. Cristina Fuertes Planas-Aleix, in *Foro. Revista de Ciencias Jurídicas y Sociales. Nueva Época*, vol. 18, issue 2, 2015, pp. 528–531. – By prof. Isabel Araceli Hoyo Sierra, in *Iuris Tantum. Revista de la Facultad de Derecho. Universidad Anahuac*, Mexico, Year XXX, no. 26, Tercera Época, 2015. There is a translation into English, *Law and Literature*, Prologue by François Ost, Leiden-Boston, Brill-Nijhoff, 2016.

Falcón y Tella, María José, *Cuestiones de Filosofía del Derecho*, Madrid-Barcelona-Buenos Aires-Sâo Paulo, Marcial Pons, 1st. ed., 2020, 2nd. expanded ed. 2025. Reviewed: – By prof. María Eugenia Pérez Montero, in *Foro. Revista de Ciencias Jurídicas y Sociales. Nueva Época*, Facultad de Derecho, Universidad Complutense de Madrid, vol. 23, issue 2, 2020, pp. 405–410. – By prof. María Ángeles Nogales Naharro, in *Dereito. Revista Xurídica da Universidade de Santiago de Compostela*, no. 2, year 2021, pp. 213–240. There is an English translation, *Challenges to Contemporary Legal Thinking*, The Haghe, Melrose Legal Publishers, 2026 (forthcoming).

Falcón y Tella, María José, *El Derecho en Cervantes y Shakespeare*, Foreword by Carla Faralli, Madrid – Barcelona – Buenos Aires – Sâo Paulo, Marcial Pons, 2021. There is a translation into English by Deirdre B. Jerry, *The Law in Cervantes and Shakespeare*, Leiden-Boston, Brill-Nijhoff, 2021. Reviewed by Christina G. Waldman, What's New on SirBacon.org, pdf. June 11, 2024.

Falcón y Tella, María José, "Hacia un Derecho penal más humano," in *Anuario de Derechos Humanos. Nueva Época*, vol. 6, 2005, pp. 247–271.

Falcón y Tella, María José, "A aboliçao do castigo," in *Revista dos Tribunais*, translated by Claudia de Miranda Avena, vol. 898, issue 2, first section, year 99, August 2011, pp. 409–423.

Falcón y Tella, María José, "Legitimidade, Validade e Eficácia do Castigo," "Legitimacy, Validity and Effectiveness of Punishment," in *Revista da AGU, Escola da Advocacia Geral da Uniao*, year IX, no. 25, Brasília-DF, July-September 2011, pp. 7–31.

Falcón y Tella, María José, "El progreso de la Humanidad: Dostoievski y Kafka," in the Tribute to Manuel Nuñez Encabo, *In varietate concordia. Anuario de Derechos Humanos. Nueva Época*, supervised by Cristina Fuertes-Planas Aleix and Fernando Falcón y Tella, Instituto de Derechos Humanos – Departamento de Filosofía del Derecho, Facultad de Derecho, Universidad Complutense de Madrid, vols. 13 and 14, 2012 (released in May 2017), my contribution in vol. 13, pp. 213–233.

Falcón y Tella, María José, "El Derecho 'de' la Literatura," in *Anuario de Filosofía Jurídica y Social. Asociación Argentina de Derecho Comparado. Sección Teoría General*, Buenos Aires, Abeledo-Perrot, Lexis Nexis, no. 35, 2015, pp. 269–309.

Falcón y Tella, María José, "Law and Literature in the novels of Robert Louis Stevenson," in *American International Journal of Humanities and Social Science*, vol. 2, no. 1, February 2016, pp. 26–32.

Falcón y Tella, María José, "Law in Literature in Classical Antiquity," in *International Journal of Education and Human Developments*, vol. 2, no. 2, March 2016, pp. 1–12.

Falcón y Tella, María José, "The Law 'of' Literature," in *International Journal of Education and Social Science*, vol. 3, no. 4, April 2016, pp. 29–39.

Falcón y Tella, María José, "Un mundo sin reglas o la capacidad de soñar," in D. Announssamy – A. Bailleux – D. Bernard – A. Botero – J. Calvo – C. Callejas – R. Estrada – M. J. Falcón y Tella – C. Gómez – C. Gómez Frode – C. Huerta – P. Louys – J. van Meerbeeck – M. Morales – F. Ost – E. de la Parra – A. san Vicente – G. Tanda – S. Zanda – O. Torres, *Iurisfictio*, compilation and foreword by Óscar Enrique Torres, Ciudad de México, Ed., Libitum, 2019, pp. 185–196. Reviewed in: – Revista El mundo del Abogado (Arienzo Zuri). https://elmundodelabogado.com/

revista/libros/item/iurisfictio. -Lex Malacitana (José Calvo): https://iurisdictio-lexmalacitana.blogspot.com/2019/08/.

Falcón y Tella, María José, "La venganza en la Literatura," in María José Falcón y Tella – Juan Antonio Martínez Muñoz (dirs.), *Estudios Jurídicos Multidisciplinares. José Iturmendi Morales, Maestro Complutense. Homenaje*, Valencia, Tirant lo Blanch, 2020, pp. 47–86. There is a translation into English, "Revenge in Literature," in María José Falcón y Tella – Juan Antonio Martínez Muñoz (eds.), *Challenges to Legal Theory. Essays in Honour of Professor José Iturmendi Morales*, Leiden-Boston, Martinus Nijhoff-Brill, 2021, pp. 15–48. Reviewed in *El Notario del siglo XXI*, Revista del Ilustre Colegio Notarial de Madrid, July 2022.

Falcón y Tella, María José, "Delito y castigo en la Literatura," in *Anuario de Filosofía Jurídica y Social. Asociación Argentina de Derecho Comparado. Sección Teoría General*, Buenos Aires, Abeledo-Perrot, Lexis Nexis, no. 40, 2020, pp. 213–240.

Falcón y Tella, María José – Falcón y Tella, Fernando, *Fundamento y finalidad de la sanción: ¿Un derecho a castigar?*, Madrid, Marcial Pons, 2005, Foreword by Antonio García-Pablos de Molina. Reviewed in *Foro. Revista de Ciencias Jurídicas y Sociales. Nueva Época*, Facultad de Derecho, Universidad Complutense, Madrid, 1, 2005, pp. 374–375. Reviewed by: María Eugenia Pérez Montero, in *Anuario de Derechos Humanos, Nueva Época*, Instituto de Derechos Humanos, Facultad de Derecho, Universidad Complutense de Madrid, 6, 2005, pp. 790–798; and Ana Valero Fernández de Palencia, in *Foro, Revista de Ciencias Jurídicas y Sociales, Nueva Época*, Facultad de Derecho, Universidad Complutense de Madrid, 2, 2005, pp. 461–463. Translated into English (*Punishment and Culture: A Right to Punish?*, by Peter Muckley, Boston-Leiden, Martinus Nijhoff, 2006. Reviewed in: *Foro, Revista de Ciencias Jurídicas y Sociales*, Facultad de Derecho, Universidad Complutense de Madrid, 2, 2005; Martinus Nijhoff Publishers, spring 2006 Catalog, "Human Rights & International Law," pp. 28 and 89; Martinus Nijhoff Publishers, spring 2007 Catalog: "Human Rights & International Law," cover and p. 34. Reviewed by: José María Carabante Muntada, in *Archiv für Rechts-und Sozialphilosophie*, Band 94, Heft 4, 2008, pp. 547–549; and Carissa Byrne Hessick, in *New Criminal Law Review*, II, 3, pp. 498–503). Also translated into Italian (*Fondamento e finalità della sanzione: diritto di punire?*, by Raffaello Dal Col, Milan, Giuffrè, 2008) and Portuguese (*Fundamento e finalidade da sançao: Existe um direito de castigar?*, by Claudia De Miranda Avena, revised by Luiz Flávio Gomes, Brazil, Revista dos Tribunais, 2008).

Faralli, Carla, *La Filosofía del Derecho contemporánea. Temas y desafíos* -from *La filosofia del diritto contemporanea. I temi e le sfide*, Bari, Laterza, 2nd ed. 2005–, translation into Spanish by José Iturmendi Morales, María José Falcón y Tella and Juan Antonio Martínez Muñoz, Madrid-Buenos Aires, Hispania Libros, 2007. Reviews: By Fernando Falcón y Tella, in *Anuario de Derechos Humanos, Nueva*

Época, Instituto de Derechos Humanos, Facultad de Derecho, Universidad Complutense de Madrid, 8, 2007, pp. 496–500. And by Cristina Fuenteseca Degeneffe, in *Revista de Derecho Privado*, January-February 2008, pp. 99–102.

Faralli, Carla, "Le origine di 'Diritto e letteratura' nel realismo americano," in *Materiali per una Storia della Cultura Giuridica*, 42, 1, 2012, pp. 81–90.

Faralli, Carla, "Diritto e letteratura nella formazione del giurista," in *Contrato e impresa*, 30, 2, 2014, pp. 535–541.

Faralli, Carla – Mittica, Maria Paola (eds.), *Diritto e Letteratura. Prospettive di Ricerca*, Rome, Aracne, 2010.

Faria, Gentil, "Dostoevsky, the Law, and the Underground Man," in *Mundo Eslavo*, no. 16, 2017, pp. 46–54.

Feinberg, Joel (1926–2004), *Doing and Deserving*, New Jersey, Princeton University Press, 1970.

Feinberg, Joel, "El argumento de la graduación moral de los castigos," in Agustín Squella (ed.), *"H. L. A. Hart y el Concepto de Derecho." Revista de Ciencias Sociales. Universidad de Valparaiso*, 28, 1986, pp. 355–366.

Ferenczi, R., *Kafka. Subjectivité, histoire et structure*, Paris, Klincksiek, 1975.

Ferguson, Robert A., "On the Judicial Opinion as a Literary Genre," in *Yale Journal of Law and Humanities*, 2, 1990, pp. 201–219.

Ferguson, Robert A., "Untold Stories in the Law," in Peter Brooks – Paul Gewirtz (eds.), *Law's Stories*, New Haven, Yale University Press, 1996, pp. 84–98.

Fernández de Avellaneda, Alonso, *Nuevas andanzas del ingenioso hidalgo Don Quijote de la Mancha: (El "Quijote" apócrifo)*, edited by Mercedes M. Villalta, with a Foreword by Emiliano M. Aguilera, Barcelona, Iberia, Diamante, 1961. Also edited by F. García Salinero, Madrid, Clásicos Castalia, 1971; reprinted in 1999.

Fersini, Maria Pina, "'El jorobado hombrecillo'. Distorsiones del cuerpo y del espacio en el universo jurídico kafkiano," in *Cuadernos Electrónicos de Filosofía del Derecho*, 36, 2017, pp. 109–126.

Fina Sanglas, Albert, *Justicia y Literatura*, Foreword by Eugeni Gay Montalvo, Barcelona, Bosch, 1993.

Floud, Jean E., "Dangerousness and Criminal Justice," in *The British Journal of Criminology*, vol. 22, no. 3, pp. 213–228.

Floud, Jean E. – Young, Warren, *Dangerousness and Criminal Justice*, London, Heinemann, 1981.

Földényi, László F., *Los espacios de la muerte viviente. Kafka, De Chirico y los demás*, Barcelona, Galaxia Gutenberg SL, 2018.

Foucault, Michel (1926–1984), *Surveiller et punir: naissance de la prison*, Paris, Gallimard, 1975; translation into English by Alan Sheridan, *Discipline and Punish: The Birth of the Prison*, New York, Vintage Books, 1979; translation into Spanish, *Vigilar y castigar*, Mexico, Siglo XXI, 1966.

Foucault, Michel, "La pussière et le nuage," in *L'impossible prison*, Paris, Du Seuil, 1980.

Francés Lecumberri, Paz, "De los pecados y las galeras en tiempos del *Quijote* hasta nuestros días," in José Francisco Alenza García (dir.), *Cervantes y el Derecho. Ideas cervantinas para el aprendizaje del Derecho*, Colección Facultad Ciencias Jurídicas UPNA, no. 2, Cizur Menor (Navarre), Thomson Reuters Aranzadi, 2016, pp. 179–198.

Frank, Joseph, *Dostoevsky: The Seeds of Revolt 1821–1849*, Princeton, Princeton University Press, 1976. Translation into Spanish, *Dostoievski: Las semillas de la rebelión, 1821–1849*, Mexico, Fondo de Cultura Económica, 1984.

Frank, Joseph, *Dostoevsky: The Stir of Liberation 1860–1865*, Princeton, Princeton University Press, 1986. Translation into Spanish by Juan José Utrilla, *Dostoievski: la secuela de la liberación*, 1860–1865, Mexico, FCE, 1993.

Frank, Joseph, *Dostoevsky: The Miraculous Years 1865–1871*, Princeton, Princeton University Press, 1995. Translation into Spanish by Mónica Utrilla, *Dostoievski: los años milagrosos, 1865–1871*, Mexico, FCE, 1997.

Frank, Joseph, *Dostoevsky: The Mantle of the Prophet 1871–1881*, Princeton, Princeton University Press, 2002.

Freud, Sigmund (1856–1939), "Criminality from a Sense of Guilt," in "Some Character-Types Met with in Psycho-Analytical Work," in *id., Collected Papers*, IV, ed. by J. Riviere, New York, 1959; original version in *Imago*, 4, 1915–1916.

Freud, Sigmund, "Dostojewski und die Vatertötung," in *Die Urgestalt der Brüder Karamazov*, Piper-Verlag, 1928. Spanish translation, "Dostoyevsky y el parricidio," in *Obras Completas*, Buenos Aires, Amorrortu Editores, 2001, vol. CLVI.

Freud, Sigmund, *Civilization and Its Discontents*; original version in London, 1930; New York, 1962.

Freud, Sigmund, *Obras completas*, translation from the German by Luis López Ballesteros y de Torres, Madrid, Biblioteca Nueva, D. L., 1983.

Friendländer, Saul, *Kafka. Poète de la honte*, translation by Nicolas Weill, Paris, Seuil, 2014.

Fromm, Erich (1900–1980), *On Disobedience and Other Essays*, London, Routledge & Kegan Paul, 1984.

Frosini, Vittorio, "Letteratura e diritto penale," in *Rivista Internazionale di Filosofia del Diritto*, 2, 1993, pp. 281–287.

Fuchs, Rudolf, "Recuerdos de Franz Kafka," in Max Brod, *Kafka*, translation by C. F. Grieben, 3rd. ed., Buenos Aires, Emecé Editores, 2000.

Füllop-Miller, René, *Der unbekannte Dostojewski*, edited by René Füllop-Miller and F. Eckstein, 1926.

Füllop-Miller, René, *Dostoïevski, le intuitif, le croyant, le poète*, translation from English by Louise Servicen, Editions Albin Michel, 1954.

Gaakeer, Jeanne, "On the Study Methods of Our Time: Methodologies of Law and Literature in the Context of Interdisciplinary Studies," in *Intersections of Law and Culture*, Switzerland, Springer, 2012, pp. 133–149.

Gaakeer, Jeanne, "Reality, Veracity, and Probability in Law and Literature," in Ives Cartuyvels – Antoine Bailleux – Diane Bernard *et. al.*, *Le droit malgré tout. Hommage a François Ost*, Brussels, Presses de l'Université Saint-Louis, 2018, pp. 559–586.

Gaakeer, Jeanne, *Judging from Experience: Law, Praxis, Humanities*, Edinburgh, Edinburgh University Press, 2019.

Gaakeer, Jeanne, "Feel, Show, Tell: Affect and Legality in the Trial as Performance," in *Law, Culture and the Humanities*, Online First, June 19, 1923.

Galateria, Daria, *Scritti galeotti: letterati in carcere*, Rome, Rai Eri, 2000.

Galdeano, Laura, "Un año de homenajes para 'sacar a Kafka de lo kafkiano' y celebrar su carácter integrador," in *Libertad Digital*, 25th Anniversary, March 21, 2024.

Gallego Ballestero, Víctor, "Introducción," in Fiódor Dostoievski, *Diario de un escritor*, Translation, introduction and notes by Víctor Gallego Ballestero, Barcelona, Alba Editorial, 2010.

Gandolfo, Pedro, "Sobre el Derecho en Kafka," in *Anuario de Filosofía Jurídica y Social*, 1985.

Garapon, Antoine, "Kafka ou le non-lieu de la loi," in *Revue Interdisciplinaire d'Études Juridiques*, 28, 1992, pp. 1–17.

García Costa, Francisco Manuel, "El Derecho constitucional en el *Quijote*," in *Anales de Derecho*, Universidad de Murcia, 23, 2005, pp. 187–202. This article is a transcript of the lecture titled "El *Quijote* y los fundamentos del Derecho," delivered at Cajamurcia Aula de Cultura on October 25, 2005, as part of the international course "La modernidad del *Quijote*."

García Martín, Pedro, "Prologue" to Various Authors, *Cervantes y el Derecho. Ideas cervantinas para el aprendizaje del Derecho*, Cizur Menor (Navarre), Thomson Reuters Aranzadi, 2016.

García-Pablos de Molina, Antonio, *Criminología. Una introducción a sus fundamentos teóricos para juristas*, Valencia, Tirant lo Blanch, 1996.

García Posada, Miguel, "El episodio quijotesco de los galeotes ambigüedad lingüística y significación," in *Hispanic Review*, 2, 1981.

García Ramírez, Fernando, "Peculiaridades kafkianas," in *Letras Libres*, May 30, 2024.

García Ramírez, Fernando, "Kafka y el sueño de Sion," in *Letras Libres*, June 14, 2024.

Garet Mas, Julio, "Sobre *Tipos delincuentes del* Quijote" (Quito, 1966), in *Revista Nacional*, Montevideo, vol. XI, April-September, 1966.

Garland, David, "Durkheim's Theory of Punishment: A Critique," in *id.* and Peter Young (eds.), *The Power to Punish*, London, 1983.

Garland, David, *Punishment and Welfare: A History of Penal Strategies*, Aldershot, Gower, 1985.

Garland, David, "The Criminal and His Science," in *British Journal of Criminology*, 25, 2, 1985, pp. 109–135.

Garland, David, "The Punitive Mentality: Its Socio-historical Development and Decline," in *Contemporary Crises*, 10, 1986, pp. 305–320.

Garland, David, "British Criminology before 1935," in *British Journal of Criminology*, 28, 1988, pp. 131–147.

Garland, David, *Punishment and Modern Society. A Study in Social Theory*, Chicago, The University of Chicago Press, 1990.

Garland, David, "Criminological Knowledge and Its Relation to Power: Foucault's Genealogy and Criminology Today," in *British Journal of Criminology*, 32, 4, 1992, pp. 403–422.

Garland, David, "Penal Modernism and Postmodernism," in T. Blomberg – S. Cohen (eds.), *Punishment and Social Control*, New York, Aldine de Gruyter, 1995.

Garland, David, "The Limits of the Sovereign State: Strategies of Crime Control in Contemporary Society," in *British Journal of Criminology*, 36, 4, 1996, pp. 445–471.

Garland, David, "Governmentality and the Problem of Crime: Foucault, Criminology, Sociology," in *Theoretical Criminology*, 1, 2, 1997, pp. 173–214.

Garland, David, *The Culture of Control. Crime and Social Order in Contemporary Society*, Chicago, The University of Chicago Press, 2001.

Garland, David – Young, Peter, *The Power to Punish: Contemporary Penalty and Social Analysis*, London, Heinemann Educational Books, Atlantic Highlands, N.J., Humanities Press, 1983.

Garrido, Luis, *La criminología en la obra de Cervantes*, speech on his induction into the Mexican Academy of Language, June 11, 1956, Mexico, 1956.

Gascón, Daniel, "El secreto de la literatura es la letra K.," in *Letras Libres*, October 20, 2024.

Gasillón, María Lourdes, "Ezequiel Martínez Estrada y Franz Kafka, narradores de la máquina burocrática," in *Cuadernos del Sur-Letras*, 44–45, 2014–2015, pp. 41–69.

Gendin, Sidney, "The Meaning of Punishment," in *Philosophy and Phenomenological Research*, XXVIII, 1967–1968, pp. 236–237.

Gibbens, "Les problèmes posés par le traitement psychiatrique des délinquants," in *Revue de Science Criminelle*, 1958.

Giddens, Anthony, *Durkheim*, Hassocks, Sussex, 1978. London, Fontana, 1986.

Gide, André (1869–1951), *Dostievski*, translation by Laura Claravall, Ediciones del subsuelo, 2016. *Dostoevsky*, 1923.

Gil, Alberto, *Un paseo por la Praga de Kafka*, Madrid, Reino de Cordelia, 2024.

Gil Bartomeu, Mariana, "Las violaciones de los derechos fundamentales del Señor K. en *El proceso* de Franz Kafka," in A. Hernández Cervantes (ed.), *Derecho y Literatura. Una alianza que subvierte el orden*, Mexico, Bonilla Artiga Editores, 2017.

Gladfelder, Hal, *Criminality and Narrative in Eighteenth-Century England: Beyond the Law*, Baltimore, John Hopkins University Press, 2001.

Glatzer, Nahum Norbert, "Franz Kafka y el Árbol del Conocimiento," published as an appendix in *Los amores de Franz Kafka*, translation by R. Vivero and P. Moure, Barcelona, Subsuelo, 2015.

Glucksmann, André (1937–2015), *Dostoievsky en Manhattan*, Barcelona, Taurus, 2002.

Godoy, Juan Manuel, "Salió a la venta una carta privada de Franz Kafka escrita en el año 1920," in *Infobae*, June 18, 2024.

Goethe, Johann Wolfgang von (1749–1832), *Fausto*, edited by Helena Cortés Gabaudan, Madrid, Universidad Autónoma de Madrid, 2010. There is also a translation into Spanish by Miguel Salmerón, Madrid, Espasa Calpe, 2009. Also in Barcelona, Océano, cop., foreword by Francisco Ayala. Also in Madrid, Santillana, 1999, translation into Spanish and notes by Emilio Tadeo Blanco. And with foreword by the Duke of Alba, Madrid, Espasa Calpe, 1998.

Goldman, Alan H., "Toward a New Theory of Punishment," in *Law and Philosophy*, vol. l, 1982, pp. 57–76.

Goldschmidt, Georges Arthur, "Avec Kafka, toujours plus loin," in *La quinzaine littéraire*, 545, 1989.

Gómez Herrera, Carlota, "El Kafka de Foucault y las habitaciones de sí mismo: tejidos biosemióticos," Chapter of the book by Mónica María Martínez Sariego – Gabriel Laguna Mariscal (eds.), *Avance en investigación sobre literatura: teoría y crítica*, Madrid, Dykinson, 2024, pp. 151–166.

González, Manuel Richard – Riaño Brun, Iñaki, "Jueces y Administración de Justicia en el *Quijote*," in José Francisco Alenza García (dir.), *Cervantes y el Derecho. Ideas cervantinas para el aprendizaje del Derecho*, Colección Facultad Ciencias Jurídicas UPNA, no. 2, Cizur Menor (Navarre), Thomson Reuters Aranzadi, 2016, pp. 253–274.

González de Ávila, Manuel, "Escenificar la presencia: O. Welles y F. Kafka, 'El Proceso'," in *Arbor. Ciencia, Pensamiento y Cultura*, no. 748, 2011, pp. 401–409.

González Echevarría, Roberto, *Amor y ley en Cervantes*, translation into Spanish by Isabel Ferrer Marrades, Madrid, Gredos, 2008. English version, *Love and the Law in Cervantes*, New Haven-London, Yale University Press, 2005.

González Echevarría, Roberto, "El amor y el Derecho en Cervantes. Love and the Law in Cervantes," in *Atenea*, 505, 2012, pp. 11–31.

González Encinar, María A., "Prologue" to Various Authors, *Tras las huellas de Don Quijote. Actas de la Jornada dedicada a* Don Quijote de la Mancha, Antwerp, Lessius Hogeschool, December 9, 2005, edition and translation by Lieve Behiels, Ministerio de Educación y Ciencia de España – Lessius Hogeschool (Associatie K. U. Leuven), 2007, pp. 1–4.

González García, José María, *La máquina burocrática* (*Afinidades electivas entre Max Weber y Kafka*), Madrid, Visor, 1989.

González García, José María, "Jaulas, máquinas y laberintos (Imágenes de la burocracia en Kafka, Musil y Weber)," in *Observaciones Filosóficas*, no. 4, 2007. http://www.observacionesfilosoficas.net/Kafkaylaneurosis.htm.

González Hernández, Óscar Jairo, "A propósito de los cien años de La Metamorfosis, de Franz Kafka," in *Ciencias Sociales y Educación*, vol. 4, no. 7, 2015, pp. 389–401.

González Vicén, Felipe, "La figura de Don Quijote y el donquijotismo en el pensamiento de Miguel de Unamuno," in *Romanische Forschungen*, Hamburg, 57, 2/3, 1943.

Goodrich, Peter, "Erotic Melancholia: Law, Literature, and Love," in *Law & Literature*, vol. 14, issue 1, spring 2002, pp. 103–129.

Granda, David, "El universo kafkiano le sienta como un guante al siglo XXI," in *El País*. Cultura, February 28, 2024.

Gray, Arthur Herbert (1868–1956), "The Christian View of the Use of Punishment," in *Howard Journal*, 2, 1929.

Greco Haro, José Manuel, *Dostoyevski. Pánico al nihilismo*, tfg supervised by Jesús Francisco De Garay Suárez-Llanos, Universidad de Sevilla, 2024.

Grisham, John (1955-), *The Firm*, 1991; translation into Spanish, *La tapadera*, by Enric Tremps, Barcelona, Planeta, 1993.

Grossman, Leonid Petrovic, *Dostoïevski*, L'Aventurine, 2003.

Grözinger, Karl Erich, *Kafka und die Kabbala: das Jüdische im Werk und Denken von Franz Kafka*, Frankfurt/M., Campus Verlag, 2014.

Grundlehner, Philip, "Manual Gesture in Kafka's Prozess," in *The German Quarterly*, LV, 1982, pp. 186–199.

Grusemann, Michael, *Dostojewski*, Munich, Rosl, 1921.

Guardini, Romano, *Religiöse Gestalten in Dostojewskijs Werk: Studien über den Glauben*, Mainz, Mattias Grünewald, 1989.

Guardini, Romano – Rossi, Maria Luisa, *Il mondo religioso di Dostojevski*, Brescia, Mercelliana, 1968. Translation into Spanish, *El universo religioso de Dostoievski*, Buenos Aires, Emecé Editores, 1954.

Guelbenzu, José María, "'Señor Kfka', de Bohumil Hrabal: humor para sobrevivir al horror," in *El País. Babelia*, January 4, 2024.

Guerard, Albert J. (1914–2000), *The Triumph of the Novel: Dickens, Dostoevski, Faulkner*, New York, Oxford University Press, 1976.

Gufé, Cristina, *99 Cartas a Kafka*, Madrid, Sial Narrativas, 2010.

Gulotta, Guglielmo, *Psicoanalisi e responsabilità penale*, Milan, Giuffrè, 1972.

Gunn, John – Maden, Anthony – Swinton, Mark, *Mentally Disordered Prisoners*, London, Institute of Psychiatry, 1991.

Gutiérrez, Rubén, "La representación de las doctrinas anarquistas en la novela 'Los demonios' de Dostoyevski. De la utopía revolucionaria a la ideología nihilista," in

Humanitas. Revista de Teoría, Crítica y Estudios Literarios, vol. 2, no. 3, July-December 2022, pp. 171–195.

Gutwirth, Serge, "Une petite réflexion sur l'importance de la flibusterie épistémologique des littéraires. Dostoïevski, la criminologie, les sciences, le droit et la littérature," in François Ost – Laurent van Eynde– Philippe Gérard – Michel van de Kerchove (dirs.), *Lettres et lois. Le droit au miroir de la littérature*, Brussels, Publications des Facultés Universitaires Saint-Louis, 2001, pp. 305–342.

Haferkamp, Hans, *Kriminalität ist normal – Zur gesellschaftlichen Produktion abweichenden Handelns*, Stuttgart, Ferdinand Enke Verlag, 1972.

Haferkamp, Hans, "Zur Notwendigkeit handlungstheoretischer Analysen der Kriminalität und der Kriminalisierung," in Arbeitskreis Junger Kriminologen (ed.), *Kritische Kriminologie*, 1974.

Haffe, Bernhard, "Hat emanzipierende Sozialtherapie noch eine Chance?," in *Seminar: Abweichendes Verhalten. III.* Edited by Lüdersen and Sack, *Die Gesellschaft Reaktion auf Kriminalität*, Frankfurt am Main, 1977.

Hancher, Michael, "Billy Budd Famous Last Words," *Symposium*, in *Cardozo Studies in Law and Literature*, vol. 1, issue 1, spring 1989.

Hauptmann, Gerhart – Gjellerup, Karl – Gide, André, *Los premios Nobel de Literatura*, Esplugues de Llobregat (Barcelona), Plaza y Janes, 1981.

Heller, Peter, "On Not Understanding Kafka," in *The Kafka Debate. New Perspectives for Our Time*, New York, 1977.

Henel, Ingeborg, "Die Türhüterlegende und ihre Bedeutung für Kafkas 'Prozess'," in *Deutsche Vierteljahrsschrift für Literaturwissenschaft und Geistesgeschichte*, vol. 37, no. 1, 1963, pp. 50–70.

Heras, Mario de las, "En el año de Kafka, ¿cuál es el verdadero significado de la palabra 'kafkiano'?," in *El Debate*, January 11, 2024.

Heras Bretín, Rut de las, "La tumba que nos acerca a Kafka," in *El País*, June 13, 2024.

Hernández, Isabel, *Introducción a* El proceso, 5th. ed., Madrid, Cátedra, 2001.

Hernández, Isabel, "¿Quién era Franz Kafka?," in *Turia. Revista Cultural*, nos. 149–150, 2024, pp. 158–173.

Hernández, Isabel – López Lizana, Alejandro (selection and translation), *Franz Kafka y el amor*, Barcelona, Vegueta, 2025.

Hernández Arias, José Rafael, "Prologue" to *Franz Kafka, Cuentos completos*, Madrid, 2003.

Herzfeld, Hermann, "Dostojewski und die russische Staatsidee," in *Universitas*, year 1, Hefts 3–4, June-July 1946.

Hessen, Serguéi, "Die Idee des Guten in den 'Brüdern Karamazov'," in *Der Russische Gedenke*, I, 1929.

Hierro, Liborio, "Libertad y responsabilidad penal," in *Anuario de la Facultad de Derecho. Alcalá de Henares*, 1991–1992, pp. 161–173.

Highton, Elena I. – Álvarez, Gladys Stella – Gregorio, Carlos G., *Resolución alternativa de disputas y sistema penal*, Buenos Aires, Ed. Ad-Hoc, 1998.

Hirst, Paul, "The Concept of Punishment," in *Law in Context*, 1984, pp. 73–88.

Hoffmann, Nina,*Th. M. Dostojewski. Eine biograpische Studie*, Hamburg, Hansebooks, 2022.

Hoffmann, Werner, *Los aforismos de Kafka*, Mexico, Fondo de Cultura Económica, 1979, 2014.

Hofstatter, Peter Robert (1913–1994), "Pena y reprochabilidad desde el punto de vista social-psicológico," in *Sexualidad y crimen*, translation into Spanish by Enrique Gimbernat, Madrid, Reus, 1969.

Holbach, Frédéric,*Justice laudative*, Brussels-Paris, Larcier, Pedone, 1904.

Holdheim, Wolfgang, "Ways of Mephistopheles," in *Cardozo Studies in Law and Literature*, vol. 1, issue 2, fall 1989.

Holzmann, Max, *Dostojewski. Sein Leben und Werden*, Musarion Verlag, 1923.

Honderich, Ted, *Punishment. The Supposed Justifications*, Harmondsworth, Baltimore, Maryland, Penguin Books, 1969, 1976 and 1984. Previous edition, London, Hutchinson, 1969; There is a revised edition, Cambridge, Polity, 1989 and 3rd. ed. 1990.

Hooft, P. F., "Filosofía del castigo," in *Boletín AAFD*, 20, 1985.

Hopenhayn, Martin, *¿Por qué Kafka? Poder, mala conciencia y literatura*, Santiago de Chile, Lom, 2000.

Hough, James Morden, "The Impact of Victimization: Findings from the British Crime Survey," Paper prepared for the *Third International Institute of Victimology*, Lisbon, 1984.

Hough, James Morden – Mayhew, Path, *Taking Account of Crime: Key Findings from the Second British Crime Survey*, London, Her Majesty's Stationery Office, 1985.

Hough, James Morden – Moxon, David, "Dealing with Offenders: Popular Opinions and the Views of Victims," in *Howard Journal*, 24, 3, 1985, pp. 160–175.

Hough, James Morden – Roberts, Julian, *Attitudes to Punishment: Findings from the British 1996 Crime Survey*, London, Home Office, 1998.

Hoyles, J. Arthur, *Punishment and the Bible*, London, Epworth Press, 1986.

Hrabal, Bohumil, *Señor Kafka*, translation by Patricia Gonzalo de Jesús, Madrid, Nórdica Libros, 2023.

Hubben, William, *Dostoevsky, Kierkegaard, Nietzsche and Kafka: Four Prophets of Our Destiny*, New York, Collier Books, 1962.

Hudson, Barbara,*Justice Through Punishment. A Critique to the 'Justice' Model of Corrections*, London, MacMillan, 1987.

Husak, Douglas N., "Why Punish the Deserving?," in *Nous*, 26, 1992, pp. 447–464.

Hussey, Frederick, "Just Deserts and Determinate Sentencing: Impact on the Rehabilitation Ideal," in *The Prison Journal*, LIX, 2, fall-winter 1980, pp. 36–47.

Hutchings, Peter J., *The Criminal Specter in Law, Literature and Aesthetics: Incriminating Subjects*, London, Routledge, 2001.

Ierardo, Esteban, "Kafka en su laberinto," in *Perfil*, June 30, 2024.

Ilardi, Emiliano, *La última frontera de la novela. El espacio metropolitano de Balzac a Ballard*, PhD dissertation supervised by Enric Sullà, Barcelona, Universidad Autónoma de Barcelona, 2004.

Iniesta López, Iván, *Enfermedad en la literatura de Dostoyevski*, PhD dissertation supervised by Luis Enrique Montiel Llorente, Universidad Complutense de Madrid, 2005.

Insua, J. (dir.), Palà Selva, Marina (dir.) Cuenca, A. (author), Ibañez, A. (author), Gomis, C. (author), Fronza, L. (author), *La ciutat de K. Franz Kafka i Praga*, Barcelona, Instituts d'Edicions. Diputació de Barcelona. Centre de Cultura Contemporània de Barcelona, 1999. Translation into English, *The City of K: Franz Kafka and Prague*, Barcelona, Centre de Cultura Contemporània de Barcelona, 2002.

Isaacson, José, *Kafka, la imposibilidad como proyecto*, Madrid, Editorial Plus Ultra, 1974.

Isaacson, José, *La realidad metafísica de Kafka*, Buenos Aires, Corregidor, 2005.

Iturmendi Morales, José, Foreword to Manuel Alonso Olea (1924–2003), *Entre Don Quijote y Sancho. ¿Relación laboral?*, Madrid, Servicio de Publicaciones, Facultad de Derecho, Universidad Complutense de Madrid, 1992.

Iturmendi Morales, José, "Proceso y muerte de Sócrates. Un sabio ante la justicia de su tiempo," in *Grandes abogados, grandes procesos que hicieron historia*, Pamplona, Aranzadi, 1997, pp. 155–159.

Ivancic, Tamara, *La relación entre Rusia y Occidente en la obra de F. M. Dostoyevski. Apuntes del subsuelo. Los demonios y Los hermanos Karamazov*, PhD dissertation supervised by Rafael Argullol Murgadas, Universitat Pompeu Fabra, 2004.

Ivanov, Venceslao, *Freedom and the Tragic Life: A Study in Dostoevsky*, New York, Noonday Press, 1960.

Izquierdo, Luis, *El autor y su obra, Kafka*, Barcelona, Barcanova, 1981.

Izquierdo, Luis, "Kafka," in Jordi Llovet (ed.), *Lecciones de Literatura Universal: siglos XII a XX*, Barcelona, 1995, pp. 901–910.

Izquierdo, Luis, "El proceso de Franz Kafka," in Jordi Llovet (dir.), *La literatura admirable. Del Génesis a Lolita*, Barcelona, Pasado y Presente, 2018.

Jackson, Robert Louis, *The Art of Dostoevsky: Deliriums & Nocturnes*, New Jersey, Princeton University Press, 1981.

Jackson, Robert Louis, *Dialogues with Dostoevsky. The Overwhelming Questions*, Stanford, Stanford University Press, 1993.

Jäger, "Strafrecht und psychoanalitische Theorie," in *Fest. Henkel*, 1974.

Janouch, Gustav, *Conversations with Kafka: Notes and Reminiscences*, London, Derek Verschoyle, 1953, translation into English by Goronwy Rees. There is a translation into Spanish, *Conversaciones con Kafka*, by R. Sala, Barcelona, Destino, 1999. 2006.

Jarauta, Francisco, "El siglo de Kafka," in *Sociología Histórica: Revista de Investigación acerca de la Dimensión Histórica de los Fenómenos Sociales*, vol. 14, no. 1, 2024.

Jiménez de Asúa, Luis, "La recompensa como prevención general – El derecho premial," in *Revista General de Legislación y Jurisprudencia*, vol. 125.

Jofré, Manuel, "Don Quijote como novela moderna y la conjunción de géneros altos y bajos. Don Quixote as a Modern Novel and the Mixture of High and Low Genres," Universidad de Chile, Facultad de Filosofía y Humanidades, http://www.scielo.cl/scielo.php?script=sci_arttext8pid=S0718-22012006000100003.

Johnson, Carroll B., *Madness and Lust: A Psychoanalytical Approach to Don Quichote*, Berkeley, University of California Press, 1983.

Jones, John, *Dostoevsky*, Oxford, Clarendon Press, 1983. Oxford, Oxford University Press, 1985.

Juárez Carrasco, Benito, in *El Quijote Virtual. Revista anual Escuela*, no. 189, Montevideo.

Kafka, Franz (1883–1924), *Sobre la cuestión de las leyes* (1915), in *La muralla china*, translation into Spanish by A. Pippig, A. Ruis Guiñázú and C. Gauger, Biblioteca Kafka, Alianza Editorial, 1999 (3rd. reprint, 2008).

Kafka, Franz, *Carta al padre* (1919), translation into Spanish by J. Parra, foreword by J. Llovet, Barcelona, Galaxia Gutenberg, 2003.

Kafka, Franz, *In the Penal Colony* (1919), trans. into Spanish by Juan José del Solar and Manuela Sáenz, *En la colonia penitenciaria*, in *Obras completas III*, ed. and prologue by J. J. Llovet, Barcelona, Galaxia Gutenberg-Círculo de Lectores, 2003.

Kafka, Franz, *El proceso* (1925), in *Obras completas de Franz Kafka*, I, edited by Jordi Llovet, translation into Spanish by M. Sáenz, biographical essay by Klaus Wagenbach, and foreword by Hannah Arendt, Barcelona, Galaxia Gutenberg-Círculo de Lectores, 1999. And in Madrid, Nórdica Libros, 2008. There is also an edition and translation by Isabel Hernández, Madrid, Cátedra, 2009. And translation by Emilio J. González García, Madrid, Akal, 2007. There is a translation into English, *The Trial*, New York, Schocken Books, 1998.

Kafka, Franz, *Diarios (1910–1923)* (1948), edited by Max Brod, translation by Feliu Formosa, Barcelona, Tusquets, 2010.

Kafka, Franz, *Aforismos, visiones y sueños*, Madrid, El Club Diógenes, Valdemar, 2024.

Karmen, Andrew, *Crime Victims. An Introduction to Victimology*, Belmont, California, Wadsworth, 1984.

Kenosian, David, *Puzzles of the Body: The Labyrinth in Kafka's* Prozess, *Hesse's* Steppenwolf, *and Mann's* Zauberberg, New York, Peter Lang, 1995.

Kittrie, Nicholas N., *The Right to Be Different: Deviance and Enforced Therapy*, Baltimore-London, The John Hopkins Press, 1971.

Kjetsaa, Geir, *Dostoyevski. La vida de un escritor*, Buenos Aires, Javier Vergara Editor, 1989.

Kleinig, John, *Punishment and Desert*, The Hague, Martinus Nijhoff, 1973.

Klimis, Sophie, "Amour, droit et harmonie cosmique dans la trilogie des Danaïdes d'Eschyle," in François Ost – Laurent van Eynde – Philippe Gérard – Michel van de Kerchove (dirs.), *Lettres et lois. Le droit au miroir de la littérature*, Brussels, Publications des Facultés Universitaires Saint-Louis, pp. 11–38.

Kohan, Haydée, "La repetición en la vida y la obra de Fiódor Mijáilovich Dostoyevski," in *Revista de Psicoanálisis*, vol. 52, no. 1, pp. 189–214.

Komarovic, Vasily Leonidovich, "Die Weltanschauung Dostojevskijs in der russischen Forschung 1914–1924," in *Zeitschrift für slavische Philologie*, vol. III, 1926, pp. 217–228.

Komarovic, Vasily Leonidovich, "Neue Probleme der Dostojevskij-Forschung, 1925–1930," in *Zeitschrift für slavische Philologie*, vol. X, 1933; vol. XI, 1934.

Koopman, Colin, "Kafka, Language, Pain," in *The Kafka Project*: http://www.kafka.org/essays/koopmanLP.htm.

Kosik, Karel, "Hasek y Kafka," in *Letra Internacional*, no. 4, 1986–1987, pp. 35–37.

Krauze, Enrique, "La elipse de Franz Kafka," in *Letras Libres*, June 1, 2024.

Lacan, Jacques (1901–1981), "La metáfora del sujeto," in *Introducción teórica a las funciones del psicoanálisis en criminología*, Buenos Aires, Homo Sapiens, 1978.

Laclau, Martín, *Law and Literature in Ancient Greece*, in María José Falcón y Tella (ed. and prologue), *International Studies in Law and Literature*, vol. 1, Leiden-Boston, Brill-Nijhoff, 2024, translation into English by Deirdre B. Jerry, from *La comprensión del Derecho en la antigua Grecia*, Buenos Aires, Editorial Astrea, 2022.

La Rubia de Prado, *Kafka: el maestro absoluto*, Granada, Universidad de Granada, 2002.

La Rubia de Prado, *Kafka y el cine. La estética de lo kafkiano en el séptimo arte*, Madrid, Biblioteca Nueva, 2011.

Lasso de la Vega, José S., *El dolor y la condición humana en el teatro de Sófocles*, CESIC (Instituto Arnaldo de Vilanova), 1958. Barcelona, 1971.

Lauth, Reinhard, *"He visto la verdad." La Filosofía de Dostoievski en una exposición sistemática*, translation into Spanish by Alberto Ciria, Seville, Thémata, 2014.

Lema Mosca, Álvaro, "Cuentos completos de Kafka," in *Revista de Literatura y Arte de la Asociación de Profesores de Literatura de Uruguay*, no. 37, 2024, pp. 180–181.

Lestapis, Stanislas de, "Le probléme de l'athéisme vu par Dostoievski," in *Études*, vol. 233, 1937.

Levi, P., "Una agresión llamada Franz Kafka," in *Entrevistas y conversaciones*, Barcelona, Península, 2003.

Lewis, C. S., *The Problem of Pain* (1940), Great Britain, Fontana Books, 1980.

Lewis, C. S., "The Humanitarian Theory of Punishment," in *Res Judicatae*, 6, 1953; and in Sir Leon Radzinowicz – Marvin E. Wolfgang (eds.), *Crime and Justice*, vol. 2, New York, Basic Books, 1971.

Lieb, F., "Das Problem des Menschen bei Dostojewskij," in *Orient und Occident*, III, 1930.

Lillie, N., "Towards a Biblical Doctrine of Punishment," in *Scottish Journal of Theology*, 21, 1968, pp. 449–461.

Lindblom, Ulf, "Smärtbehandling under Omprövning," in *Nordisk Medisin*, 95, 1980.

Litowitz, Douglas E., "Franz Kafka's Outsider Jurisprudence," in *Law & Social Inquiry*, 27, 2002.

Litowitz, Douglas E., *Kafka's Indictment of Modern Law*, Kansas, University Press of Kansas, 2017.

Lombardo Radice, Lucio, *El acusado Kafka*, translation into Spanish by J. Zulueta, Barcelona, Icaria, 1977.

Londoño, Julio César, "Kafka, la mirada, el estilo y la fractura," in *El Espectador*, June 15, 2024.

Londoño Hidalgo, Julio Mauricio, *Introducción al Derecho en la obra de Franz Kafka*, Pontificia Universidad Javeriana. Work developed in the seminar "Literatura y ley" (2001–2002) organized by Carmena Kline and Gustavo Zafra.

López, Guillermo Héctor, "Kafka y la comedia: una lucha formal contra la opresión," in *Araucaria. Revista Iberoamericana de Filosofía, Política, Humanidades y Relaciones Internacionales*, year 24, no. 49, First quarter of 2022, pp. 57–74.

López Aranguren, José Luis, *El cristianismo de Dostoievski*, Madrid, Librería Castrejón, 1969. Madrid, Taurus, 1970.

Löwy, Michael, "De Mendel Beilis, el judío paria, a Joseph K., la víctima universal. Una interpretación de 'El proceso' de Kafka," in *Acta poética*, 24–2, fall 2003.

Löwy, Michael, *Franz Kafka, rêveur insumis*, Paris, Stock, 2004.

Lucas, Antonio, "Franz Kafka, el triunfo de la angustia," in *El Mundo*, January 21, 2024.

Lucka, Emil, *Dostojewski*, Deutsche Verlag-Anstalt, 1924.

Luzón Peña, Diego-Manuel, "Prevención general y Psicoanálisis," in *Derecho Penal y Ciencias Sociales*, Barcelona, Ed. Mir, 1982.

Llera Cantero, Luis – Calvin Palomares, Juan, "Kafka, el exilio del reino," in *Miscelánea Comillas. Revista de Ciencias Humanas y Sociales*, vol. 81, nos. 158–159, 2023, pp. 299–308.

Llinares Chover, Joan B., "La crítica de F. Dostoievski a la antropología de N. Chernyshevski. Memorias del subsuelo como réplica a ¿Qué hacer?," in J. San Martín – T. Domingo Moratalla (eds.), *La imagen del ser humano. Historia, literatura y hermenéutica*, Madrid, Biblioteca Nueva, 2011, pp. 131–141.

Llovet, Jordi, "Prologue" to Franz Kafka, *Bestiario. Once relatos de animales*, Barcelona, 1990.

Llovet, Jordi, "Introducción," in Franz Kafka, *La metamorfosis y otros relatos*, Barcelona, España, 1992.

Llovet, Jordi, "Franz Kafka y su proyecto de una pequeña literatura nacional," in Elisa Martínez Salazar – Julieta Yelin (eds.), *Kafka en las dos orillas: Antología de la recepción crítica española e hispanoamericana*, 2013, pp. 282–287.

Maceina, Antanas – Szylkarski, Wladimir (Postface), *Der Grossinquisitor: Geschichtsphilosophische Deutung der Legende Dostojewskijs*, Heidelberg, Kerle, 1952.

Mack, Alexis Paiva, "¿Qué significa el adjetivo 'kafkiano' y qué nos dice del célebre escritor de La metamorfosis?," in *La Tercera*, July 2, 2024.

Madariaga y Rojo, Salvador de (1886–1978), *Guía del lector del* Quijote, Madrid, 1926. Madrid, Espasa Calpe, 2005.

Madaule, Jacques, *Le Christianisme de Dostoievski*, 1939. There is a translation into Spanish, *El cristianismo de Dostoievski*, Buenos Aires, Losada, 1952.

Magris, Claudio, *Literatura y Derecho. Ante la Ley*, foreword by F. Savater, translation into Spanish by M. T. Meneses, Madrid, Editorial Sexto Piso, 2008.

Mahrholz, Werner, *Dostojewski. Ein Weg zum Menschen, zum Werk, zum Evangelium*, Berlin, Furche Verlag, 1922.

Malý, Radek, *Franz Kafka. El hombre que trascendió su tiempo*, illustrated by Renáta Fucíková, translation into Spanish by Núria Mirabet i Cucala, Barcelona, Libros del Zorro Rojo, 2019.

Manlowe, Colin, "Closer than an Eye: The Interconnection of Stevenson's Doctor Jekyll and Mr. Hyde," in *Studies in Scottish Literature*, XXIII, Columbia, South Carolina, University of South Carolina, 1988.

Marchamalo, Jesús, *Kafka con sombrero*, illustrated by Antonio Santos, Madrid, Nórdica Libros, 2015.

Marfany, Gemma, "El sueño de Kafka," in *El Nacional.Cat*, April 13, 2024.

Marlowe, Christopher (1564–1593), *Doctor Faustus: The A-Text*, edited by David Ormerod – Christopher Wortham, Nedlands, University of Western Australia Press, 1989. *Doctor Faustus*, edited by Linda Cookson, with an essay by Jan Kott, Harlow, Essex, Longman, 1984. Also edited by Roma Gill, New York, Hill and Wang, 1966.

Marqués, Rosa, "2024: el año kafkiano," in *Traveler*, April 22, 2024.

Marson, Eric Lawson, *Kafka's Trial. The Case Against Josef K.*, St. Lucia, Australia, University of Queensland Press, 1975.

Marsot, Elsa, "La Main et l'esthétique du geste chez Kafka. Postures," in *Critique Litteraire*, 1, 1997, pp. 21–35.

Martí Mingarro, Luis, Foreword to Antonio Martín Gamero, *Jurispericia de Cervantes. Pasatiempo literario*, Toledo, Imprenta y Librería de Fando e Hijo, 1870, reprint in ICAM, 2002.

Martí Mingarro, Luis, Foreword to Enrique San Miguel, *Abogacía, justicia y Derecho en Shakespeare*, Madrid, ICAM, 2004.

Martí Mingarro, Luis, "El año de Cervantes y la construcción europea," in *ABC*, January 17, 2005.

Martí Mingarro, Luis, Foreword to Quintiliano Saldaña, *La criminología de "El Quijote,"* Reprint in ICAM, 2013.

Martí Mingarro, Luis, Introduction and chapter I, "Leer el *Quijote*," in *Los abogados de Madrid y el* Quijote, Madrid, ICAM-Tirant lo Blanch, 2023.

Martí Mingarro, Luis, *Estudios sobre Derecho, Cultura y Justicia*, Foreword by Eugenio Ribón Seisdedos, Madrid, Ilustre Colegio de la Abogacía de Madrid, Aranzadi, 2025.

Martín, José F., "Diálogo y poder en la liberación de los galeotes," in *Cervantes*, 11, 1991.

Martín Arnedo, Santiago, "Ante la ley y la experiencia del sentido en F. Kafka," in *Álabe. Revista de Investigación sobre Lectura y Escritura*, no. 23, January–June 2021.

Martín Arnedo, Santiago, "El estilo vertical en Franz Kafka," in *Revista de Filología Alemana*, vol. 31, 2023, pp. 65–77.

Martínez Cazares, Germán, *Kafka: el Derecho como amenaza*, Universidad Lasalle, 2005.

Martínez Estrada, Ezequiel, *En torno a Kafka y otros ensayos*, Barcelona, Seix Barral, 1967.

Martínez Estrada, Ezequiel, "Intento de señalar los bordes del mundo de Kafka" (1944), in Elisa Martínez Salazar – Julieta Yelin (eds.), *Kafka en las dos orillas. Antología de la recepción crítica española e hispanoamericana*, Zaragoza, Prensas de la Universidad de Zaragoza, 2013, pp. 11–118.

Martínez Estrada, Ezequiel, "Acepción literal del mito en Kafka" (1950), in Elisa Martínez Salazar – Julieta Yelin (eds.), *Kafka en las dos orillas. Antología de la recepción crítica española e hispanoamericana*, Zaragoza, Prensas de la Universidad de Zaragoza, 2013, pp. 176–182.

Martínez Estrada, Ezequiel, "Apocalipsis de Kafka" (1960), in Elisa Martínez Salazar – Julieta Yelin (eds.), *Kafka en las dos orillas. Antología de la recepción crítica española e hispanoamericana*, Zaragoza, Prensas de la Universidad de Zaragoza, 2013, pp. 195–199.

Martínez Fernández, Isabel, *Dostoievski*, Madrid, Ediciones del Orto, 1996.

Martínez Fernández, Isabel, *Dostoievski: de la igualdad a la diferencia. Ensayo sobre la burocracia*, Madrid, Biblioteca Nueva, 2003.

Martínez Ortigosa, Iñaki, "El último gesto de Josef K. Una reflexión filosófica en torno a su muerte," in *Espéculo. Revista de Estudios Literarios*, Madrid, Universidad Complutense de Madrid, 2009. http://www.ucm.es/info/especulo/numero41/josephk.html.

Martínez Salazar, Elisa, "¿Hay que quemar a Kafka? La recepción española de Franz Kafka en su contexto internacional," in María Cecilia Trujillo Maza (ed.), *Lectores, ediciones y audiencia: La recepción en la literatura hispánica*, 2008, pp. 357–364.

Martínez Valero, José Luis, "Una lectura de Franz Kafka. 1883–1924," in *Agora: Papeles de arte gramático*, no. 25, 2024, pp. 49–62.

Massó Castilla, Jordi, "Kafka, la Hermenéutica y otros modos de leer," in *Ecos*, 7, 2, 2017.

Matl, Josef, "Dostoievski y la crisis de nuestro tiempo," in *Revista de Estudios Políticos*, 57, 1951, pp. 35–54.

Mayoral, Carlos, "Prepárense para el año más kafkiano," in *Zenda XI Semanal*, January 16, 2024.

McPherson, Thomas, "Punishment: Definition and Justification," in *Analysis*, 28, 1967, pp. 21–27.

Mead, George Herbert (1863–1931), "The Psychology of Punitive Justice," in *American Journal of Sociology*, 23, 1918, pp. 577–602.

Meier, Martha, "Releer a Kafka," in *Expreso*, January 21, 2024.

Melville, Herman (1819–1891), *Billy Budd, Sailor*, edited by Harold Beaver, Harmondsworth, Penguin, 1967. There is a translation into Spanish, with notes, by José María Valverde, Madrid, Fascículos Planeta, 1984. *Billy Budd, marinero*, Madrid, El Mundo y la Revista, Unidad Editorial, 1998. Also in Madrid, Compañía Europea de Comunicación e Información, 1991, translation into Spanish by Julia Lavid. Also in Barcelona, Salvat, 1971; and in Madrid, Alianza, 1971.

Mereszhkovski, Dmitri, "Rodion Raskolnikoff," in *Dostojewski-Gesamtausgabe*, Piper & Co., vol. 1, 1920.

Mereszhkovski, Dmitri, *L'âme de Dostoievski*, Paris, 1922.

Merivale, Patricia, "Audible Palimpsests: Coetzee's Kafka" in Graham Huggan – Stephen Watson, *Critical Perspectives on J. M. Coetzee*, New York, St. Martin Press, 1996, pp. 98–112.

Meyer, Priscilla – Rudy, Stephen, *Dostoevsky & Gogol: Texts and Criticism*, Ann Arbor, Ardis Publishers, 1979.

Meyer, P. N., "Convicts, Criminals, Prisoners, and Outlaws: A Course in Popular Storytelling," in *Journal of Law & Education*, 42, 1992, pp. 129–137.

Milgram, Stanley (1933–1984), "Some Conditions of Obedience and Disobedience to Authority," in *Human Relations*, 18, 1965, pp. 57–75.

Milgram, Stanley, *Obedience to Authority*, New York, Harper and Row, 1974.

Millar, Jonathan, *The Uses of Pain*, Introduction by Peter Cadogan, London, South Place Ethical Society, 1973.

Miller, Jeffrey, *The Structures of Law and Literature: Duty, Justice, and Evil in the Cultural Imagination*, Montreal, Ithaca, McGill-Queen's University Press, 2013.

Miller, J. Hillis, "Laying down the Law in Literature: The Example of Kleist," in *Derecho Natural*, 1985, pp. 1491–1514.

Miller, Orest, "Materialen zur Lebensgeschichte Dostojewskis," in *Dostojewski-Gesamtausgabe*, Piper & Co., vol. 11, Russian edition, 1882.

Minson, Jeffrey, *The Genealogy of Morals: Nietzsche, Foucault, Donzelot and the Eccentricity of Ethics*, London, 1985.

Miralles Kontijoch, Francesc, *Franz Kafka*, Barcelona, Océano Grupo Editorial, 2000.

Mittica, M. Paola, *Il divenire dell'ordine. L'interazione normativa nella società omerica*, Milan, Giuffrè, 1996.

Mittica, M. Paola, *Raccontando il possibile. Eschilo e le narrazioni giuridiche*, Milan, Giuffrè, 2006.

Mittica, M. Paola, *Cantori di* nostoi. *Estrutture giuridiche e politiche delle comunità omeriche*, Roma, Aracne, 2007.

Mittica, M. Paola, *Il pensiero che sente. Pratiche di Law and Humanities*, Turin, Giappichelli, 2022. There is a translation into English by Mark Byrne, in María José Falcón y Tella (ed.), *International Studies in Law and Literature*, vol. 5, Leiden-Boston, Brill-Nijhoff, 2026.

Mittica, M. Paola, *Diritto e Letteratura e Law and Humanities. Elementi per un'estetica giuridica*, Turin, Giappichelli, 2024.

Modern, R., "Franz Kafka y Georg Trakl: una comparación," in *Revista de Occidente*, 26, 1983.

Moeller van den Bruck, Arthur, "Dostojewski, der Nihilismus und die Revolution," in *Dostojewski-Gesamtausgabe*, Piper & Co., vol. 5, 1922.

Moeller van den Bruck, Arthur, "Dostojewski als Dichter der Grossstadt," in the *Dostojewski-Gesamtausgabe* de Piper & Co., vol. 20, 1922.

Moldes, Diego, *Cuando Einstein encontró a Kafka. Contribuciones de los judíos al mundo moderno*, Barcelona, Galaxia Gutenberg, 2019.

Molina, César Antonio, "'Tú eres la tarea. Aforismos', de Franz Kafka: inquietudes kafkianas," in *ABC Cultural*, April 16, 2024.

Mont, E., "Una velada con Franz Kafka," in *Cuando Kafka vino hacia mí*, edited by Hans-Gerd Koch, translation into Spanish by Berta Vías Mahou, Barcelona, Acantilado, 2009.

Montero Bosch, David, "El asalto a la razón de Dostoievski," in *Daimon, Revista Internacional de Filosofía*, no. 68, May–August 2016, pp. 115–129.

Montiel Figueiras, Mauricio, "Breve Diccionario Kafka," in *Letras Libres*, June 3, 2024.

Montiel Figueiras, Mauricio, "El tribunal invisible de Franz Kafka," in *El Universal*, June 9, 2024.

Montoya Melgar, Alfredo (1937–2025), *El trabajo en la literatura y el arte*, Madrid, Civitas, 1995.

Montoya Melgar, Alfredo, *Amos y criados en el teatro clásico: (Cuatro ensayos con el Derecho del Trabajo al fondo)*, Madrid, Civitas Thomson-Reuters, 2022.

Mora, Jaime G., "Kafka después del fuego: todas las novedades editoriales del centenario," in *ABC Cultural*, June 6, 2024.

Moreno Ruffinelli, José, "El *Quijote* y el Derecho (I)," in *ABC Color*, October 2, 2005.

Moreno Salamanca, Astolfo Ricardo, "Dostoyevski en la Teología rusa del exilio y en la Teología católica del siglo XX," in *Cuadernos doctorales: Teología*, 73, 2023, pp. 79–158.

Morillas Esteban, Jorge, "La imagen de Cristo en Dostojewskij," in *Espíritu: Cuadernos del Instituto Filosófico de Balmesiana*, year 51, no. 126, 2002, pp. 287–295.

Morillas Esteban, Jorge, "La redención a través del amor: la Biblia en la vida y obra de Dostoievski," in *Mundo Eslavo*, no. 5, 2006, pp. 77–94.

Morillas Esteban, Jorge, "F. M. Dostoievski en España," in *Mundo Eslavo*, no. 10, 2011, pp. 119–143.

Morillas Esteban, Jorge, "Bases filológicas para una comparación entre F. M. Dostoievski y F. Nietzsche," in *Estudios Nietzsche: Revista de la Sociedad Española de Estudios sobre Friedrich Nietzsche*, no. 11, 2011, pp. 163–187.

Morillas Esteban, Jorge, Review to Javier Alcoriza Vento, *Dostoyevski y su influencia en la cultura europea*, in *Mundo Eslavo*, 2013, pp. 172–175.

Morris, Herbert (1928-2022) (ed.), *Freedom and Responsibility*, Stanford, Stanford University Press, 1961.

Morris, Herbert, "Persons and Punishment," in *The Monist*, 52, 1968, pp. 475–501.

Morris, Herbert, "Guilt and Punishment," in *Personalist*, 52, 1971, pp. 305–321.

Morris, Herbert, *On Guilt and Innocence: Essays in Legal Philosophy and Moral Psychology*, Berkeley, University of California Press, 1976.

Morris, Herbert, "A Paternalistic Theory of Punishment," in *American Philosophical Quarterly*, 18, 4, 1981, pp. 263–271.

Mosés, Stéphane, *Exégesis de una leyenda. Lecturas de Kafka*, Barcelona, Subsuelo, 2012.

Mosto, Marisa, "Empatía y compasión en la obra de Fiódor Dostoievski," in Various Authors: Martín Susnik – Cynthia Fox – Marisa Mosto – Marcos Jasminoy – Alejandro Bertolini, *Manantial en el desierto. Ensayos multidisciplinarios sobre empatía y compasión*, Buenos Aires, Ediciones El Rastro, 2016.

Moyano, Manuel, *El amigo de Kafka*, Valencia, Editorial Pre-Textos, 2001.

Muñagorri Laguía, Ignacio, *Sanción penal y política criminal. Confrontación con la nueva defensa social*, Foreword by Antonio Beristain, Madrid, Reus, Biblioteca Jurídica de Autores Españoles y Extranjeros, 1977.

Muñoz Conde, Francisco, "El principio de culpabilidad," in *III Jornadas de Profesores de Derecho Penal*, Santiago de Compostela, 1975.

Muñoz Machado, Santiago, "Sobre literatura, historia y procesos," Foreword to *Los grandes procesos de la historia de España*, Barcelona, Editorial Crítica, 2002.

Murakami, Haruki, *Kafka en la orilla*, Barcelona, Maxi-Tusquets, 2002.

Murphy, Jeffrie G. – Hampton, Jean, *Forgiveness and Mercy*, New York, Cambridge, 1989.

Murray, Nicholas, *Kafka*, translation by S. Kot, Buenos Aires, El Ateneo, 2006.

Nabokov, Vladimir (1899–1977), *Curso de Literatura europea*, Barcelona, Ediciones B., 1996. Barcelona, Ediciones Grupo Zeta, 1997.

Nabokov, Vladimir, "Franz Kafka y La metamorfosis," in *La metamorfosis*, Bogotá, Grupo Editorial Norma, 1998.

Nabokov, Vladimir, "Franz Kafka (1883–1924)," Foreword to *La metamorfosis*, translation into Spanish by J. J. del Solar, Madrid, Gredos, 2011.

Narbona, Rafael, "Dostoievski, el hombre que no perdió la esperanza," in *Nueva Revista*, 2022.

Naugrette, Jean-Pierre, "The Strange Case of Dr. Jekyll and Mr. Hyde: pour une relecture ecossaise," in *Cahiers Victoriens et Edouardiens*, Montpellier, Université Paul Valéry, 54, October 2001.

Navarro Adam, Susana, *Narrativa de transgresión: Nabokov – Dostoievski: Intertextualidad en Lolita*, PhD dissertation supervised by María de los Llanos Kasheeva, José Luis Falcó Gens and Santiago Renard Álvarez, Valencia, Universidad de Valencia, 2014.

Nava Tovar, Alejandro, "Franz Kafka y el estado de indefensión," in *Fuentes Humanísticas*, vol. 18, no. 33, July-December 2006, pp. 153–164.

Nelken, David, "Why Punish?," in *The Modern Law Review*, 53–6, November 1990, pp. 829–834.

Neufeld, Jolan, *Dostojewski. Skizze zu seiner Psychoanalyse*, Vero Verlag, 1919.

Nietzsche, Friedrich Wilhelm (1844–1900), "The Genealogy of Morals," in *The Birth of Tragedy and the Genealogy of Morals* (1887), New York, 1956.

Nistal, Francisco Javier, "La percepción del delincuente, por Don Quijote de La Mancha. Su posible traslado a la sociedad actual," in https://cj-worldnews.com/index.php/criminologia-30/historia-de-la-criminologia/item/1738-la-percepci/C3/B3n-del-delincuente-por-don-quijote-de-la-mancha.

Noriega, Carlos Gutiérrez, *Contribución de Cervantes a la Psicología y a la Psiquiatría*, Lima, Lumen, 1944.

Nóvikova, Olga, *Rusia y Occidente: N. Karamzin, P. Chaadáev, A. Jomiakov, Y. Kireevski, K. Leóntiev, F. Dostoievski, V. Soloviov, N. Berdiáiev, G. Fedótov, D. Lijachev*, Introduction by Olga Nóvikova, translation and notes by Olga Nóvikova and J. Carlos Lechado, Madrid, Tecnos, 1997.

Nozick, Robert (1938–2002), *Anarchy, State and Utopia*, Oxford, Basil Blackwell, 1974.

Obarrio Moreno, Juan Alfredo, "La tortura judicial en Franz Kafka: En la colonia penitenciaria," in *Revista de la Inquisición, Intolerancia y Derechos Humanos*, 2019.

Obarrio Moreno, Juan Alfredo – De las Heras Vives, Luis, *El mundo jurídico en Franz Kafka. El proceso*, Series "Monografías de Derecho Romano y Cultura Clásica," directed by prof. Antonio Fernández de Buján, Foreword by Fermín Morales Prats, Madrid, Dykinson, 2019.

Olmeda, Mauro, *El ingenio de Cervantes y la locura de Don Quijote*, Mexico, Editorial Atlante, 1958; and Madrid, 1973.

Ors, Javier, "Nada de cuentos con Franz Kafka," in *La Razón*. Cultura, April 27, 2024.

Ortega y Gasset, José (1883–1955), "Meditaciones sobre el *Quijote*," in *Obras Completas*, vol. I, Madrid, Alianza Editorial (1914), 2014. Also in Madrid, Cátedra, 2001.

Orwell, George (1903–1950), *Animal Farm* (1945), translation into Spanish, *Rebelión en la granja*, by Rafael Abella, Barcelona, Destino, 2010. Also in Barcelona, Unidad Editorial, 1999, with foreword by Juan Pedro Aparicio.

Orwell, George, *1984* (1949), Epilogue by Thomas Pynchon, translation into Spanish by Miguel Temprano García, Barcelona, Penguin Random House, 2014. Also in Barcelona, Destino, 2012, introduction by Fernando Galván, Reading guide by Francisco Alonso.

Orwell, George, "Lear, Tolstoy, and the Fool," in Sonia Orwell – Ian Angus (eds.), *The Collected Essays, Journalism and Letters of George Orwell*, vol. 4, 1968.

Orwell, George, "Politics vs. Literature: An Examination of *Gulliver's Travels*," in Sonia Orwell – Ian Angus (eds.), *The Collected Essays, Journalism and Letters of George Orwell*, vol. 4, 1968.

Ossorio Morales, Juan (1901–1964), *Derecho y Literatura*, Foreword by Julia Ruiz-Rico Ruiz Morón, Preliminary study by José Antonio López Nevot, Granada, Editorial Universidad de Granada, Colección Archivum, 2016.

Ost, François, "Antigone, encore," in *Journal des Procès*, no. 355, October 2, 1998, pp. 10–11.

Ost, François, "Kafka ou l'en deça de la loi," in François Ost – Laurent van Eynde – Philippe Gérard – Michel van de Kerchove, *Lettres et lois. Le droit au miroir de la littérature*, Brussels, Publications des Facultés Universitaires Saint-Louis, 2001, pp. 127–186.

Ost, François, "Le pacte faustien ou les avatars de la liberté," in *Faust ou les limites du savoir*, Brussels, Publications F.U.S.L., 2002, pp. 263–316.

Ost, François, *Raconter la loi. Aux sources de l'imaginaire juridique*, Paris, Odile Jacob, 2004.

Ost, François, *Sade et la loi*, Paris, Odile Jacob, 2005.

Ost, François, "L'invention du tiers, Esquyle et Kafka," in *Esprit*, no. 8, August–September 2007, pp. 147–165.

Ost, François, "Sade ou la contrefaçon des lois," in *Imaginer la loi*, supervised by Antoine Garapon and Denis Salas, Paris, Éd. Michalon, 2008, pp. 69–96.

Ost, François, "Sade ou la politique du pire," in *Droit politique et littérature. Mélanges en l'honneur du professeur Yves Guchet*, Brussels, Bruylant, 2008, pp. 587–611.

Ost, François, "Shakespeare, la comédie de la loi," in *Revue Interdisciplinaire d'Études Juridiques*, no. 66, 2011, pp. 131–175.

Ost, François, *Shakespeare. La Comédie de la Loi*, Paris Michalon; Collection "Le bien commun," 2012. There is a translation into Spanish, *Shakespeare. La comedia de la ley*, Buenos Aires, Jusbaires Editorial, 2016.

Ost, François, "To Avenge, to Forgive or to Judge? Literary Variations," in *NoFo*, no. 9, 2012, pp. 1–13.

Ost, François, "A vingar, punir, perdoar. A literatura como espaço de possiveis jurídicos," in *I.H.U., Revista do Instituto Humanitas Unisinos*, Porto Alegre, no. 435, December 2013, pp. 63–68.

Ost, François, "Entretien sur Victor Hugo et William Shakespeare," in *Victor Hugo. Homme de lettres, homme de droit*, supervised by Pierre Mazeaud and Catherine Puigelier, Paris, Mare et Martin, 2013, pp. 33–53.

Ost, François, "La justice, ses alternatives et ses symboles. Venger, pardonner ou juger? Variations littéraires," in *Les figures du procès au-delà des frontières*, supervised by Wanda Pastor and Lionel Miniato, Paris, Dalloz, 2013, pp. 137–155.

Ost, François, "Cher William Shakespeare," in *Lettres à Shakespeare*, supervised by Dominique Goy-Blanquet, Paris, Éditions Thierry Marchaisse, 2014, pp. 115–124.

Ost, François, "Le théâtre de William Shakespeare, mine d'or pour les études de 'droit et littérature'; certes, mais en quel sens?," in *Clio@Thémis*, no. 7, 2014, pp. 1–28.

Ost, François, *"Le marchand de Venise*: le pari et la dette, le jeu et la loi," in *McGill Law Journal. Revue de Droit de McGill*, no. 62–4, 2017, pp. 1103–1151.

Ost, François, "'*Measure for Measure*': Are Criminal Laws Made to Be Applied?," in François Ost – Daniela Carpi (eds.), *As you Law it. Negotiating Shakespeare*, Berlin-Boston, De Gruyter, 2018, pp. 183–198.

Ost, François, "Tempo e contrato: Critica ao pacto faustico," in *Redes – Revista Electronica Direito e Sociedade*, vol. 6, 1, May 2018, pp. 93–115.

Ost, François, "'Coimbra', le livre ultime. Variations kafkaïennes," in *Revue Interdisciplinaire d'Études Juridiques*, no. 82, 2919, pp. 105–113.

Ost, François, *Le procès de Socrate*, Brussels, Editions Samsa, 2024.

Ost, François, *Contes de la rue Soufflot*, Paris, Dalloz, 2024, Reprint of the 3 vols. by Dalloz: *Si le droit m'était conté* (2019. There is a translation into Brasileiro, *Contos juridicos*, by Fernando Herren Aguilar, London, Editions Thoth, 2024.), *Nouveaux contes juridiques* (2021), and *Le Congrès et autres contes juridiques* (2024).

Ost, François, *Legal Tales. Once Upon a Time, the Law*, vol. 4 of the *International Studies in Law and Literature*, edition and foreword by María José Falcón y Tella,

Leiden-Boston, Brill-Nijhoff, 2025. There is a translation into Spanish by María José Falcón y Tella, *Cuentos jurídicos. Érase una vez el Derecho*, foreword by María José Falcón y Tella, Valencia, Tirant lo Blanch, 2026.

Ost, François (with L. Couloubaritsis), *Antigone et la résistance civile*, Brussels, Éd. Ousia, 2004.

Ost, François (with Jeanne Gaakeer), *Crossing Borders: Law, Language and Literature, Proceedings of the Special Workshop on Law and Literature held at the 23rd World Conference of Philosophy of Law and Social Philosophy (IVR), August, 2007, Cracow*, Nijmegen, Wolf Legal Publishers, 2008.

Ost, François (with S. van Drooghenbroecke), "George Orwell à la Cour de Cassation (note sous Cass. Fr. 9 octobre 2001)," in *Journal des Tribunaux*, 2002, pp. 1–57.

Ost, François (with L. van Eynde), "Faust ou les frontières du savoir," in *Faust ou les limites du savoir*, Brussels, Publications F.U.S.L., 2002, pp. 7–10.

Ost, François (with L. van Eynde, Philippe Gérard and Michel van de Kerchove), *Lettres et lois. Le droit au miroir de la littérature*, Brussels, Publications F.U.S.L., 2001.

Ost, François (adapted by J.-Cl. Idée), *La nuit la plus longue. Sade et Portalis au pied de l'échafaud*, Louvain-la-Neuve, Anthemis, 2009.

Ost, François – Carpi, Daniela (eds.), *As you Law It. Negotiating Shakespeare*, Berlin-Boston, De Gruyter, 2018.

Ovelar, María, "Las visiones de Kafka en su centenario: claves para entender el mundo," in *20 Minutos*, June 26, 2024.

Pardo Gato, José Ricardo, "El Derecho en la época del *Quijote*," February 10, 2009, https://aranzadiycivitas.wordpress.com72009/02/10/el-derecho-en-la-epoca-del-quijote/.

Pareyson, Luigi, *Dostoevskij: filosofia, romanzo di esperienza religiosa*, Turin, Einaudi, 1993. There is a translation into Spanish, *Dostoievski. Filosofía, novela y experiencia religiosa*, Madrid, Encuentros, 2008.

Parra, Marco Antonio de la, "El lector de Kafka," in *Estudios Públicos*, no. 79, 2000, pp. 437–449.

Pascal, Roy, *Kafka's Narrators, A Study of His Stories and Sketches*, Cambridge, Cambridge University Press, 1980.

Pasik, Daniela, "¿De pronto te sentís un bicho? En 'La metamorfosis' Kafka mostró el efecto de los cambios sobre nosotros," in *Infobae*, February 26, 2024.

Passage, Charles E., *Dostoievski the Adapter: A Study in Dostoievski's Use of the Tales of Hoffmann*, Baltimore, Maryland, H. G. Roebuck & Son, 1963.

P. C., "La asombrosa lucidez de Kafka, Zweig y Roth para vaticinar el fascismo y la guerra," in *El Confidencial*, June 29, 2024.

Peces, C., "Sobre el deseo y sus paradojas: Una aproximación a Franz Kafka," in *Clinical and Health Journal of Empirical Research in Psychology*, vol. 11, no. 2, 2000, pp. 257–271.

Penella, Manuel, *Franz Kafka*, Madrid, Ed. Urbión Hispamérica, 1984.

Pérez de los Cobos Orihuel, Francisco, *Kafka o la miseria del Derecho*, Madrid, Trotta, 2026.

Pérez García, A., "La aventura de los galeotes," in María Ángeles Varela Olea – J. L. Hernández Mirón (dirs.), *Huellas de Don Quijote: La presencia cultural de Cervantes*, Madrid, Universidad San Pablo CEU, 2005.

Pérez Márquez, Raquel, "'El proceso' de Kafka desde la retórica," in *Foro Interno: Anuario de Teoría Política*, 7, 2007, pp. 93–122.

Pérez-Prendes Muñoz-Arraco, José Manuel (1933–2017), *Leopoldo Alas "Clarín" y el espíritu de las leyes*, Oviedo, 2002.

Pérez-Prendes Muñoz-Arraco, José Manuel, "Cervantes y los juristas (esbozo de una guía historiográfica)," in *Foro, Nueva Época*, 2, 2005, pp. 47–130.

Perrot, Jean, *Crime and châtiment de Dostoievski – analyse critique*, Paris, Hatier, 1970.

Persak, Christine, "Spencer's Doctrines and Mr. Hyde: Moral Evolution in Stevenson's 'Strange Case'," in *The Victorian Newsletter*, University of Kentucky, 86, fall 1994.

Persky, Serge, *La vie et l'oeuvre de Dostoievski*, Paris, Payot, 1924.

Pestaña Castro, Cristina, "Intertextualidad de Franz Kafka en J. L. Borges," in *Espéculo. Revista de Estudios Literarios*, no. 7, 1997–1998.

Pether, P., "Trouble with Iphigenia: Feminist Critiques of Feminist Crime Fiction and the Case against Sara Paretsky," in *Australian Journal of Law and Society*, 9, 1993, pp. 3–18.

Pevear, Richard, "Foreword" to Dostoevsky, *Demons*, Vintage Books, 1995, pp. vii–xxiii.

Pfau, Thomas, "The Pragmatics of Genre: Moral Theory and Lyric Authorship in Hegel and Wordsworth," in *Cardozo Arts & Entertainment Law Journal*, 10, 1992, pp. 397–422.

Picatoste Bobillo, Julio, "La sombra de Kafka es alargada," in *Faro de Vigo*, September 11, 2016.

Picatoste Bobillo, Julio, "J. Kierkegaard y Kafka (I y II)," in *Faro de Vigo*, October 9 and 10, 2016.

Picatoste Bobillo, Julio, "Más Kafka," in *Faro de Vigo*, June 9, 2019.

Picatoste Bobillo, Julio, *Kafka y el Derecho*, Cizur Menor (Navarre), Thomson Reuters, Aranzadi, 2021.

Poggioli, Renato, "Kafka and Dostoyevski," in A. Flires (ed.), *The Kafka Problem*, New York, Gordiam Press, 1975, pp. 69–83.

Politzer, Heinz, *Franz Kafka. Parable and Paradox*, Cornell University Press, 1966.

Politzer, Heinz, "Franz Kafka's Language," in *Modern Interpretations Franz Kafka's* The Trial, New York, 1987.

Posner, Richard A., "Law and Literature: A Relation Reargued," in *Virginia Law Review*, 72, 1986, pp. 1351–1392.

Posner, Richard A., *Law and Literature. A Misunderstood Relation*, Cambridge, Massachusetts, Harvard University Press, 1988. 1998. 3rd. ed. 2009. There is a translation into French by Christine Hivet and Philippe Jouary, *Droit et Literature*, Paris, PUF, 1996. And a translation into Spanish by Pilar Salamanca y Marina Muresán, *Ley y Literatura*, Valladolid, Cuatro y el Gato, Colegio de Abogados de Valladolid, 2004.

Posner, Richard A., "Comment on Richard Weisberg's Interpretation of Billy Budd," *Symposium*, in *Cardozo Studies in Law and Literature*, vol. 1, issue 1, spring 1989, pp. 71–82.

Posner, Richard A., *Cardozo: A Study in Reputation* (1990), Chicago, University of Chicago Press, 1993.

Posner, Richard A., *The Problems of Jurisprudence* (1990), Cambridge, Massachusetts, Harvard University Press, 2007.

Posner, Richard A., "When Is Parody Fair Use?," in *Journal of Legal Studies*, 21, 1992.

Posner, Richard A., *Overcoming Law*, Cambridge, Massachusetts, Harvard University Press, 1995.

Posner, Richard A., "Judicial Biography," in *New York University Law Review*, 70, 1995.

Posner, Richard A., "Judges' Writing Styles (And Do They Matter)," in *University of Chicago Law Review*, 70, 1995.

Posner, Richard A., "Legal Narratology," in *University of Chicago Law Review*, 74, 1997.

Posner, Richard A., *The Little Book of Plagiarism*, New York, Pantheon, 2007.

Potter, Parker B., Jr., "Ordeal by Trial: References to the Nightmare World of Franz Kafka," in *Pierce Law Review*, 3, 2004, pp. 195–330.

Prager, Hans, *Die Weltanschauung Dostojewskis*, Foreword by Stefan Zweig, Hildesheim, Verlag Borgmeyer, 1923.

Pulver, Max, "Paseo con Franz Kafka," in *Cuando Kafka vino hacia mi...*, edited by Hans-Gerd Koch, translation into Spanish by Berta Vías Mahou, Barcelona, Acantilado, 2009.

Purdy, Gilbert Wesley, "A Talmudic Analogy to Kafka's Parable 'Vor dem Gesetz'," in *Papers on Language and Literature*, vol. 4, no. 4, 1968.

Quezada, José, "'Kafka es un experto en el poder': Reiner Stach," in *El Universal*, June 9, 2024.

Quintano Ripollés, Antonio (1905–1967), "Culpabilidad y retribución como premisas de la justicia penal," in *Homenaje al profesor Luis Legaz y Lacambra. Estudios Jurídico-Sociales*, Universidad de Santiago de Compostela, 1950.

Quintano Ripollés, Antonio, "La evolución del Derecho penal moderno ('contra corriente')," in *Anuario de Derecho Penal y Ciencias Penales*, 1957.

Quintero Olivares, Gonzalo, "La llamada privatización del Derecho penal," in *Revista de Derecho y proceso penal*, 2001, 6, pp. 13–21.

Quintero Olivares, Gonzalo, "La imagen de la justicia en el *Quijote*, en Cervantes y en su tiempo," in *Quaderns Forum*, IX, *Revista del Colegio de Abogados de Tarragona*, December 2005.

Ranulf, Svend (1894–1953), *Moral Indignation and Middle-Class Psychology: A Sociological Study*, Copenhagen, Levin & Munksgaard, 1938.

Rawls, John (1921–2002), *A Theory of Justice*, Belknap Press (1971). There is a translation into Spanish by María Dolores González Soler, *Teoría de la Justicia*, Madrid, Fondo de Cultura Económica de España, 1979. 2nd. ed. 1995.

Rebón, Marta, "Milena Jesenká, la sombra de la amante de Kafka entre la niebla del campo de exterminio de Ravensbrück," in *El Mundo*, El Libro de la Semana, February 26, 2024.

Redondo, Agustín, "De las terceras al alcahuete del episodio de los galeotes en el *Quijote* (I, 22). Algunos rasgos de la parodia cervantina" (1989), in *Actas del X Congreso de la Asociación Internacional de Hispanistas, I*, 1989.

Redondo Reyes, Pedro, "La tradición clásica en la obra de Franz Kafka," in *Estudios Clásicos*, vol. 49, no. 132, 2007, pp. 107–126.

Reichenberger, Theo – Reichenberger, Kurt, "El alcahuete condenado: un detalle enigmático en el episodio de los galeotes," in Kurt Reichenberger – Darío Fernández Morera (dirs.), *Cervantes y su mundo*, vol. I, 2004.

Requena, Eva, "Dostoievski. 200 años de actualidad," in *Alternativas económicas*, 98, 2022, pp. 62–63.

Resnik, Judith, "Singular and Aggregate Voices: Audiences and Authority in Law & Literature and in Law & Feminism," in Michael Freeman – Andrew Lewis (eds.), *Law and Literature. Current Legal Issues*, volume 2, London–New York, Oxford University Press, 1999, pp. 687–728.

Resnik, Judith – Heilbrun, Carolyn, "Convergences: Law, Literature and Feminism," in *Yale Law Journal*, 99, 1990, pp. 1913–1953.

Rica Aranguren, Álvaro de la, "Kafka y la Historia," in *Revista de Libros*, 107, 2005, pp. 25–26.

Rica, Álvaro de la, "Una puerta para el centenario de Kafka," in *Las Terceras de ABC*, January 19, 2024.

Richard González, Manuel – Riaño Brun, Iñaki, "Jueces y Administración de Justicia en el *Quijote*," in José Francisco Alenza García (dir.), *Cervantes y el Derecho. Ideas cervantinas para el aprendizaje del Derecho*, Colección Facultad Ciencias Jurídicas UPNA, no. 2, Cizur Menor (Navarre), Thomson Reuters Aranzadi, 2016, pp. 253–274.

Rieff, Philip (1922–2006), *The Triumph of the Therapeutic: Uses of Faith After Freud*, Chicago, University of Chicago Press, 1966.

Rivera León, Lorena, "Dostoievski: Del héroe romántico al héroe de nuestro tiempo, o de la imposibilidad de ser Napoleón," in *La Torre del Virrey: Revista de Estudios Culturales*, no. 15, 2014, pp. 49–58.

Rivera León, Lorena, "El eterno marido que no sabía amar: Un parásito del deseo en la novelística de Dostoievski," in *Los retos de la filosofía en el siglo XXI*, vol. 2, 2015, pp. 21–33.

Rivera León, Lorena, *El amor en Dostoievski. Un estudio desde la antropología filosófica*, PhD dissertation supervised by Faustino Oncina Coves and Joan B. Linares Chover, Universidad de Valencia, 2016.

Rivera León, Lorena, "Dostoievski: Una lección de anatomía desde el subsuelo," in *Daimon. Revista Internacional de Filosofía*, no. 5, issue 5, 2016, pp. 867–875.

Rivera León, Lorena, "Entre Escila y Caribdis: Razón y fe al hilo de 'Los demonios' de Dostoievski," in *Antropología filosófica y Literatura*, supervised by Joan B. Llinares Chover, 2019, pp. 113–150.

Rivera León, Lorena, "Enfermedad y mal moral en el primer Dostoievski: El caso de Nétochka Nezvánova," in *Interessos filosòfics del present*, supervised by Elena Nájera Pérez, Antonio de Murcia Conesa and Jorge Pulla González, 2019, pp. 323–333.

Robert, Marthe, *Introduction à la lecture de Kafka*, Editions de l'Éclat, 1946.

Robert, Marthe, *L'Ancien et le Nouveau. De Don Quichotte à Franz Kafka*, Paris, Bernard Grasset, 1963. There is a translation into Spanish, *Lo viejo y lo nuevo. De Don Quijote a Franz Kafka*, Monte Ávila Latinoamericana Editores, 1993, and Trifaldi Editorial, 2006. And a translation into English by Carol Cosman, *The Old and the New: From Don Quixote to Kafka*, University of California Press, 1977.

Robert, Marthe, "Don Quichotte ou le présent obscur," in *La Semaine Cervantès, France Culture*, 1966.

Robert, Marthe, *Kafka*, Buenos Aires, Paidós, 1969.

Robert, Marthe, *Seul, comme Franz Kafka*, 1969. There is a translation into English, *As Lonely as Franz Kafka*, Harcourt, 1982, and Schocke, 1986. And a translation into German, *Einsam wie Franz Kafka* (1982), Fischer Verlag, 1987.

Robert, Marthe, *Acerca de Kafka. Acerca de Freud*, Barcelona, 1970. 2nd. ed., Anagrama, 1980.

Robert, Marthe, *Franz Kafka's Loneliness*, Faber & Faber, 1982. There is a translation into Spanish, *Franz Kafka o la soledad*, by J. Ferreiro Santana, Mexico, Fondo de Cultura Económica, 1993.

Robertson, Ritchie, "Introduction and Notes," in Ritchie Robertson, *Kafka. A Very Short Introduction*, Oxford-New York, Oxford University Press, 2004.

Robertson, Ritchie, "Introduction and Notes," in Franz Kafka, *The Metamorphosis and Other Stories*, translated by Joyce Crick, Oxford, Oxford University Press (World's Classics), 2009.

Robertson, Ritchie, *Kafka: A Brief Insight*, New York, Sterling Pub., 2010.

Robinson, Martha S., "The Law of the State in Kafka's *The Trial*," in *American Legal Studies Association Forum*, 6, 1982, pp. 127–144.

Robles Morchón, Gregorio, *Crimen y castigo. (Ensayo sobre Durkheim)*, Madrid, Civitas, 2001.

Robles Morchón, Gregorio, "Émile Durkheim (1858–1917)," in *Juristas universales*, supervised by R. Domingo, Madrid, Marcial Pons, 2002.

Rodríguez Criado, Francisco, *Mi querido Dostoievski*, Alpedrete (Madrid), Ediciones de La Discreta, 2012.

Rodríguez Devesa, José María (1916–1987), "Tratamiento psiquiátrico en la delincuencia," in *R. E. P.*, 1970.

Rodríguez Guerrero, Ignacio, *Tipos delincuentes del* Quijote, 2 vols., Foreword by Carlos López Narváez, Quito, Ed. Casa de la Cultura Ecuatoriana, 1966. Also in Medellín, Bedout, 1974.

Rodríguez Romero, Matías Germán, "Principios procesales del Derecho en El Proceso de Franz Kafka. ¿Qué tan lejos estamos del proceso del autor austriaco?," in *Revista Derechos en Acción*, year 5, no. 17, spring 2020, pp. 487–494.

Rojas, Ricardo Manuel, "El poder represivo del Estado: ¿Se justifica la existencia del Derecho penal?," in *Themis*, 35, 1997.

Rojo, José Andrés, "Canetti lee a Kafka," in *El País. Babelia*, July 11, 2023.

Rojo, José Andrés, "Diccionario Franz Kafka: el universo del escritor de la A a la Z," in *El País. Babelia*, May 4, 2024.

Rosell Villasevil, José, "Los galeotes, espejo de Cervantes vapuleado," in *Toletum: Boletín de la Real Academia de Bellas Artes y Ciencias Históricas de Toledo*, 43, 2000.

Royo Villanova, Ricardo, "La locura de Don Quijote," in *III y IV Centenario de "El Quijote" en la Real Academia Nacional de Medicina*, Madrid, Real Academia Nacional de Medicina, 2005, pp. 75–104.

Rózanov, Vasili, "La leyenda del gran inquisidor. F. M. Dostoievski," in Alexandr Nikolayevich Nikolyukin (ed.), *Ensayos literarios. Sobre escritores y escritura*, Moscow, República, 1996.

Ruescas, Aída, "¿Qué significa de algo es 'kafkiano'?," in *Infobae*, February 28, 2024.

Ruiz Fernández, Jesús, "El *Quijote* y el fenómeno del quijotismo," in *Revista de Humanidades*, 20, January-December 2013.

Runfola, Patrizia, *Praga en tiempos de Kafka*, translated into Spanisy by A. Becciu, Barcelona, Bruguera, 2006.

Sadurski, Wojciech, *Giving Desert Its Due*, Dordrecht, D. Reidel Pub. Co., 1985.

Sadurski, Wojciech, "Distributive Justice and the Theory of Punishment," in *Oxford Journal of Legal Studies*, 5, 1, 1985.

Safranski, Rüdiger, *Kafka*, Barcelona, Tusquets Editores, 2024.

Salas, Denis, *Kafka. El combate con la ley*, translated into Spanish by V. Lofiego, Buenos Aires, Poder Judicial de la Ciudad de Buenos Aires. Consejo de la Magistratura, 2015.

Saldaña, Quintiliano (1878–1938), "La criminología de el *Quijote* (notas para su estudio)," in *Revue Hispanique*, 68, 1926, pp. 552–581.

Saldaña, Quintiliano, "Picardía y criminología españolas en Cervantes," in *Filosofía y Letras*, 1, 4, 1916, Madrid, Universidad Central; and in "La criminología de el *Quijote*," in *Revue Hispanique*, 68, 1926.

Saleilles, Raymond (1855–1912), *L'individualisation de la peine*, Paris, F. Alcan, 1898, 3rd. ed. 1927, introduction by Gabriel Tarde; *The Individualization of Punishment*, translation into English from the 2nd. French edition by Rachel Szold Jastrow, with an introduction by Roscoe Pound, Boston, Little Brown, 1911.

Salillas, Rafael (1854–1923), "La criminalidad y la penalidad en el 'Quijote'," in *El Ateneo de Madrid en el III Centenario de la Publicación de "El Ingenioso Hidalgo Don Quijote de la Mancha," Conferencias*, Madrid, Imprenta de Bernardo Rodríguez, 1905, pp. 85–118.

Sánchez Trujillo, Guillermo, "Crimen y castigo de Franz Kafka," in *The Kafka Project*: http://www.kafka.org/essays/crimen.htm.

Sandel, Michael, *Liberalism and the Limits of Justice*, Cambridge, Cambridge University Press, 1982.

Sanmartín Arce, Ricardo, *De Job a Kafka, El sentido en nuestro tiempo*, Valencia, Tirant lo Blanch, 2020.

Saraskina, Ludmila, *Fiodor Dostoïevski. Une victoire sur les démons*, translated into French by Bruno Bisson, Lausanne, L'Age d'Homme, 2008.

Sarrailh, Jean, "Lesage, adaptateur d'Avellaneda," in *Bulletin Hispanique*, Faculté des Lettres de Bordeaux, LXVI, July-December 1964, pp. 359–362.

Scanlan, James P., *Dostoevsky, the Thinker*, Ithaca (New York), Cornell University Press, 2002.

Scarry, Elaine, *The Body in Pain. The Making and Unmaking of the World*, Oxford, Oxford University Press, 1988.

Sciacca, Fabrizio, "La legge nascosta. Il paradosso di Kafka," in *Rivista Internazionale di Filosofia del Diritto*, 2, 1993, pp. 222–236.

Schaffner, Anna Katharina, "Masochism: Franz Kafka and the Eroticization of Suffering," in *Modernism and Perversion Sexual Deviance in Sexology and Literature*, 1850–1930, 23, 3, September 2014.

Schloezer, Boris de, "Les Brouillons des Frères Karamasov," in *Mesures*, October 1935.

Schmidhäuser, Elsbeth, "Die Verhaftung des Josef K. Zum Verständnis von Kafkas Roman 'Der Process'," in *Neue Juristische Wochenschrift*, 1991, pp. 1455–1460.

Schmill Ordoñez, Ulises, *La conducta del jabalí. Dos ensayos sobre el poder: Kafka y Shakespeare*, Mexico, UNAM, Instituto de Investigaciones Jurídicas, 1983.

Schockweiler, Fernand, "Fondement du droit de punir. Réflections sur l'évolution des conceptions," in *Revue de Droit Penal et de Criminologie*, 1982, pp. 467–482.

Schubart, Walter, *Dostoyevski y Nietzsche: seguido de Ensayos sobre la relación spiritual entre Rusia y Europa*, translation into Spanish by María Stock, foreword by Dalmacio Negro Pavón, CEU Ediciones, 2024.

Seksik, Laurent, *Kafka no quiere morir*, translated by Adolfo García Ortega, Barcelona, Seix Barral, 2024.

Seoane, Andrés, "En busca del Kafka desconocido: un escritor alegre, tierno, bromista… y hasta muy ligón," in *El Mundo*. La Lectura, June 3, 2024.

Serrano Martínez, Jorge, "Influencia literaria de Dostoyevski en la obra de Unamuno," 2020. There is a translation into English, "On the Influence of Dostoyevsky in Unamuno's Work," in *Revista Científica Electrónica de Ciencias Gerenciales*, no. 45, year 15, 2020, pp. 35–42.

Serrano-Plaja, Arturo, *Realismo "mágico" en Cervantes: "Don Quijote" visto desde "Tom Sawyer" y "El idiota,"* Madrid, Gredos, 1967.

Serrano Poncela, Segundo, *Dostoievski menor*, Madrid, Taurus, 1959.

Serrano Poncela, Segundo, *Estudios sobre Dostoievski*, Caracas, Universidad Central de Venezuela, Ediciones de la Biblioteca, 1968.

Shakespeare, William (1564–1616), *The Merchant of Venice* (1600), Ed. Molly M. Mahood, Cambridge, Cambridge University Press, 1987. *El mercader de Venecia*, foreword by Vicente Molina Foix, Madrid, Alianza Editorial, 2010. There is also a Spanish ed. and translation by the Instituto Shakespeare, supervised by Manuel Ángel Conejero Dionis-Bayer, Madrid, Cátedra, 2007.

Shakespeare, William, *King Lear* (1606). There is a bilingual edition English-Spanish, with translation into Spanish by Luis Astrana Marín, Madrid, Imagine Ediciones, 2002. *El Rey Lear*, foreword by G. K. Hunter, translation into Spanish by Javier Montes, Madrid, Gredos, 2011. There is also a Spanish edition by the Instituto Shakespeare supervised by Manuel Ángel Conejero Dionis-Bayer, Madrid, Cátedra, 2008. And a Spanish translation, with foreword by Enrique Moreno Castillo, Barcelona, DVD Ediciones, 2001.

Shakespeare, William, *Hamlet* (1623), Ed. Philip Edwards, Cambridge, Cambridge University Press, 1985. There is a bilingual edition English-Spanish by Luis Astrana Marín, Madrid, Imagine Ediciones, 2002. There is also a Spanish translation edited by the Instituto Shakespeare, supervised by Manuel Ángel Conejero Dionis-Bayer, Madrid, Cátedra, 2011.

Sheinbaum, Diego, *Kafka, Defoe y Dostoievski en la escritura de J. M. Coetzee*, Mexico, Elefanta Editorial, Colección Ensayo, Series Editor, Emiliano Becerril Silva, 2017.

Sher, George, *Desert*, New Jersey, Princeton University Press, 1987.

Shestov, Lev (1866–1938), *Dostoievski y Nietzsche. Filosofía de la tragedia*, translated into Spanish by D. J. Volgelman, Buenos Aires, Emecé Editores, S. A., 1949. And also a Spanish translation by Alejandro Ariel González, Hermida Editores, 2022.

Silos, L., "Kafka, Franz: 'La transformación y otros relatos'," in *Estudios de Traducción*, 2, 2012, pp. 201–210.

Silva, Amador de Lorenzo, *El Derecho en la obra de Kafka. Una aproximación fragmentaria*, Breviarios de Rey Lear, 2008. Madrid, Ediciones Complutenses, 2025.

Simakov, Pavel, "Kafka, ese ilustre desconocido Arte TV, 2024, 52 min.," in *Mientras Tanto*, no. 235, 2024.

Singer, Isaac Bashevis, *Un amigo de Kafka (y otros relatos)*, translation by Andrés Catalán, Madrid, Nórdica Libros, 2025.

Singer, Richard G., *Just Deserts: Sentencing Based on Equality and Desert*, Cambridge, Massachusetts, Ballinger, 1979.

Smith, Adam (1723–1790), *The Theory of Moral Sentiments* (1759), Oxford, 1976.

Smith, Alan E., "Galdós, Kafka y Rosa Montero," in *Revista Hispánica Moderna*, vol. 48, no. 2, 1995, pp. 265–273.

Smokti, Eugenia, "La sed de crecer produce herejía: reflexiones sobre 'La leyenda del Gran Inquisidor' de F. M. Dostoievski," in *Revista de la Inquisición*, 10, 2001.

Smolin, Justin, "Before the Law: An Introduction to Kafka," in *The Kafka Project*: http://www.kafka.org/essays/smolin.htm.

Sontag, Susan (1933–2004), *Contra la interpretación y otros ensayos*, translation by H. Vázquez Rial, revised by A. Major, Barcelona, Penguin Randome House Grupo Editorial, 2014 (reprint 2019), pp. 19–20.

Sophocles (496 B.C.–406 B.C.), *Antígona*, in Colección Clásicos Inolvidables, 2nd. ed., Buenos Aires, El Ateneo, 1950. There is also a Spanish translation by Francisco Miguel del Rincón Sánchez, Madrid, Escolar y Mayo, 2013.

Spierenburg, Petrus Cornelis, *The Spectacle of Suffering: Executions and the Evolution of Repression*, Cambridge, Cambridge University Press, 1984.

Stach, Reiner, "Kafka y sus ediciones," in *Revista de Libros*, no. 51, 2001, pp. 3–6.

Stach, Reiner, *Kafka: Die Jahre der Entscheidungen*, Frankfurt/M. Fischer, 2010. Translation into Spanish, *Kafka. Los años de las decisiones*, Madrid, Siglo Veintiuno de España Editores, 2003.

Stach, Reiner, *Kafka. Los primeros años. Los años de las decisiones. Los años del conocimiento*, translation into Spanish by Carlos Fortea Gil, Barcelona, Acantilado, 2016.

Stach, Reiner, *¿Éste es Kafka? 99 hallazgos*, translation into Spanish by Luis Fernando Moreno Claros, Barcelona, El Acantilado, 2021.

Steiner, George, *Tolstoy or Dostoevsky: An Essay in Contrast*, London, Faber & Faber, 1989. There is a translation into Spanish by Agustí Bartra, *Tolstói o Dostoievski*, Madrid, Siruela, 2002.

Steiner, George, "Introduction," in Franz Kafka, *The Trial*, New York, Knopf/Everyman's Library, 1992.

Steiner, George, "Pasión intacta. Ensayos 1978–1995," in *Notas sobre* El proceso *de Kafka*, translated into Spanish by M. Gutiérrez and E. Castejón, Madrid, Siruela, 1997. 2001.

Steinmann, Jean, "Dostoievsky. Romancier de notre temps," in *La Vie intellectuelle*, year 15, no. 2, February 1947.

Stellino, Paolo, "El descubrimiento de Dostoievski por parte de Nietzsche," in *Contrastes. Revista Internacional de Filosofía*, vol. XIII, 2008.

Stellino, Paolo, *Nietzsche y Dostoievski. Psicología, resentimiento y moral*, PhD supervised by Jesús Marcial Conill Sancho, Universitat de València, 2010.

Stern, Joseph Peter, "The Law of *The Trial*," in *On Kafka: Semi-Centenary Perspectives*, London, 1976.

Stern, Laurence, "Deserved Punishment, Deserved Harm, Deserved Blame," in *Philosophy*, 45, 1970, pp. 317–329.

Stevenson, Robert Louis (1850–1894), *The Works of Robert Louis Stevenson*, Swanston Edition, London, Chatto and Windus, in association with Cassell and Company Limited, William Heinemann and Longmans Green and Company, 1911–1912. Vol. V: *Strange Case of Dr. Jekyll and Mr. Hyde*. Vol. VI: *Treasure Island*.

Stevenson, Robert Louis, *Dr. Jekyll y Mr. Hyde*, translation into Spanish by Carmen Criado, Madrid, Alianza, 2004.

Strachow, Nikolai, "Über Dostojewskis Leben und literarische Tätigkeit von 1860–1881," in *Dostojewski-Gesamtausgabe*, Piper & Co., vol. 12, Russian edition, 1882.

Stratenwerth, Günter, "Strafrecht und Sozialtheraphie," in *Festschrift für Bockelmann*, 1979.

Strathern, Paul, *Kafka en 90 minutos*, translation into Spanish by Sandra Chaparro Martínez, Madrid, Siglo XXI de España Editores, 2016.

Strawson, Peter Frederick, "Freedom and Resentment," in *Proceedings of the British Academy*, XLVIII, 1962.

Stringfellow, Franz, "Kafka's Trial: Between the Republic and Psychoanalysis," in *Cardozo Studies in Law and Literature*, vol. 7, issue 2, fall-winter 1995, pp. 173–206.

Talavera, Pedro, *Derecho y Literatura*, Foreword by Adela Cortina, Granada, Comares, 2006.

Talavera, Pedro, *Law and Literature: A Still-thriving Relationship*, in *International Studies in Law and Literature*, vol. 3, María José Falcón y Tella (ed.), Javier de Lucas (foreword), Deirdre B. Jerry (translator), Leiden-Boston, Brill-Nijhoff, 2025.

Terras, Víctor, *A Karamazov Companion, Commentary on the Genesis, Language and Style of Dostoevsky Novel*, London, University of Wisconsin Press, 1981. Madison, The University of Wisconsin Press, 2002.

Terras, Víctor, *Reading Dostoevsky*, London, University of Wisconsin Press, 1998.

Tezanos, José Félix, "Los límites de la obediencia. Consideraciones sobre el experimento de Stanley Milgram," in *Sistema*, 12, 1976, pp. 99–114.

Thompson Oenning, Diane, *The Brothers Karamazov and the Poetics of Memory*, Cambridge, Cambridge University Press, 1991.

Thurneysen, Eduard, *Dostojewski*, Chr. Kaiser, 1921. There is a translation into English by Keith R. Crim, *Dostoevsky*, Richmond, Va., John Knox Press, 1964. And a translation into French by P. Maury, *Dostoeivski ou les confins de l'homme*, Paris, Je Sers, 1934.

Tierno Galván, Enrique (1918–1986), "Un tema de Dostoyevski: la preocupación," in *Monteagudo: Revista de Literatura Española, Hispanoamericana y Teoría de la Literatura*, no. 1, 1953, pp. 11–17.

Tierno Galván, Enrique, "Concepción del mundo e ideas políticas en la obra de Dostoyevski," in *Revista de Estudios Políticos*, no. 70, 1953, pp. 83–106.

Timmermann, Freddy, "Dolor, identidad y poder. Franz Kafka, Cartas a Milena," in *Revista Temas Sociológicos*, no. 8, 2002, pp. 208–236.

Tomain, Joseph P., *Creon's Ghost: Law, Justice, and the Humanities*, Oxford, Oxford University Press, 2009.

Torres Muro, Ignacio, "Clarín, jurista," in María José Falcón y Tella – Juan Antonio Martínez Muñoz (dirs.), *Estudios Jurídicos Multidisciplinares. José Iturmendi Morales, Maestro Complutense. Homenaje*, Valencia, Tirant lo Blanch, 2020, pp. 1015–1026. There is a translation into Englisy by Deirdre B. Jerry, "Clarín, Jurist," in María José Falcón y Tella – Juan Antonio Martínez Muñoz (eds.), *Challenges to Legal Theory. Essays in Honour of Professor José Iturmendi Morales*, Leiden-Boston, Brill-Nijhoff, 2021, pp. 67–78.

Troyat, Henri, *Dostoievski*, 1940, Barcelona, Salvat, 1986.

Trueba Mira, Virginia, "Los infiernos de lo abstracto (Kafka en Zambrano)," in *ENDOXA*, no. 41, 2018, pp. 195–212.

Ugrinski, Alexej – Lambasa, Frank S. – Ozolins, Valija K. (eds.), *Dostoievski and the Human Condition After a Century*, London, Praeger-Greenwood Press, 1986.

Umbreit, Mark S., *Crime and Reconciliation: Creative Options for Victims and Offenders*, Nashville, Abingdon Press, 1985.

Unamuno, Miguel de (1864–1936), "Sobre la lectura e interpretación del *Quijote*," in *La España moderna* (April 1905), in *Obras Completas*, Madrid, 1958.

Unamuno, Miguel de, *Vida de Don Quijote y Sancho* (1905), Madrid, Cátedra, edited by Alberto Navarro, 1988.

Unseld, Joachim, *Franz Kafka. Una vida de escritor: Historia de sus publicaciones*, translation into Spanish by José María Mínguez, Barcelona, Anagrama, 2006. 1st. ed. 1989.

Val Macé, Maéva, *El Derecho en la literatura. Análisis filosófico de la obra* Crimen y castigo, Tfg supervised by María José Bernuz Beneitez, Zaragoza, Facultad de Derecho, Universidad de Zaragoza, 2017.

Valls Boix, Juan Evaristo, "Sobre Kafka. Textos, discusiones, apuntes," in *Laoconte. Revista de Estética y Teoría de las Artes*, no. 1, 2014, pp. 192–195.

Vandelli, Luciano, *Papeles y papeleo. Burocracia y literatura*, foreword by Santiago Muñoz Machado, translation into Spanish by G. M. Díaz González, Pozuelo de Alarcón (Madrid), Portal Derecho-Iustel, 2015.

Van den Haag, Ernest, *Political Violence and Civil Disobedience*, New York, Harper & Row, 1972.

Van Dusen, H., Jr., "Civil Disobedience, Destroyer of Democracy," in *American Bar Association Journal*, vol. 55, February 1969.

Various Authors, *Historia de las literaturas eslavas*, Madrid, Cátedra, 1997.

Various Authors, *Cuando Kafka vino hacia mi…*, edited by Hans-Gerd Koch, translated into Spanish by Berta Vías Mahou, Barcelona, Acantilado, 2009.

Various Authors, *Kafka en las dos orillas: Antología de la recepción crítica española e hispanoamericana*, edition and introduction by Elisa Martínez Salazar and Julieta Yelin, Zaragoza, Prensas de la Universidad de Zaragoza, 2013.

Various Authors, *Philosophy and Kafka*, edited by Brendan Moran and Carlo Sazani, Plymouth, Lexington Books, 2013.

Various Authors, *Imaginar la ley. El Derecho en la Literatura*, Directed by Antoine Garapón and Denis Salas, translation into Spanish by A. Dilon, Poder Judicial de la Ciudad de Buenos Aires, Consejo de la Magistratura, 2015.

Various Authors, *A medio camino. Intertextos entre la literatura y el derecho*, edited by Diego Falconi Trávez, Valencia, Tirant Humanidades, 2016.

Vásquez Coronel, Luis, "Don Quijote constitucionalista, adalid de la libertad," June 12, 2017, in http://legis.pe/don-quijote-constitucionalista-adalid-libertad/.

Vela Treviño, Sergio – Vela Martínez, Sergio, "Don Quijote y el Derecho penal," Symposium on "El concepto del Derecho en el *Quijote*," in the meeting at Guanajuato, *Actas*, VI, 1994.

Venzon, Rubén, "Kafka apócrifo: fototextualidad y reescritura en 'Proyecto K.' de Paco Gómez," in *Anales de Literatura Española*, vol. 42, 2025, pp. 117–143.

Verdú de Gregorio, Joaquín, "Huellas de la inocencia en la creación artística (Cervantes-Dostoievski-Velázquez-Dreyer)," in *Miscelánea Comillas, Revista de Ciencias Humanas y Sociales*, vol. 65, no. 126, January-June 2007.

Vergès, Jacques, *Justicia y Literatura*, Barcelona, Ediciones Península-Atalaya, 2013. Translation into Spanish by Loles Oliván, from *Justice et littérature*, Paris, Presses Universitaires de France, 2011.

Vialatte, Alexandre, *Kafka ou l'innocence diabolique*, Paris, Les Belles Lettres, 1998.

Vialatte, Alexandre, *Mon Kafka*, Paris, Les Belles Lettres, 2001.

Viana Navarro, Jorge, "Kafka, el precursor que se adelantó a nuestro tiempo," in *Barcarola. Revista de Creación Literaria*, nos. 105–106, 2024, pp. 199–204.

Vidal, Augusto, *Dostoievski*, Barcelona, Barral Editores, 1972.

Vila, Juan Diego, "Delincuencia e imaginario femenino en el *Quijote* de 1605: Don Quijote, Ginés de Pasamonte y los galeotes," in Edith M. *et al.* (eds.), *La cultura hispánica y Occidente. Actas del IV Congreso Argentino de Hispanistas*, 1995.

Vila-Matas, Enrique, "Los hijos de Kafka," in *Letras Libres*, June 1, 2024.

Vilas, Manuel, *Dos tardes con Franz Kafka*, Madrid, Alianza Editorial, 2025.

Vil'mont, Nikolai Nikolaevich, *Dostoievski y Shiller*, 1984.

Villoro, Juan, "Dostoievski: el aprendizaje del éxtasis," in *Revista de la Universidad de México*, no. 89, 2011, pp. 11–21.

Víquez Jiménez, Alí, "Los hombres de Dostoievski," in *Revista de Filología y Lingüística de la Universidad de Costa Rica*, 35, 1, 2012, pp. 87–110.

Vismann, Cornelia, "Rejouer les Crimes Theater vs. Video," in *Cardozo Studies in Law and Literature*, vol. 11, issue 2, winter 1999, pp. 161–178.

Vitoria, Francisco de, *Relectio de potestate civili. Estudios sobre su Filosofía Política.* Edition by Jesús Cordero Pando, Madrid, Consejo Superior de Investigaciones Científicas, 2008.

Vives Antón, Tomás Salvador – Carbonell Mateu, Juan Carlos – González Cussac, José Luis – Alonso Rimo, Alberto – Roig Torres, Margarita (eds.), *Crímenes y castigos: Miradas al Derecho penal a través del arte y la cultura*, Valencia, Tirant lo Blanch, 2014.

Von Hirsch, Andrew – Ashworth, A., "Not Just Deserts: A Response to Braithwaite and Pettit," in *Oxford Journal of Legal Studies*, 13, 1992, pp. 83–96.

Von Kleist, Heinrich (1777–1811), *Michael Kohlhaas*, Barcelona, Pomaire, 1980.

Vullierme, Jean Louis, "La fin de la justice pénale," in *Archives de Philosophie du Droit*, 1983, pp. 155–180.

Wagenbach, Klaus, *Kafka*, Madrid, Alianza Editorial, 1981.

Wagenbach, Klaus, "Franz Kafka: una biografía," in *Obras Completas de Franz Kafka*, vol. I, translation into Spanish by J. Parra, Galaxia Gutenberg, Círculo de Lectores, 1999.

Wahnón, Sultana, "Una sentencia justa para Josef K.: Sobre *El proceso* de Kafka," in *Isegoría, Revista de Filosofía Moral y Política*, 25, 2001.

Wahnón, Sultana, "Josef K. era inocente: Sobre *El proceso* de Kafka," in *Raíces: Revista Judía de Cultura*, 49, 2001–2002.

Wahnón, Sultana, *Kafka y la tragedia judía*, Barcelona, Riopiedras Ediciones, 2003.

Walser, Martin, *Descripción de una forma. Ensayo sobre Franz Kafka*, Buenos Aires, Editorial Sur, 1969. Editorial Fontamara, 2000. Mexico, E. Coyoacán S. A., 2006.

Wasik, Martin – Von Hirsch, Andrew, "Non-custodial Penalties and the Principles of Desert," in *Criminal Law Review*, 1988, pp. 555–572.

Wasserstrom, Richard, "Some Problems in the Definition and Justification of Punishment," in A. Goldman – J. Kim (eds.), *Values and Morals*, Dordrecht, Reidel, 1978.

Weber, Susanne Maria, "El Derecho en la obra de Kafka," in *Psikeba: Revista de Psicoanálisis y Estudios Culturales*, 5, 2007.

Weiner, Susan, *Law in Art. Melville's Major Fiction and Nineteenth-Century American Law*, Frankfurt am Main, Peter Lang, 1992.

Weisberg, Richard H., "Law, Literature, and Cardozo's Judicial Poetics," in *Cardozo Law Review*, 1, 1979, pp. 283–342.

Weisberg, Richard H., *Literature as Negativity: Ressentiment in Dostoyevski and Flaubert*, Univ. Microfilms Internat, Ann Arbor, Mich., 1982.

Weisberg, Richard H., *The Failure of the Word: The Protagonist as Lawyer in Modern Fiction*, New Haven-London, Yale University Press, 1984. Translation into Italian, *Il fallimento della parola. Figure della legge nella narrativa moderna*, Bologna, Il Mulino, 1990. Translation into French, *La "parole défaillante": L'homme du droit au coeur du roman modern (Dostoïevski, Flaubert, Camus, Melville)*, Editions L'Epitoge, 2019.

Weisberg, Richard H., *When Lawyers Write*, Boston, Little, Brown, 1987.

Weisberg, Richard H., "The Law-Literature Enterprise," in *Yale Journal of Law and the Humanities*, 1988, pp. 1–67.

Weisberg, Richard H., "Accepting the Inside Narrator's Challenge: Billy Budd and the Legalistic Reader," *Symposium*, in *Cardozo Studies in Law and Literature*, vol. 1, issue 1, spring 1989, pp. 27–48.

Weisberg, Richard H., *Poethics and Other Strategies of Law and Literature*, New York, Columbia University Press, 1992.

Weisberg, Richard H., "The Codification of Western Law and the Poetics of Disclosure," in *Cardozo Studies in Law and Literature*, vol. 6, issue 2, fall-winter 1994, pp. 157–170.

Weisberg, Richard H., "Literature's Twenty-Year Crossing into the Domain of Law: Continuing Trespass or Right by Adverse Possession?," in Freeman, Michael – Lewis, Andrew (eds.), *Law and Literature. Current Legal Issues*, vol. 2, London-New York, Oxford University Press, 1999, pp. 47–61.

Weisberg, Richard H., "Fish Takes the Bait: Holocaust Denial and Post-modernist Theory," in *Law & Literature*, vol. 14, issue 1, spring 2002, pp. 131–142.

Weisberg, Richard H., "Wigmore and the Law and Literature Movement," in *Law & Literature*, vol. 21, issue 1, spring 2009, pp. 129–145.

Weisberg, Richard H., *Law, Literature, and History. A Fateful Rendezvous with the Shoah*, vol. 2 of the *International Studies in Law and Literature*, María José Falcón y Tella (series ed.), Leiden-Boston, Brill-Nijhoff, 2025.

Weisberg, Richard H. – Barricelli, Jean-Pierre, "Literature and the Law," in Gibaldi, Joseph – Barricelli, Jean-Pierre (eds.), *Interrelations of Literature*, New York, The Modern Language Association of America, 1982, pp. 150–175.

Wellek, René, *Dostoevsky: A Collection of Critical Essays*, Englewood Cliffs, N. J., Prentice-Hall, 1962.

White, James Boyd, *The Legal Imagination: Studies in the Nature of Legal Thought and Expression*, Boston, Little, Brown and Co., 1973; *The Legal Imagination*, 2nd abridged ed., Chicago, University of Chicago Press, 1985. Wolters Kluwer brought out a *45th Anniversary Edition* of this book, Aspen Publishing, 2018, with a new preface written by the author.

White, James Boyd, *Heracles' Bow: Essays on the Rhetoric and Poetics of the Law*, Madison, University of Wisconsin Press, 1985.

White, James Boyd, *When Words Lose Their Meaning. Constitutions and Reconstitutions of Language, Character, and Community*, Chicago, University of Chicago Press, 1985.

White, James Boyd, "Law and Literature: 'No Manifesto'," in *Mercer Law Review*, 39, 1988.

White, James Boyd, "Book Review: What Can a Lawyer Learn from Literature?," in *Harvard Law Review*, 102, 1989, pp. 2032–2047.

White, James Boyd, *Justice as Translation: An Essay in Cultural and Legal Criticism*, Chicago, University of Chicago Press, 1990.

White, James Boyd, "Essays in Law and Literature," in *Connecticut Law Review*, 1991, pp. 669–742.

White, James Boyd, *Acts of Hope: Creating Authority in Literature, Law and Politics*, Chicago, University of Chicago Press, 1995.

White, James Boyd, *From Expectation to Experience: Essays on Law & Legal Education*, Michigan, University of Michigan Press, 1999. 4th. reprint 2002.

White, James Boyd, "Writing and Reading in Philosophy, Law and Poetry," in Freeman, Michael – Lewis, Andrew (eds.), *Law and Literature. Current Legal Issues*, vol. 2, London–New York, Oxford University Press, 1999, pp. 1–21.

White, James Boyd, *When Language Meets the Mind: Three Questions*, Wolf Legal Publisher, 2007.

White, James Boyd, *Living Speech. Resisting the Empire of Force*, Princeton, New Jersey, Princeton University Press, 2008.

White, James Boyd, *The Gospel as Conversation: Texts, Sermons, and Questions for Reflection: A Study Guide*, Wipf & Stock Publishers, 2013.

White, James Boyd, *Keep Law Alive*, Carolina Academic Press, 2019.

Wigmore, John Henry (1863–1943), "A List of Legal Novels," in *Illinois Law Review*, II, 1908, pp. 547–593.

Wigmore, John Henry, "A List of One Hundred Legal Novels," in *Illinois Law Review*, 17, 1922, pp. 26–41.

Wolff, Kurt, *Autores, libros, aventuras. Observaciones y recuerdos de un editor, seguidos de la correspondencia del autor con Franz Kafka*, translation into Spanish by Isabel García Adánez, Barcelona, Acantilado, 2010.

Wolynski, Akim Wowitch, *Das Reich der Karamasows*, Jazzybee Verlag, 1924.

Yarmolinsky, Abrahan, *Dostoievsky. La vida y la obra*, Introduction by Aníbal Castelnuovo, Buenos Aires, Zamora, Colección Los Genios, no. 3, 1947.

Zambrano, María (1904–1991), "Franz Kafka. Mártir de la miseria humana," in *Espuela de Plata* (Havana), August 1941, pp. 3–8. Also in Various Authors, *Kafka en las dos orillas*, edition and introduction by Elisa Martínez Salazar and Julieta Yelin, Zaragoza, Prensas de la Universidad de Zaragoza, 2013, pp. 101–111.

Zambrano, María, "Franz Kafka, un mártir de la lucidez," in *Asomante* (Puerto Rico), 1, January-March 1947, pp. 5–17. Also in *Aurora. Papeles del Seminario María Zambrano*, no. 3, 2001, pp. 124–132.

Zambrano, María, "La novela-tragedia: El castillo de Kafka," in Various Authors, *Kafka en las dos orillas. Antología de la recepción crítica española e hispanoamericana*, Zaragoza, Prensas de la Universidad de Zaragoza, 2013.

Zehnhoff, Hans-Werner am, "*Don Quijote* y la parodia," in Various Authors, *Tras las huellas de Don Quijote. Actas de la Jornada dedicada a* Don Quijote de la Mancha, Antwerp, Lessius Hogeschool, December 9, 2005, edition and translation by Lieve Behiels, Ministerio de Educación y Ciencia de España – Lessius Hogeschool (Associatie K. U. Leuven), 2007, pp. 57–65.

Zilboorg, Gregory (1890–1959), *The Psychology of the Criminal Act and Punishment*, New York, Harcourt, Brace, 1954; London, Hogarth Press, 1955; New York, Greenwood Press, 1968.

Zolezzi Ibárcena, Lorenzo, "El Derecho en *Los hermanos Karamazov*. The Law in *The Brothers Karamazov*," in *Derecho PUCP* (*Pontificia Universidad Católica del Perú*), 74, 2015, pp. 355–395.

Zweig, Stefan (1881–1942), *Tres maestros* (*Balzac-Dickens-Dostoievski*), translation into Spanish by J. Fontcuberta, Barcelona, De Juventud, 1941. Barcelona, Acantilado, 2011.,

Index

www.ingramcontent.com/pod-product-compliance
Ingram Content Group UK Ltd.
Pitfield, Milton Keynes, MK11 3LW, UK
UKHW020822290926
15470UKWH00003B/1309

9 789004 765993